Agovino's text is a valuable addition to a burgeoning American soccer canon that will continue to grow with the sport's popularity."
 Matthew Tettleton, *Aethlon: Journal of Sports Literature*

"An intimate and wonderfully written account of a sport that is increasingly shaking America's soul out."
 Colum McCann, author of the National Book Award winner *Let the Great World Spin*

"An always-readable, always-engaging journey through the life of a football-mad New Yorker. . . . Truly fascinating."
 Andi Thomas, sb *Nation*

"A funny and affecting account of one American's stubborn embrace of soccer."
 Esquire

"A gripping narrative . . . offering insights into the growth of soccer's popularity in America."
 Souvik Naha, *Journal of Sport History*

"Those who lived through this barren time for the game in America during the '80s will see a lot of themselves in this diary, while for the new mls era, this will be an eye opener on how things used to be."
 The Football Pink

"Here is a delightful, briskly readable memoir of sports obsession that deftly cuts across decades and cultures—with one manic, maddening, miraculous sport at its center."
 Hampton Sides, best-selling author of *Ghost Soldiers*

THE SOCCER DIARIES

FIFA WORLD ALL·STAR

FOR THE BENEFIT OF UNICEF

AUGUST 7, 1982/GIANTS STADIUM/EAST RUTHERFORD, NEW JERSEY

THE
SOCCER
DIARIES

AN AMERICAN'S THIRTY-YEAR PURSUIT
OF THE INTERNATIONAL GAME

Michael J. Agovino

UNIVERSITY OF NEBRASKA PRESS | LINCOLN AND LONDON

Portions of this book originally appeared
in *Tin House* and *Howler*. Images courtesy
of United States Soccer Federation (Team
America-Italy game program), the New York
Cosmos (Cosmos yearbook), FIFA and Roger
Huyssen (FIFA-UNICEF World All-Star Game
program), Transatlantic Challenge Cup,
ticket stubs, press passes (from author).

Library of Congress
Cataloging-in-Publication Data
Agovino, Michael J.
The soccer diaries: an American's
thirty-year pursuit of the international
game / Michael J. Agovino.
pages   cm
ISBN 978-0-8032-4047-6 (hardback: alk. paper)—
ISBN 978-1-4962-0597-1 (paper: alk. paper)—
ISBN 978-0-8032-5566-1 (epub)—
ISBN 978-0-8032-5567-8 (mobi)—
ISBN 978-0-8032-5565-4 (pdf)
1. Soccer—History. 2. Soccer—
United States—History. I. Title.
GV942.5.A43 2014
796.3340973—dc23
2013045092

Set in Minion by Lindsey Auten.
Designed by N. Putens.

For Adria, my sister and first
Soccer Made in Germany companion

Football, bloody hell.

SIR ALEX FERGUSON

CONTENTS

ACKNOWLEDGMENTS

Many thanks to my agent, the wonderful Jennifer Gates. And thank you to my new friends in Nebraska: the great Rob Taylor, editor of many a fine baseball book and who I suspect will soon be searching for soccer on Saturday mornings in Lincoln; and his associate, Courtney Ochsner, who is so efficient and kind they named a sporting goods chain for her in Switzerland (where you can buy all of your soccer gear!). Thanks also to Karen H. Brown for a fine copy edit (her hometown of Boulder, Colorado, was flooding as she gamely completed her work). Thank you also to Joeth Zucco, who managed the project through to the end, to Nathan Putens for the beautiful book design, and Acacia Gentrup and the marketing team. Finally, I thank all of you who spent time playing soccer with me, talking soccer with me, and watching soccer with me. This is for you.

INTRODUCTION

To quote Ryszard Kapuscinski, who makes a cameo in these pages, "This is a very personal book, one about being alone and being lost." Well, maybe not about being lost in my case—though my poor sense of direction has tripped me up a time or two—but certainly about being alone. Alone, that is, while pursing a friend, the friend being the sport of soccer.

This friend has been full of contradictions: it's been simple but nuanced; endearing but tedious; often inspiring though sometimes dark; intellectual but primal; sometimes stylish and poetic, other times ugly and crude; at one time it was elusive, but now it's ubiquitous.

But it's always been there for me—often after I had to look long and hard—and it's always been generous. It takes but it gives—and shares and teaches, too.

We met in 1982, almost by accident, thanks to what was then known as SIN, the Spanish International Network. Befriending soccer back then almost felt sinful in this country. It was a punch line, made fun of as foreign, less than masculine, possibly communist.

For me, it didn't matter. I was hooked in the summer of 1982, and have doggedly pursued the sport, and the culture that surrounds it, ever since. This book is about that pursuit, from foreign games on snowy UHF channels and Toby Charles on PBS's *Soccer Made in Germany* to the 24/7 coverage of today.

It's also about the people I met—while playing, watching, discussing, and arguing about soccer—and the places I visited along the way. I've seen games in seven countries, which might seem like a lot to some, or not very many to others. What I saw delighted me, sometimes frustrated me, but always fascinated me. It ends, thirty years and one day later, where it began, in the Bronx.

In between, there are stops in Rome, London, Munich, and many in Zurich. There are World Cup matches, European Championships (just one game and the dullest of all time, but still), UEFA Cup, Champions League, international and club friendlies. There are the NASL, MLS, USMNT, EPL, and FIFA.

From great stadiums (Berlin's Olympiastadion, Rome's Stadio Olimpico, Dortmund's Westfalenstadion, and Yankee Stadium—well, almost) to brilliant national teams (Brazil, Germany, Argentina, Italy). From great clubs (the Cosmos, Bayern Munich, AC Milan, Benfica, Liverpool, Feyenoord, Roma) to clubs I'd never heard of (MyPa?).

From the Bundesliga to Serie A, from the Recreation Ground in Aldershot to FIFA's gleaming headquarters overlooking Zurich; the Great Lawn in Central Park to a training facility on Spain's Costa del Sol, ground zero of Europe's economic collapse.

But this book is also where I've discovered and grappled with soccer in the most unlikely of places: the Waldorf-Astoria, the Plaza Hotel, the Public Theater, Film Forum, the Tate Gallery, the Guggenheim Museum, Sonny Mehta's apartment, Lincoln Plaza

Cinema, the TriBeCa Film Festival, a conference room in the Hilton Hotel, the Dolder Grand Hotel, the Brooklyn Academy of Music, and Dia:Beacon. And to places that no longer exist: the Palladium, Foxboro Stadium, Giants Stadium—so much in Giants Stadium—and a social club in Queens.

This is not an official history of the sport but, rather, my own observations, opinions (many unpopular, that you're welcome to disagree with), musings, and wonderings as an American fan and occasional journalist.

Despite this being my own take, I'd like to think it shows the evolution of soccer—how it's been perceived, presented, and processed—in this country over the last thirty years. It's for the hardened fan, but also for the newcomer who's just discovered the sport, and for anyone who's curious about soccer, just the way I was in the summer of 1982. You might make a new friend. All are invited, and it's my hope that all will find places throughout to smile. May you enjoy the journey as much I as did.

February 1, 2013

Prologue

It is not just a simple game; it is
a weapon of the revolution.

CHE GUEVARA

August 7, 1982
FIFA-UNICEF World All-Star Game
Giants Stadium
East Rutherford, New Jersey

The day of my first soccer game began in the Bronx, where I was from. We didn't have a car, my father didn't drive (nor did he make any apologies for that), so we took a city bus, the QBX1, to the No. 6 subway at Pelham Bay Station. This didn't take us to any game or stadium, but first to 125th Street, where we, the only white people, crossed the platform for the 4/5 express, to Grand Central, then to the shuttle, and finally to the Port Authority Bus Terminal.

The steps from the subway, menacing and dark in those years, to whatever was above—a street, a plaza, a square, light, safety in numbers—usually brought an exhale and relief, but at the Port Authority, it was the opposite. It was an ascension into still more, and diverse, rings of despair—and the pent-up energy of wants and needs. It was at once the most alive of spaces and the most

1

terrifying, besides, that is, the No. 6 train that we had just taken, a portable mural of affirmation and rage, the elevated tracks buttressed by tenement carcasses.

Weeks before, this ad had appeared in the *New York Times*: "For the first time in history, the world's greatest soccer players—selected on the basis of their performance in the 1982 World Cup—will collide in an international all-star match. Above all else, they'll be fighting for one goal: to help the world's children." The game was sponsored by UNICEF; tickets were pricey at fifteen, eleven, and seven dollars. If you couldn't make it, the ad read, be sure to make a donation to UNICEF on East Thirty-Eighth Street. It was billed as "Europe vs. the Rest of the World."

My father, who understood little about soccer but encouraged my newfound interest in it, bought us tickets high in the upper deck. It would be hard to get to, he said, but there would be buses from the Port Authority. We'd been to Shea and Yankee Stadiums together, and Madison Square Garden, but never to Giants Stadium and never on such a journey, across three rivers, to see a game.

The bus to Giants Stadium was crowded, unlawfully so I'm certain, not an inch of standing room to be wriggled. But the law likely didn't care about us; we were "other." If there were white people, and there were a few, none aside from us appeared to be speaking English. Mostly, though, there were nonwhite people, with every texture and curlicue of hair, every shade of skin, from caramel to onyx, but different, it was clear—through speech, gait, stance—from the black people I lived among in Co-op City, or on the No. 6 train, or at the 125th Street station.

It may have reeked of an admixture of perspiration and, with windows wide open, bus exhaust, but it was the most comfortable uncomfortable coach ever to depart from Forty-Second Street and Eighth Avenue, everyone giddy, full of smiles and harmonies. They couldn't wait to see their countryman, or neighboring countryman, or someone at least from their part of the world, in performance: Thomas N'Kono of Cameroon, Faisal Al-Dakhil of Kuwait, Julio

César Arzú and Roberto Figueroa of Honduras, Lakhdar Belloumi of Algeria, Jaime Duarte of Peru, and Júnior and Sócrates of Brazil. Soccer was the game of Europe—Italy, young men with names and faces and noses like mine, had just won the World Cup, beating, to the delight of everyone it seemed, the West Germans—but this was also the game of the third world, of poor people. For that, I liked it more.

Outside the stadium, soccer balls ping-ponged up and down, to and fro, off feet, thighs, and foreheads all over the vast parking lot, which appeared interminable—concentric circles of sterility in middle-of-nowhere New Jersey, brought to life by people from every latitude. If there were "real Americans"—*whatever that means*—they were the minority and arrived in cars.

It was intimidating, the sheer size of the crowd and the steep incline of the upper deck. Yankee and Shea hadn't been like this. They usually had no more than ten or twenty thousand, maybe forty if the Yankees had a key rival in town. I'd never sat so high up in those stadiums. On this night, it felt as though we'd all spill out of the upper tiers.

Just before kickoff, Danny Kaye, the entertainer and UNICEF ambassador, told us, on behalf of all the world's children, to scream. He said, "Make the loudest noise ever heard!" And we did, the 76,891 of us, the second-largest crowd in the history of U.S. soccer, and Giants Stadium shook.

The game program, like everything from that night, was different in the best of ways. It was sophisticated, worldly, and informative, not merely photos of Mr. Met juxtaposed with Schaefer Beer ads. The first page had a letter from President Ronald Reagan. When my father saw his picture, he said, in his East Harlem Italian inflection, "Disgrazia." It had a letter from João Havelange, as stately as any UN Secretary-General, who was the president of the world governing body known as Fédération Internationale de Football Association, FIFA for short, in Zurich, Switzerland. It had a profile of UNICEF, of its mission, and photos of handicapped kids—about my age, at around fourteen—in Rwanda, at the Gatagara Mission Center, trying their best to kick the ball on a dusty patch. Another photo showed starving children in Somalia's Sabaad Refugee Camp. Rwanda, Somalia—now I'd have to find them in the *Britannica Atlas*, my favorite book, just the way I'd had to find Cameroon, its capital Yaoundé, Kuwait, Honduras (and Tegucigalpa—*But Daddy, how do you pronounce Tegucigalpa?*), Vigo, Gijón, La Coruña, and Zaragoza in the previous weeks when I'd come across this game I knew little of that now obsessed me.

Someone named Brian Glanville, "a soccer correspondent for the *London Sunday Times*," wrote about the different national styles of soccer. (What a thought. I never heard of this in baseball. There was no Brazilian way of playing baseball or an English way; they didn't play baseball.) Glanville declared that the Scots had changed their style—to a fault—and that the Czechoslovaks were known for their "Danubian deliberation and pattern weaving." There was a byline from someone named Juvenal, just Juvenal, who wrote for the Argentine magazine *El Gráfico*, and Rob Hughes, another "correspondent" for the *London Mail on Sunday*. I loved how they used that word, *correspondent*, and how these pieces read like serious, global concerns. It made sense that there were soccer correspondents. *Could I be a soccer correspondent?*

The program had profiles and a photo of each player: Rossi, the hero; Keegan; Rummenigge; Platini; Camacho; and Antognoni, who scored the winner past the great N'Kono in the final minutes. They played for wonderful-sounding teams; not the London Lions or Paris Panthers but Tottenham Hotspur, Juventus, Alianza Lima, Canon Yaoundé, Corinthians, Flamengo. There was a World Cup quiz and primers of great players from days past. It was all there, in this Baedeker of the game, its past, present, and future. Another headline read, and this delighted me, "U.S. Soccer: The Time Is Now." There was a photo of an American player for the Portland Timbers of the NASL who represented U.S. soccer's future. His name was Glenn Myernick.

My mother had pulled me out of religious instruction the year before; we weren't churchgoers anyway. This would be my bible, and I would memorize every word of it, every thought, every fact.

I read the game articles the next day in the *New York Times*. One claimed that Belloumi, the Algerian who'd helped shock West Germany a few weeks earlier, had left his honeymoon early to be there. Falcão, the lanky Brazilian, attended despite his father having just suffered a heart attack. I clipped these articles and attached them, with the ticket stubs, to the program. I'd keep them forever, even if it turned out to be worth something, no matter how much I might need the money.

We made the loudest sound ever—you should've heard us—just like Danny Kaye wanted. And then, over the public address system, they played John Lennon's "Imagine."

Part 1

. . . .

Five days shalt thou labor, as the Bible
says. The seventh day is the Lord thy
God's. The sixth day is for football.
ANTHONY BURGESS

OSMOS

s-Atlantic Challenge Cup

C CHALLENGE

83

SOUN

ITALY

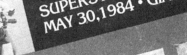

Spring 1982
IS 181
Bronx, New York

This was eighth grade, gym class. I was a small kid, normally the kind who would get picked on, but because of luck, and a little pluck, was spared. Probably because I loved sports, knew a lot about it, and was good in gym class, except when they tried to teach us how to swim, but that's another story. None of us could swim. Our junior high school, IS 181, named after the great Catalonian cellist Pablo Casals, didn't have an actual gym, so phys ed was conducted in the field house of the adjacent, and notorious, New York City high school, this one named after Give 'em Hell Harry. Every six weeks or so we'd rotate sports. Touch football outside in the asphalt yard; running and sprinting on Truman's track; and volleyball and basketball, our favorite, in the field house with actual nets, which was something the outdoor courts never had. And then, in the spring, this new thing, soccer, which really wasn't that new at all. Just to kids like us, urban kids, who after school played more basketball or handball or two-hand touch football, always on asphalt to a soundtrack of Afrika Bambaataa and Kurtis Blow or the Black British R&B Invasion of Central Line, Junior, Imagination, and Jimmy Ross.

Soccer? We'd kind of heard about the Cosmos from the sports highlights on the news, but the games were far away, in New Jersey. There was a thing called indoor soccer, the New York Arrows, but that was even farther away, at the Nassau Coliseum, and looked more like hockey.

But every spring, our gym teacher, Mr. Chiarello, who was just like your gym teacher—hairy, bearish, loud—but a bit more streetwise, held up a black-and-white ball with hexagons and pentagons and said, "Yo, listen up, fellas. This right here is a soccer ball. Soccer is the most popular sport in the world."

The tough kids, usually the best athletes, were allowed to refer to him simply as "Chee," and would say, "So Chee, why ain't no one here play it?"

"Yo, I'm tellin' you, they will be soon. Now, listen up, get into two lines."

So we did just that, one class stretched out across the length of a volleyball baseline, and another class, the opponent, on the opposite baseline. Then he told us to pick five players who were good with their feet to step out of the line to actually kick and maneuver with the ball. The rest would stay spread out every few feet and that would be the goal. In other words, there were ten goalkeepers spanning about thirty feet and anything the opposing five field players could manage to get between them was a goal. All on comfy hardwood. This was more ridiculous than the indoor soccer on TV news highlights, where someone named Steve Zungul seemed to score five goals a game for the New York team. Ridiculous, but we played. We loved to play anything, we loved being in gym. There was never any locker-room anxiety of being naked in front of your classmates. The only anxiety was the possibility of the high school kids passing through and bullying us or, more likely, invading bands from our rival IS 180, also connected to the Truman field house, but in the other direction. *Yo, we got each other's back, right?* And anyway, the fashion was to wear your gym shorts under your jeans, above the belt line, with your gym shirt tucked into the shorts. The shirt read "Northeast Bronx Education Park"—blue lettering on orange, the colors of our city, and of the Knicks and Mets.

We did this every spring; but this time something different happened. Someone passed the ball in my direction, and I kicked it between two of the ten goalies strung across that final line. A goal!

Hugs from teammates, my classmates, who liked me already, but now liked me a little more. Then it happened again. A second goal, the winning goal. We won, my homeroom class, 2–1. I was the hero. Then it happened the next week, I scored more goals, we made it to the championship game, and then I don't remember what happened. And then it was done. There was no team or league to join, no one to play with in the street, on the tower-in-the-park grass, or the asphalt, where we played most of our games. That was that. There were no possibilities, no opportunities to improve, not here in the Bronx.

June 13, 1982
Argentina vs. Belgium
Live on SIN

The *New York Times* was in our apartment everyday; we had home delivery. I would look at the sports section first, and I saw that today was the first game of this thing called the World Cup. There was a photo of the referees weighing the game ball, whose design looked wildly different from the black-and-white panels I was used to seeing. I was curious. There had been New York Cosmos games on Channel 9, but my father never watched; he had no money riding on it. On some weekends ABC would show an NASL game and I'd watch for a few minutes once in a while. I had rooted once or twice for the Minnesota Kicks, the only reason being that they played in the greatest stadium in all the world, Metropolitan Stadium in Bloomington, Minnesota, home to my Vikings. My thinking was that it was necessary to support any team that shared this hallowed ground, whether it be the Twins (Rod Carew!), the Kicks, or the Golden Gophers. The Twins were a baseball team; baseball I understood. I was raised on baseball; my father taught me baseball. The Kicks, in these few telecasts on *Wide World of Sports*, they never really sank in. I only remember an African player named Ace Ntsoelengoe. What a name. But this World Cup game I thought I'd

11

check out. It was on TV, on SIN, the Spanish International Network, and there was nothing else to do.

Holy shit! What is this? Marching out in single file, exchanging banners, each team posing for a team photo just before the game; those uniforms, like the very flags themselves. Everyone is overcome with emotion, the fans, the players; the Argentine coach can't stop smoking. And this beautiful moment as soon as the final whistle sounded: players took off their jerseys and exchanged them with an opponent. I wanted to be part of that. It was less than two hours, shorter than a baseball game, or football, basketball, and hockey, but it was exhausting—and exhilarating.

I couldn't wait until tomorrow. And the day after and the day after that.

Tomorrow
June 14, 1982

Every game was on TV, live on SIN in our mornings and afternoons. PBS would show a shortened, seamlessly edited sixty-minute version at eleven o'clock at night, under the program title *Soccer Made in Germany.* "Shame," by Evelyn Champagne King—of the Bronx, by the way—was, for whatever reason, the theme music.

Italy played Poland the next day, the morning game, in a place called Vigo. I had been to Spain, on a family vacation, six years before, but I hadn't heard of Vigo. Since we were one of the few families in my corner of the Bronx to travel, I was always drawn to our massive *Britannica Atlas.* And no short cuts, either, no looking at the index in the back with the longitudinal and latitudinal coordinates with the corresponding page number. Maybe that was efficient, less time consuming, but it was no fun. It was like peeking at the answer key in the back of the teacher's version of a textbook. The fun was in the journey of running my finger up the Portuguese-Spanish border or west to east, along the Pyrenees, to try to find this place. Where the hell was it?

So with the game underway, I searched for Vigo. Madrid is easy, we were in Madrid, and Barcelona, we were supposed to go to Barcelona; I find that, too. But where's this Vigo? I ran my finger over the two-page spread that shows Spain, Portugal, southern France, and northern Morocco. Granada, Valencia, Sevilla, Bilbao. Ah, here, in the left-hand corner, right above Portugal. It looks small; no wonder I missed it.

The game went on, sometimes in the background as my eyes combed the atlas, sometimes in the foreground, when the Spanish announcer grew in urgency, which on this morning was rare. This wasn't like yesterday's game, with the pageantry; that massive, majestic stadium; the emotion; the burst of intensity after the goal was scored; the Belgian, Erwin Vandenbergh, dropping to his knees, not out of contrivance but because he was overcome. No, this was—quiet. The stadium looked small; it had the musical name of Estadio Balaídos. The tempo was much slower, even slower than baseball. *Is that possible?* There was the constant blare of air horns even if nothing of consequence was happening. When I finally found Vigo and put the atlas to the side, I remained glued to the TV, even as nothing continued to happen. The Poles were dressed exactly like their flag—white shirts, red shorts—but why were the Italians in blue shirts and white shorts? I may have been a self-hating Italian, but I knew the flag: red, white, and green. I'd have to find out.

The final score was 0–0. So how to explain this enthralled feeling? I shifted, and accepted, this new biorhythm, and quite easily. At the end of seventh grade, I found two FM stations, WBAI and WLIB, which played reggae music. It was different to what I normally listened to: soul, funk, R&B, and a new thing called rap. "Shame," with its saxophone solo, was an anthem in these parts of the Bronx, before I'd ever heard of *Soccer Made in Germany*. Reggae was black music but its core felt different. You were drawn into it, or, I was told by other seventh-graders, black seventh-graders, you weren't. *Mike, man, how can you listen to that island-mon shit?* Soccer, lilting, more ebb then flow, with spells of soaring lyricism, felt something like this.

Then came the Brazilians. This was still another rhythm, another feel altogether. They played in the second game that day, against the USSR. I had a couple of friends over and we watched it in my room. They were older, my two best friends, my only two friends in Co-op City who hadn't moved away or gotten into the wrong crowd, one black, the other Indian. They were bored by it. *Yo, let's go out and play some ball.* Ball, in the Bronx in 1982, meant only one thing. *Wait, it's almost over, let me just see the end of this game.* Brazil was losing, but look at them. There were the same air horns blown from the crowd but this game had a constant drumbeat and brass harmony from the stands—and it wasn't coming from Soviet fans. They may have been winning, but everyone knew what was coming. Even my best friend, Calvin, who was black, said, "Brazil's gonna win. Ain't they the best at soccer?" Our other best friend, Ravi, who was Indian and knew nothing about soccer, agreed with him.

They were right. A player named Sócrates, so skinny, all arms and legs in those short shorts, delicately skipped past two Soviets and blasted a shot into the corner of the goal. It was said that Sócrates was criticized for not celebrating after goals. This was a soccer player my father could love. Not only did he have, for some reason, the name of the ancient philosopher—my father loved the ancient Greeks, the ancient Egyptians, Sumerians, Etruscans, Romans, all the ancients, and anything historical—but he was indeed a serious man. His club team in Brazil was Corinthians. Not the Jets or the Mets, the Giants or even the Yankees, but *Corinthians*. With his close-cropped beard, black curls, and unsmiling face, he *was* biblical. He could've been a bust in the antiquities wing of Metropolitan Museum. But he was prebiblical, too—he was Sócrates after all—and postmodern, as he was a doctor who chain-smoked. He was twenty-eight years old, but he had the demeanor of a sixty-year-old.

My father would rail against contemporary baseball players who would soak up congratulations after throwing to the right base or moving the runner over. *They're supposed to do these things! It's their job! Rizzuto did that in his sleep!* Sócrates he would embrace, if he'd had the patience for this game. Sócrates had more urgent matters on his mind. A goal, and a spectacular one, like the one he just scored? It was his job and an important one, securing the midfield and aiding in the attack of what appeared to be the best team in the world. No dropping to his knees, like Erwin Vandenbergh. No jumping up and down. Not even a smile, just raising his arms to the gods.

That wasn't the case for his teammate Éder, just Éder—*where did they get these names?*—who scored the spectacular winner. He was so delighted he did a somersault in front of the frenzied crowd. Brazil would be my team. Then we played basketball, the three of us, Calvin, Ravi, and me, a game called "Twenty-One," a game you could play with an odd number of people.

Later, at our dinner table, I said to my parents, "When we went to Spain, how come we didn't go to Vigo?"

"Where's that?" My mother said. "Barcelona, we were supposed to go to Barcelona or Valencia or Sevilla but we got sick."

"Vigo would have been nice for the food," my father said. "It's in the region of Galicia, and they're known to be the best cooks in Spain. Maybe next time. Why? Where did you see Vigo?"

"There was a soccer game there today. Italy played Poland."

"How'd the Italians make out?" he asked.

"It was a tie, 0–0," I said.

"Oh, soccer can end in a tie?"

"I guess so. The regular team that plays in Vigo is called Celta Vigo, like the Boston Celtics—isn't that funny?"

His eyes lit up. "Do you know why that is?" He didn't wait for a response. "The Celts were an Indo-European people who settled in this part of Spain, Galicia, before they eventually found their way to Ireland and the British Isles. I don't pretend to know soccer, but I'd bet it's a historical reference."

I didn't want a history lesson. I wanted to talk soccer. This game wouldn't be passed down to me. I'd have to learn the hard way—or the best way. On my own.

June 23, 1982
Italy vs. Cameroon
Live on SIN

The following week, Italy played, again in Vigo, and this time against a country I'd never heard of: Cameroon. What was immediately striking was not that the team was all black, the first one I'd seen in these first two weeks, but their uniform colors: green shirts, red shorts, gold socks, nearly all the liberation colors, which I knew from my early eavesdropping into reggae on WBAI and WLIB—David Hinds with Steel Pulse singing "Worth His Weight in Gold," *rally round the flag, rally round the red, gold, black, and green.* There was no white anywhere. Where was this place, Cameroon? Out came the *Britannica Atlas.* No cheating. I'd have to run my finger over the continent of Africa until I'd find it. The way some kids my age were comic-book geeks, I always had my head in the atlas. There it is, Cameroon or Cameroun. The capital city is Yaoundé. How is that even pronounced? With the game on in the background—not much was happening—I studied its shape, something like a big Idaho, but flipped. Cameroon was medium in size. It wasn't as big as Zaire, the heart or more the belly of Africa. Nor was it as big as the massive nations to its north: Sudan, Chad, Libya, and the oddly shaped Mali. Who made these borders anyway? I was only a kid, but the way they were drawn up didn't seem to make sense. And what of these tiny countries that bordered it or were nearby? Gabon, Equatorial Guinea, Togo, Benin, and the oddest of all, Gambia, which was virtually completely surrounded by another country, Senegal. How many countries were there in Africa? It was almost impossible to count them from the map without counting some twice. Anyway, I'd try, starting from the northwest and Morocco, since we'd been there in 1976, and moving eastward, then south and west, spiraling down: Morocco, Algeria, Libya, no wait, Morocco, Algeria, Tunisia, Libya . . . Did I count that? Let me get a pen.

Then something happened: Italy scored a goal, which seemed to be inevitable. Then, a minute later, the Spanish announcers appeared to be in shock, as did the Italian players: Cameroon, just like that, scored a goal themselves, their first in the tournament, their first ever in the World Cup finals. They were bursting with joy. The Italians were yelling at each other and making very Italian hand gestures. Those I recognized. The two hands held together, as in prayer, and shaken up and down: "You've got to be kidding." That's how the game ended, like so many had in the past week, in a tie. How could a tie be so riveting? It was enough, barely, for Italy to advance to the second round. Cameroon appeared thrilled to have scored against these legendary Italians and would have to go back home. To Yaoundé.

July 11, 1982
World Cup Final
Italy vs. West Germany
Live on ABC

The World Cup ended, but it felt like a new, refreshing beginning, one possibility after the next. Something else was out there—and my father didn't have the rent money riding on it, like with my other favorite sports and teams. And it helped that my team won. First, I have to tell you, I switched teams. I went with the winner, which is something I'd never done. Well, I went with more than the winner. I went with blood, really. Blood over trend.

I was a Vikings fan precisely because they'd lost Super Bowl XI to the Oakland Raiders. And they didn't just lose; they were pummeled, bullied. When Sammy White was hit so hard by Raiders safety Jack Tatum that his helmet flew off, I thought he'd been decapitated. The Vikings, then, the losers, were my team. Someone had to love them. And I was a Mets fan in the Bronx, during the 1970s glory years of the home-borough Yankees. The Knicks were nothing special, not anymore. I only began following the Knicks during Red Holzman's second, and far less glamorous, tour of duty. So I didn't go with the winner. But when I saw those Brazilians, in canary yellow shirts, against the enemy, the Soviets, with the imposing CCCP on their jersey, I was for Brazil. Éder was the man I wanted to grow up to be. He was dashing, cool, sinewy—I could get all the girls I wanted if I looked like that. But then the impossible happened: Italy beat Brazil. I didn't see it live; my family went to Boston that Fourth of July weekend to get out of the steamy city and also to visit colleges for my sister, who would soon be graduating high school.

We got back on the night of the game and I watched the rebroadcast on PBS. I still had to see it to believe it. I loved all kinds of sports announcers—the CBS boxing team of Tim Ryan and Gil Clancy; ABC's boxing (and bowling) man, Chris Schenkel; Vin Scully on NBC's *Game of the Week*; Al McGuire for college basketball; Verne Lundquist; Cal Ramsey for the Knicks; Al Michaels; Marv Albert; even Cosell. But Toby Charles was quickly developing into my newest hero, more even than Éder, more than any New York Met or Minnesota Viking. Early in the match, he said that the Italians were "switching positions well." I didn't know what this meant exactly, but it sounded like sharp, precise analysis, and Toby sounded confident. The score, the one that had already happened, held up. Italy still won, 3–2. The Brazilians were out, and the Italians would move on to the semifinals. They beat the Poles, the same Poles they'd tied with a few weeks earlier, and beat the West Germans in the final. The Germans were about as evil as the Soviets. Early in the tournament, they had colluded with the Austrians to eliminate the skillful, upstart Algerians. Algeria had the best uniform in the tournament, the colors of their flag: white, a shock of red, and a most perfect shade of green, the color, I found out, of Islam. They upset West Germany, 2–1, and they were punished for it. This sport had conspiracy theories, gamesmanship, out-and-out cheating.

I saw those games, all of them. I saw the epic semifinal against France, saw how they sent a Frenchman off on a stretcher, saw the

French blow a two-goal lead, and a German bicycle kick. I saw the great Michel Platini kiss the ball for luck. And Italy stood up to the Germans, the bigger, badder Germans. I liked Italy's shortest player, Bruno Conti. When Uli Stieleke looked down at him and got in his face, he pushed him back. He was now my favorite player.

But to continue my growing obsession with soccer, I'd have to wait four full years, four interminable years. Colombia would be the next host, in 1986. *Where is Colombia exactly?* I hadn't even started high school; by the time the next World Cup came around I'd be finished with high school. That was hard to fathom—and scary. This sport—during a game, between games, between World Cups—taught patience. It transcended the Gregorian. It taught the meaning of the word *quadrennial.* "Wait till next year," in World Cup time, meant wait four years, which gave it the heft of a political cycle or a lunisolar episode.

I may have been in thrall, but not everyone was. A local sports-writer, Phil Mushnick, of the *New York Post,* wrote a great column titled "Ugly Americanism in Cup Coverage." It read, "While America's soccer fans were thrilled that TV gave as much video attention as it did to the World Cup, it was often both laughable and revolting to hear some of our local sportscasters treat the planet's most popular sport with an ignorance they seemed genuinely proud of. They knew nothing about soccer, therefore, how could you?"

He then went on to list some of the jokes at soccer's expense in the past month:

From WDVM (CBS), Washington DC, June 16: "In another match today, England beat France 3-1. England jumped off to a 1-0 lead and France came back to tie it on this goal. Then England came back, however, to take the lead for good. After some . . . nice setup pass here to Robson. Now he makes it 2-1 on the header. You'll see the replay here. I don't know why I give these guys names; we don't know who they are."

And this from WBZ (NBC), Boston, June 13: "Now I know there are a lot of soccer fans out there because both of them called up after the [six o'clock news] and said, 'Why did you not have highlights from the World Cup?'"

Continued Mushnick: "The same mistakes will probably be made in 1986 and a few sportscasters will wonder aloud next year why the World Cup was cancelled."

I applauded Mushnick, cut out the article, and was determined not to let ignorance ruin my new-found obsession. The question now was where to take it from here.

And then there was a ball.

July 1982
Harry S Truman High School Athletic Field
Bronx, New York

C'mon, we'll go down to Herman's. That's what my father said when I begged him for a soccer ball after the World Cup ended. Herman's was the great sporting-goods chain store in the city. I had a ball; now I had to teach myself to play. There was no one else. Chiarello, the gym teacher, only told us to kick with the inside of the foot, not the toe, but beyond that I didn't know anything. I watched the players closely during the World Cup games and would try to mimic their kicking motion, their movements, their technique. There was a commercial on SIN during the games where someone kicked the ball to himself while keeping it in the air. I could try to do this.

I was in luck, for two reasons. PBS, Channel 13, basically repeated the entire tournament, on weekday mornings, again with Toby Charles's commentary. He'd start off every broadcast, with his brother introducing him, poking a little fun, saying something like, "And now, the man who said, 'O'Neill is in the net, and the ball is offside,' my brother Toby Charles." Apparently, Toby Charles was famous for making the odd nonsensical remark, instead of saying, "O'Neill is offside and the ball is in the net." Daft as he was, I was learning the game through him. So I'd watch all the games over again, like a student, every feint and gesture, every action and inaction.

Then in the afternoon I'd go out with my ball. There I often joined a friend from my huge thirty-three-story building. His name was Amani. He was super smart, two years older than me, same as Ravi, but went to a prestigious boarding school in Connecticut. He was a natural athlete and terribly self-critical. When I scooted under the fence of Truman High School's massive, chain-link-enclosed baseball and football field, a few steps from the back of my building, I saw Amani practicing by himself. He invited me to join and taught me the basics.

He'd run laps around the quarter-mile track for stamina, keep the ball in the air with feet, thighs, and head—that's called juggling, he said—and then to work on his long-distance shooting and passing, he'd drive the ball into the empty grandstand seats. Most times, the ball would slowly dribble down the steps and back to us. If it didn't, we'd have to climb the steps and get it, but that would strengthen our legs, he said. He had it all figured out and could care less if he practiced all by himself. He always did his own thing and never cared what anyone thought. I would be the same, then.

He told me what it was like to play on his high school team. They ran so much in practice they'd throw up, he said. *Word?* Yes, he said, you'll have to be ready for that. But he encouraged me to try out for my high school team. I wouldn't be going to Truman, and they didn't even have a team. But he knew of the New Rochelle school I would be attending—another black kid on his floor went there—and said I should practice every day and maybe I'd be able to play.

One hot afternoon that summer I was there before he was. Soon I saw him approaching the field, but with two men on either side of him, one with a mane of salt-and-pepper dreadlocks. These are my uncles, he said, visiting from Jamaica. Come practice with us, Amani said. Ya mon, the dreadlocked uncle said encouragingly, let's have a trainin' session. We formed a small conceptual circle with the aim of juggling the ball between the four of us. Jugglin' is key, Amani's uncle said. And don't let no one tell you it's not important or that you don't use it in a game. If they say that, it means they can't do it. It teaches touch and ball control, and soccer is all about touch and control.

This was my first juggling with a group. I had been practicing obsessively for several weeks now, but this was the most difficult form of ball control, so more times than not the string ended with me. I'm sorry, I'd say and say again and again, I'm sorry. Finally the dreadlocked uncle said, No problem, mon, no problem. You just learnin'. And remember: never say you're sorry.

Our practice session, my first with anyone besides Amani, ended, and the uncles were headed back to Jamaica.

I listened to everything Amani told me that summer, but in a few weeks, he was gone, too—back up to his fancy Connecticut private school, where no one had heard of Co-op City. I played, in hundreds of yards of empty space, alone, beside a notorious city high school with identical tower buildings looming.

September 5, 1982
New York Cosmos vs. San Diego Sockers
Giants Stadium
East Rutherford, New Jersey

In the days that followed the FIFA-UNICEF World All-Star Game a month earlier, I begged my father to take me to another soccer game. He relented. Giants Stadium was still the home of the land's greatest team: the Cosmos. As luck would have it, the playoffs were upon us and my father got tickets for game two in the second-round series against the unfortunately named San Diego Sockers.

The North American Soccer League (NASL) had many silly names for its teams—the Kicks, the Philadelphia Atoms, the Montreal Manic (pronounced man—EEK, with a French inflection)—but the Sockers lacked even a geographical pun, like the Seattle Sounders or Vancouver Whitecaps.

This was, as announcer Jim Karvellas called it on WOR Cosmos telecasts and radiocasts, "Cosmos Country." Pelé—the DiMaggio of soccer, my father called him, even if he didn't know this game—and Franz Beckenbauer, the most elegant of Germans, had both retired. But Giorgio Chinaglia, this Italian no one seemed to like, even local Italians, was still there, as was Carlos Alberto, the epitome of grace. Was it soccer he was playing or warming up for a ballet performance? There was Ricky Davis, the endearingly boyish Californian, who was the poster boy for the future of American soccer. And a worthy one. He was not only *our* best all-around player, he became a very good all-around midfielder, period; not flashy but hardworking, reliable, tireless, positive. American. He held his own at the UNICEF game; he belonged. An American could excel at this game.

How could he not get better playing and practicing with all these great players on an everyday basis? Andranik Eskandarian, aka Eski, an Armenian who played for Iran in the 1978 World Cup. Vladislav Bogicevic, aka Bogie, who was a starter in the '74 World Cup for Yugoslavia, appeared uncaring, even lazy, but had a freakish kind of peripheral vision. So if he didn't run it was because he didn't have to; he would anticipate his teammates' movements in advance. They would receive his passes in perfect stride, in open space, with opportunity, with gratitude. He was thirty-two now, past his soccer prime as I was learning and playing on artificial surfaces—a plastic abomination not sanctioned by FIFA—but he was still as expert as I suspect he ever was. There were not one, but two Dutch players from the Total Football 1974 and '78 teams: Wim Rijsbergen and Johan Neeskens, who more resembled a seventeenth-century Flemish aristocrat than athlete.

They had the great silent German goalkeeper Hubert Birkenmeier, and there was his perennial backup, David Brcic—like Davis, an American, perhaps as good as Birkenmeier, perhaps better. He was agile, athletic, with dazzling reflexes, always in the right place at the right time—on the field, that is. Career-wise, he was wrong place, wrong time, on a team that didn't appreciate him, in a country that didn't appreciate him, in an era that didn't appreciate him. Like so many of his teammates: Ricky Davis, Steve Moyers, Chico Borja, Jeff Durgan, Darryl Gee.

The Sockers had Julie Veee (yes, Julie, though he was a man, and Veee with three *e*'s), Ade Coker, and Kaz Deyna. What spectacular names.

The crowd wasn't what it was for the UNICEF match, about thirty-four thousand, filling less than half the stadium. It was still thirty-four thousand people, though; substantially more than the Mets drew, a lot more than the Mets drew, but was it half full or half empty? The entire upper deck, where we sat last time, was empty, a massive section of empty seats in bright red. That section alone was the size of some entire stadiums, like the Estadio Balaídos in Vigo.

Gone was that bursting intensity, the sense of levitation, the feeling of this being a gathering of an in-the-know tribe. It was the playoffs, it meant something, it meant a lot, but it was against the Sockers, with a late-summer chill in the air. And it was getting late. My father never wore a wristwatch but he kept glancing at the clock on the scoreboard. We had to make sure we got a bus back to the Port Authority, and the Port Authority being what it was—a space of decadent possibility on the one hand, I suppose, and the despair of extinguished hope on the other—the earlier the better, even if there was never a good time to be at the Port Authority.

But this game was tied and it looked as if it was headed, not for "extra-time," as Toby Charles called it in the epic France–West Germany semifinal, but "overtime." It wasn't the only Americanization the NASL used. One was obvious: in two weeks' time, the Cosmos or the Sockers would play in the final, known as the Soccer Bowl. There were others: in the box score, the goal scorer was listed with two assist-makers, as in the NHL; and the time of the goal, also as in hockey, was listed by the minute and second. To break a tie at the end of "overtime," a game would go into a "shootout," a more skillful rendition of the penalty-kick round, in which a player began at the thirty-five yard line—another NASL wrinkle—and had five seconds to advance the ball and shoot past the oncoming keeper, who was more often than not referred to here as the "goalie" (again, as in ice hockey).

Shootouts had their pluses, but please, not tonight. My father wanted to get back. Then I had a flashback: I had been to two NFL games, both in 1979—one on a Monday night at Shea Stadium with my father and another here at Giants Stadium, where the Giants had played the St. Louis Cardinals on a frigid Sunday afternoon. Somehow, with my sister and two cousins, a few years older than us, we'd missed the last bus and were stranded outside Giants Stadium past dark, in the middle of god-damned nowhere, freezing and hungry. No taxis, no subways or trains, no more buses, no stadium officials that I can remember. Was there even a pay phone? There must've been because we called a relative who picked us up hours later. That feeling of being stranded was as traumatic as I'd had as a kid, more than the New York City subways or the Port Authority, simply because there was no one and nothing around, which is why suburbia, with its lawns that came to the curb, its cul-de-sacs, its artifice, its silence, always gave me the willies. When we would visit friends in Westchester who moved out of Co-op City, it was nice—for a day, maybe an overnight.

I never wanted to get stranded again, here at Giants Stadium or anywhere. On the way out, the bus from Port Authority had been, like the stadium, half empty. How many buses would even be heading back? It wasn't clear at the Port Authority; there was no schedule and little in the way of customer service. We couldn't leave a contest that was tied late in the game. My father may have been indulging me in my new soccer addiction, as he had years earlier with my Star Trek enthusiasm, but he valued sports competition too much to leave a game before a winner was decided. It's why he always held baseball in higher esteem: it couldn't end in a tie and, most of all, unlike the other American sports, it was not managed by a clock. So we watched the action—the San Diego Sockers hanging in there against the mighty Cosmos—nervous, glancing up at the clock, both the game clock and the actual clock.

Please someone score, someone score. Thank god for Jeff Durgan. He was the fierce young American central defender from the Pacific Northwest, built like a Pac 10 tight end, who was part of the bright future of American soccer. He didn't have the boy-next-door charm of Ricky Davis but the edgier look of a rock star. He went up high for a header, I think off a corner kick, and scored—89:02 Durgan (Bogicevic). Game, essentially, over. Time to run for that bus.

When we arrived at the Port Authority, my father had to run, literally, to the bathroom; stadium food often worked on his stomach. He told me to wait outside the men's room, that I shouldn't look at or talk to anyone, that he'd be right out. He came out a minute later with a facial expression that I'd never seen. It was one of repulsion and disgust, with his hand over his nose and mouth. Was it a smell, a sight? Was there blood, vomit, shit, other bodily fluids? Was it on the floor, on the walls, on the ceiling? I asked. "What? What is it?" He didn't say. Let's just get the hell out of here as fast as possible, he said. And we did, onto Seventh Avenue, whatever Cosmos fans there were on the buses, long since scattered in the entropy.

September 1982
Bronx, New York

The Cosmos went on to beat the Tulsa Roughnecks—speaking of silly nicknames—in the next round of the playoffs and defeated the Seattle Sounders in the Soccer Bowl. It was at Jack Murphy Stadium in San Diego in front of just twenty-two thousand people. Why so few? Chinaglia, this man everyone loved to hate, scored the only goal. After the game, the players sang "Guantanamera," but instead of the familiar lyrics, substituted each player's name. This was reported in the *New York Times* the next day by George Vecsey, who appeared as transfixed and transformed from the World Cup that just ended as I had. He was reliving it—Paolo Rossi's improbable hat trick, the West Germany-France semifinal, the peculiar details, the joyous idiosyncrasies—in his mind and by extension his column, as if he didn't want it to end.

The Cosmos were at least at a good place stateside, and somewhat closer to home, for us to resume our enthusiasm. They weren't what they were; Giants Stadium not as full, the international stars not as glittering, but you were still watching men of great skill, with international "caps"—a new soccer word learned—on their CVs. Maybe they played in the 1974 or 1978 World Cups, but there were newer Cosmos who might still become stars on the international scene. There was Richard Chinapoo, a former standout for Long Island University now with the Cosmos who was, as WOR radio analyst Seamus Malin sophisticatedly put it, a Trinidadian international.

Seamus was a beacon. While I loved the enthusiasm of his Cosmos play-by-play man, Jim Karvellas, my father soon informed me that Karvellas was an announcer, and a good one, of all trades, mainly professional basketball. Seamus was just soccer—my father hadn't heard of him. He went to Harvard, it was brought up more than once, and brought a level of depth to his color commentary that most other American announcers didn't, never mind the sport. Maybe because he wasn't very hyperbolic in the "Holy Cow," "going, going, gone goodbye" vain that I was used to and that he wasn't American, but Irish, even if his brogue was barely detectable. He always said what country a player was from, how many caps they had, and if they'd played in a World Cup. He provided a context. It had only been a couple of months, but I was learning more through him. He loved the expression "That's a good ball," not "That's a good pass." Another one was "Play on, says the referee," meaning a foul was called but the referee, with arms outstretched, would not disrupt the flow of play if the fouled team had an advantage.

Seamus would praise the Englishman Steve Hunt, the "ex-Coventry man," he'd call him, for being a classic winger, stretching the field wider, creating space in the middle of the field—he may have said "middle of the park." And he praised Hunt for his uncanny ability to cross the ball from nearly anywhere at any angle, especially

from "the touchline." I, on the other hand, liked Hunt for the way
he wore his socks: down around his ankles, without shin guards
like so many players in the West Germany-France semifinal. It was
strange that WOR would break away to a commercial while the game
was being played, sometimes missing a goal. ABC did this, too, for
the World Cup final. Not that I was complaining.

And there was still Toby Charles on PBS. With the World Cup
over now, he called the weekly German game, which was known as
the Bundesliga. He still talked about things like "switching positions"
and he taught us all how to pronounce Borussia Mochengladbach.
I even learned through Tony Tirado on SIN, which didn't break
for commercials until half time. I didn't speak Spanish, even if my
mother insisted that I should, that "it was the future," but I was
learning *futbol* Spanish. *Tiro de esquina, mediocampo, la derecha,
izquierda, el arbitro, muy cerca, directo, indirecto, tiro libre, falta,
penal (penal, penal, sí señor!)*. But more than that, I was learning just
from his cadence and intonation when something of consequence
was happening. His voice was the cue, like music in a movie. I
learned the word *peligroso*. Toby Charles would say it a different
way: "There's danger there."

On the newsstand, there wasn't much soccer coverage. The local
papers had short Cosmos game reports, if that, and the occasional
musings of George Vecsey, still depressed the World Cup was over.
A little magazine called *Soccer Digest*—there was also *Baseball Digest*
and *Football Digest*—was a formulaic monthly. The magazine *Soccer
America* had NASL news, some international coverage, college soccer,
and a lot on grassroots leagues, which seemed to be everywhere.
Apparently, there was a thriving local club called the Brooklyn Ital-
ians. What a hilarious name, I thought, the Brooklyn Italians. New
Jersey was a hotbed, maybe *the* hot bed, but so was, of all places, St.
Louis. *St Louis?* But there was nothing that covered these foreign
leagues, where great men like Sócrates played, on these teams, Real
Madrid—pronounced rey-al, not real—Internazionale, Arsenal,
Boca Juniors, Argentinos Juniors, VfB Stuttgart. *What could the vfB*

stand for? And why is the f lowercase? It was foreign and off-limits, unless you could read a foreign-language paper.

In one of these publications, or maybe after the *Soccer Made in Germany* telecast, there was an ad for a book on the just-completed World Cup by Franz Beckenbauer. It wasn't cheap; it was published in hardcover with color photography. With the help of my sister, I begged my father for the book. He got us a money order and within weeks we received it. There was a four-hundred-word recap for each game with great photos. Like the program for the FIFA-UNICEF All-Star game, I memorized every word. I came across the phrase "The ball is round," for the first time. It read: "'The ball is round.' This short and precise phrase is still true, even in the computer age, as the final results of the first round proved."

If only I could buy more stuff: books, T-shirts, replica jerseys, shorts, anything. But there was just this book. Access was limited. It was time to play.

Fall 1982
New Rochelle, New York

As it turned out, making my high school soccer team wasn't very difficult. *Everyone made it.* This was not done out of any altruistic reasons—of giving every kid a chance, improving their self-esteem, their self-worth through sports. No, nothing like that. We just needed bodies. The school was pathetically small, literally thirty students per grade. Each team—baseball, basketball, and especially soccer—needed every able-bodied boy.

There was little choice of where I could go to high school. I wasn't smart enough for Stuyvesant, where my father attended forty years before, or Bronx High School of Science, due west across the Borough Beautiful, so it was either the biggest high school in the city's public school system, Harry S Truman, a five-minute walk, or the smallest private school in the history of the world, New Rochelle Academy, a private school with no cachet, no influence, no prestigious alumni, no nothing except a "headmaster" with delusions of grandeur. By 1982 Truman was a ghetto high school. It was one thing to practice soccer in its open, desolate field in the summer; it was something else to attend classes there. (Catholic school was out of the question; my mother had lived through a Catholic school education in Brooklyn and forbade it for my sister and I). No learning or college preparation would happen at Truman, only a day-to-day grind of survival, of not getting beat up, of honing the social skill—or antisocial skill—of not being seen, of preserving self-respect and dignity. And there was no soccer team.

I don't, for the life of me, remember who the coach was my freshman year except that he knew nothing about soccer. He was a gym teacher, basically, and coached the basketball and baseball teams, which somehow were competitive. The soccer team had long been a joke in the school and had gone several years since they'd won a game or even scored a goal. We didn't have proper uniforms. They looked like gym uniforms in the city public schools, in all-tomato red. Before we touched a ball, we were put through grueling running drills. Amani was right; I could've thrown up.

I tried to engage my new teammates, and classmates, in soccer conversation. Did you watch the World Cup? *Did you see France-West Germany? Algeria's cool uniforms? Did you see the Paolo Rossi hat trick against Brazil? Who's your favorite player? Zico? Falcão? Zoff? Keegan? Rummenigge? Platini?* No one had, nor did they seem to care that they had missed the greatest spectacle in sport. All they talked about on our team was who was going to play fullback or halfback.

I'm going to play right fullback.

Okay, if you play right full, I'll play right halfback.

I've got center back.

I'm right halfback.

I'll be center half.

Who's going to play goalie this year?

From Toby Charles, I knew just forward, midfield, defense, sweeper, wingers, and "keeper," not "goalie." He used the term fullback, but rarely. Here, now, with these new kids, everyone was a fullback or halfback as in the NFL. I was waiting to hear someone call out, "I have first dibs on quarterback." They seemed to be Americanizing the sport. Maybe that made sense, but I didn't know what any of this actually meant or where I would play, if I would play. *Everyone plays, right?*

I was used sparingly that first season. I was tiny, even by soccer standards, probably just a little over a hundred pounds. For our "home games," we played in another part of New Rochelle, on a rancid public field, with no nets on the goals, barely visible white lines, bumps and depressions, little actual grass, and most alarming, broken glass. The only thing we were taught to do by the coach/gym teacher, in our practices and now in games, was to "boot it." That or "put a boot in it" or "stick a head in it." I'd never heard the great Toby Charles use that expression on *Soccer Made in Germany.* Or Seamus Malin.

If you couldn't boot it long enough or far enough—forget if it went to a teammate—you didn't play. If you didn't put a good enough boot in it, you were seen as not quite masculine enough to play, possibly homosexual. *Don't play like a faggot, boot it!*

When I did play, I was in the completely wrong position of left fullback. I had only started to develop my right foot over the summer, but I had little or no ability with my left foot. *Please, don't let the ball come to me.* This was Little League baseball all over again. When the ball did come to me, and the opposing players, all much bigger than I was, set upon me, I tried to clear it down the wing with my left foot so, at worst, it would go out of bounds or at best a teammate might run on to it. I'd seen the top players do this in the World Cup. But I didn't kick it very far. *Mike, boot it! That's not the way to boot it!* Next time down—*please ball, don't come to me*—in the same position, knowing I couldn't boot it, I tried to dribble past this massive oncoming forward. It didn't work; he easily stripped it from me. *Mike! What are you doin'? Don't try that fancy shit, boot it! This isn't the Cosmos.* I nodded to the sidelines. This was turning into a nightmare. One more time, the ball rolled into this massive area I had to cover and I shifted the ball to my strong right foot but sent the ball to the opposition in the middle of the field. *Mike! Mike! That's no way to boot it!*

That was the whole season. I didn't play much, and when I did, I said "sorry" a lot. *Never say you're sorry.* We lost every game without scoring a goal. When we played away games, the other schools, which did have prestige, had real soccer uniforms, their own fields, with smooth grass, and even cheerleaders. They even gave us snacks and beverages at half time; and when the game ended, orange slices and granola bars. My school didn't even do that for us, its own players. We had one water cooler. The thrill of this new game was gone. Organized play wasn't what I had hoped.

November 1982
Lorenzo's Barbershop
Park Avenue South
New York, New York

My father had good news: he found someone he knew who liked soccer. It was his barber, Lorenzo, on Twenty-Eighth Street and Park Avenue South. Lorenzo was from "the other side," Sicily, and apparently looked like the Italian actor Michele Placido. *He's some actor that Michele Placido.* I was a teenager now, and it was time to change barbers anyway; the place across the street was for kids and old men.

He took me on Saturday mornings. It was silent; more a funeral home than the raucous barbershop my black friends told me about in Co-op City's Section 5, where there was communal conversation and snapping. Lorenzo was a man of few words and not only because his English was limited. Before I got on the chair, I heard my father talk to him, what little talk there was, in a combination of English and Southern Italian dialect. My father did most of the talking.

I had always been shy, so when I got on the chair, I didn't say much, just something like, Not too short.

Just a little trim?

Well, short but not too short.

He repeated, Short but not too short.

Yes, I said, short but not too short.

I felt stupid already. How could I ask him about soccer? It took several visits for me to work up the courage to ask the simplest of questions: So, you like soccer?

He quickly perked up, and looked straight at me, though the mirror. Yes, he said. But that's all he said. This wouldn't be easy.

Did he like the Italian national team? Yes, of course. And what was his favorite club team? Juve, he said. Who? Juve, Juventus—you know Juventus? Yes, I said. I knew they had Paolo Rossi, Dino Zoff, Marco Tardelli, and Claudio Gentile.

And now Platini and Boniek, he said. You know Platini and Boniek?

Yes, from the World Cup and the World All-Star Game. Did he go to the World All-Star Game?

No, he shrugged, almost dismissively, as if to suggest, why bother?

Then, as he dusted me off, he asked in a broken English mumble: Do you watch the game on Sunday?

Watch what game on Sunday? I asked.

The game from Italy, Sunday morning. (There was a live game from Serie A, on WYNC Channel 31.)

Oh wow, I said. I'll watch.

And *Novantesimo* at about 1:15, he said.

Nova-what? I said.

Novantesimo Minuto, the Ninetieth Minute, was the highlight show of all the goals and key plays in every Serie A game. It was supposed to begin at 1:15, but this being the feed from RAI in Italy, it started, just like Lorenzo said, at about 1:15; it might also begin at 1:13 or 1:17 or even more toward 1:25. It wasn't listed in the *New York Times* TV guide; it was a secret bit of knowledge.

When my father took me for a coffee-shop hamburger on the next corner at eleven in the morning, I told him that Lorenzo was a quiet man. Yes, my father said, but you have to understand, he's had tragedy in his life: he's a widower, he recently lost his wife. All he has is his son. I suspect soccer is the only thing that gives him any kind of joy in life.

February 1983
Mexico City, Mexico

In the winter of early 1983, we went on a family vacation, though not to Puerto Rico where my father had gambling associates who let us stay in their apartments for free in lieu of paying my father what they actually owed him. We'd been there six times from 1974 to 1982, and being we didn't swim or scuba dive or sail or jet ski, there was only so much we could do at the city beach in Condado, only so many drinks to sip, so many walks in Old San Juan. We loved Puerto Rico but with my father able to afford a midwinter trip, my parents decided we would go to Mexico for the first time. There were all sorts of bounced-checks drama—my father couldn't really afford this trip after all—but this was no particular surprise to us. We were accustomed to his odd ways with money—irresponsible yet charming; always short yet always generous. What shocked us most in Mexico City was the air quality, or lack thereof. We hadn't known anyone who had been there, and the pollution—despite us being from New York City, despite the exhaust of the four different city buses puffing away in front of our building—jarred the system. That, combined with the altitude—we'd never been so high—made breathing, the most essential of acts, seem like a gift, one we were lucky to have.

But life in Mexico City went on, without anyone seeming to notice. In Chapultepec Park on a sunny afternoon—or was it Alameda?—couples strolled hand in hand, grandparents played with children, clowns performed. No one played soccer; there didn't appear to be room. Mexico hadn't made it to the last World Cup, but I knew they loved this sport. SIN would televise games from Estadio Azteca, a massive structure that had hosted many matches in the 1970 World Cup (one whose transcendence had been alluded to in the FIFA World All-Star Game program). Azteca always looked packed, and bright and sunny, and it always seemed as if Club América, in its all-yellow uniform, was shown every week. Club América—were they the Yankees of Mexican soccer? I begged my father to go see Club América. But he was short of money, especially hard cash, and no, we'd have to go next time if we ever came back to Mexico. Or back in New York for the Cosmos. We did ask the concierge at the hotel how many teams there were in Mexico City, and if he liked Club América. He shook his head no—Club América were bad; you must like Cruz Azul. And by the way there were four teams in Mexico City. *Four teams?!* My father thought it would be a two-team city, but this was even more than Yankees/Dodgers/ Giants. We did see the stadium from a distance, in a taxi. I couldn't keep my eyes off it, the ring of the upper deck a halo in haze. I did the next best thing; I bought postcards of it, and on the back wrote, "Home of the 1970 World Cup Final." I placed these cards—of the interior and exterior of the Azteca, a place I had almost been to, that I'd seen from a distance—on the cork board above my bed.

March 3, 1983
New Rochelle, New York

Next to my cork board, there was something new, all jagged shapes and pastels: a giant map of Africa. It had been a gift. Six months before, on the first day of soccer practice, I made my first high school friend. His name was Lau, in my grade but two years younger; he had been accelerated ahead. He was from Africa. I approached him and asked questions. Where was he from? Tanzania, he said. Tan-zania, it was clear from his pronunciation, not Tan-ZANE-ia. Where was that in relation to Cameroon? Nowhere near, he said, Tanzania is in the East, near Kenya. Cameroon was in the west, where most of the

African soccer powers were. Did he watch the World Cup? A little, he said, but he didn't seem to share my enthusiasm, for soccer or any sport. As a player, he was no worse than me, but no better either. He seemed more concerned with geopolitics; his father worked at the United Nations and had once ran for president of Tanzania. *Word?* He also liked reggae music. That, too, we had in common.

Did I like Bob Marley?

Of course.

He loved soccer, you know.

No, I didn't. Wow.

Did I like Jimmy Cliff?

Yes, "The Harder They Come."

Did you see the movie?

No, I didn't know it was a movie.

I was fifty-fifty on this mini-quiz he gave me.

Then I came back with one: What about Scientist? I asked.

Who's that?

I heard him on WBAI, on the Hapte Selassie show, I said. He did a series of songs called Ten Dangerous Matches on the album called *Scientist Wins the World Cup.*

Yeah? How does it go?

Man, I can't sing, and there aren't many words. *Love, it's confidential and love it's universal and love it's international, love* . . . But I'll bring it in. I taped it from the radio.

I was quick to ask more questions about Tanzania, and he was more than willing to answer; he seemed to appreciate it, as no one else seemed to care. The name Tanzania came from a combination of the words Tanganyika, the large mainland territory, and Zanzibar, the small island off the coast. *Wow!* The language was Swahili, which he spoke at home. His family was from Mwanza, on the southern coast of Lake Victoria. Was that the capital? No, the capital had been Dar es Salaam, on the coast, but was moved to Dodoma, inland. Dar es Salaam, Haven of Peace, was still the most important city. He called it Dar, just Dar.

Six months after that first practice, on my birthday—the same day as Zico's, which I still remembered from the FIFA World All-Star Game program—Lau gave me a present: the map, folded up in tidy squares. I loved it, and up it went on my bedroom wall next to the cork board. It was as good as a soccer gift, and in a way it was. Now I could learn the map of Africa by osmosis, while I was sleeping, with the flags and headshots of each country's leader. There was Tanzania, right there, lower right, and there was Dar. No longer would I need the *Britannica Atlas*, whose spine was coming undone. I'd look around Tanzania from my bed. There's Rwanda, I can barely see it from here, where those kids in the game program photo were from. And Burundi, another tiny place, and Zaire, the massive Zaire. And there was Uganda, another neighbor. Uganda I knew. I knew Kampala was the capital. I knew this because of a man named Cornelius Boza Edwards, a prize fighter, and a good one, a champion in one of the lighter-weight divisions. When Tim Ryan and Gil Clancy announced his fights on CBS they said he was from Kampala, Uganda, fighting out of London, England. This sounded like the coolest place on earth, Kampala, Uganda.

On the map's border were the flags, all bright with diagonals, stars, triangles, crescent moons, torches, eagles, sometimes all in one, not like Europe's redundant tricolors and sideways crosses. In morning daydream, fading in geometry class, I'd figure out how these colors and patterns would be implemented into a national soccer team uniform.

The map was dated. Rhodesia, for one, was still Rhodesia, not Zimbabwe, and for Uganda's leader, there was still a headshot of Idi Amin Dada. I knew Amin as a grotesque figure from the TV trailer of a recent movie called *Amin: The Rise and Fall*. But so what if the map was dated? It was still invaluable, even if more countries might change their names, their capitals moved inland. There were still things to learn, lakes to run my finger around—there's Lake Victoria, the Serengeti Plain to its south and east, Kilimanjaro east of that, hovering over the border. There were names of presidents and prime ministers that needed to be pronounced just so, with the great care that only comes with deep familiarity and frequency, with the emphasis on the right syllable—it's Tan-zan-ia, I'd now tell people, not Tan-ZANE-ia. Just the fact that it listed Idi Amin as Idi Amin *Dada* gave me an extra kernel of knowledge that might somehow, somewhere, be useful, even if he was, Lau told me this, in exile in Saudi Arabia.

Tanzania was led by an anti-Amin, Lau assured me, a kindly-looking man with gray hair, Julius K. Nyerere. He was a genteel socialist. He was my favorite African president now, like his name-sake Julius Erving, the good doctor.

But more to the point, Lau, will Tanzania make the next World Cup? Maybe, I hope, he said, but not likely. Organization was lacking, no infrastructure was in place to nurture and cultivate talent, the country so poor, with malaria, which he would have recurrences of, an ongoing problem. So don't count on it, he said. In fact, it'll probably never happen.

Sometime in 1983
Victory

I had a new favorite movie. I didn't know what my previous favorite movie was. My parents were movie buffs, especially of foreign films from France, Italy, Sweden, India, Japan, and West Germany. It hadn't been passed down yet. I was between kids' movies and real movies. *Star Wars*? Eh, it was okay, but so long ago. And I preferred *Star Trek*, still shown on WPIX, Channel 11, which seemed to show only Yankees games and repeats of old TV shows and movies. *Close Encounters*? Didn't even see it. *Rocky*? Nah, I was rooting for Apollo Creed. I'd seen *Downhill Racer* on TV late at night once, with Robert Redford, this guy my mother and father always talked about, as an Olympic skier. I liked that. And I liked the *Airport* series with George Kennedy and *Capricorn One* with O. J. Simpson. But nothing, nothing, would come close to *Victory*, a masterpiece.

It had been released in 1981 but now was making the rounds on TV. My parents agreed to watch it this night, on Channel 11, if I'm not mistaken, because not only was it helmed by a worthy director—John Huston of *The Maltese Falcon*, *The Treasure of the Sierra Madre*—but it starred Michael Caine, who they loved in so many films, and the great, and they emphasized great, Max von Sydow, *a giant, an absolute giant.* I don't know what shocked them more, the fact that he was in a movie about soccer or that he was in a movie with Sylvester Stallone. More importantly, for me, it starred Pelé and other real soccer players.

It's the story of an American prisoner of war named Hatch (played by Stallone) who intends to escape with a team of Allied soccer greats drafted to play in an exhibition match against the Third Reich's all-stars. Of course, Hatch being American, he can't play soccer, though he must be good with his hands, and Michael Caine, the cockney coach and former West Ham United player, appoints him as goalkeeper. During a practice, Stallone asks Caine, "Where do I stand for a corner kick?" *Yeah where do you stand for a corner kick?* I had a year of game experience, if you could call it that, under my belt and still didn't know. And I was a left fullback, a very right-footed one, but I should know where my own keeper is positioned. Sly doesn't get a straight answer; three times he asks, until finally, Caine says, "The far post."

Von Sydow is a good Nazi, preferring the poetry of the game to propaganda. Pelé plays the harmonica on the top bunk, is the object of Nazi on-field viciousness, and plays on with a dislocated shoulder. The crowd—and the game is in Paris—chants "Vic-toire! Vic-toire! Vic-toire!"

When they have a chance to escape at half time from the bowels of the stadium through the Parisian sewer system, they decide to go out for the second half instead. Pelé scores on a bicycle kick to tie the game, but when the Nazis are gifted a penalty kick in the dying seconds, it's the goalkeeper, Hatch, Stallone, Rocky—*Vic-toire! Vic-toire!*—who makes the save. The game ends in a tie, 4–4; the war won.

My parents were ready to get up and change the channel—maybe something better was on one of the three major networks now—as the Parisian fans stormed the field, kicked open the gates, and hid their heroes under coats and bowler hats, but no, there were still credits, and these weren't just credits, this was a roster, and John Huston, brilliant director that he was, did the credits just like that, a roster: Pelé, Brazil; Osvaldo Ardillas, Argentina, the same Ardillas from the Argentine World Cup team, who was in my FIFA All-Star Game program, incredible; Kaz Deyna, Poland (and the San Diego Sockers, I wanted to shout); John Wark, Scotland; Bobby Moore, England.

Well, that was cute, my mother said. Yeah, it was funny, my father said.

Cute? Funny? Were we watching the same movie, I mean film? This was a cinematic achievement that would stand the test of time! *And you're supposed to be film buffs?!*

June 5, 1983
Fiorentina vs. São Paulo
Cosmos vs. Seattle Sounders
Giants Stadium
East Rutherford, New Jersey

It was a new year, a new season. It was time, again, to beg. Never underestimate the act of begging. Soon we—all four of us, my parents, sister, and me—were off to the Port Authority, in the sunshine of high noon, blinding and warm, with the final destination being Giants Stadium.

Was the Port Authority any less what it was—name the adjective: decadent, seedy, intimidating, vile—on a Sunday, awash in deep spring sunlight? We took a taxi, across town, through the muck, the Deuce, like the Kurtis Blow record. Why I don't remember, probably because my mother, whose ideal afternoon was shopping in Lord & Taylor or wandering through the Metropolitan

Museum, refused to walk west of the New York Public Library; Bryant Park was a park in name only. There was unshakable traffic on Forty-Second Street, maybe something happened, and we took a detour, up Sixth Avenue west on Forty-Third or Forty-Fifth and down Seventh, each square block more seamy than the next, something about sex everywhere—and drugs, though not advertised. While some people were in church finishing mass, clasping hands, *peace be with you*, people here, were just finishing their Saturday night, pursuing or succumbing to vice, which they may have hated themselves for. That or caressing their pain. They were, on Sunday morning, now early afternoon, running away, or running toward, their shame and relief.

Do you look away? And where do you look? Being fifteen, I wanted to look, at all of it, but felt I should look away; my mother and sister were there in the backseat with me, my father on the jump seat of one of the dowdy old checker cabs. I thought my mother was going to cover my eyes as we drove past great big marquees with SEX SEX SEX; PEEP PEEP PEEP; GIRLS GIRLS GIRLS; LIVE LIVE LIVE; all apparently for twenty-five cents. *Oh god, what this looks like.* She'd never been to a soccer game in her life; we'd only seen the Mets, Yankees, and Knicks as a family, but she couldn't get to Cosmos Country fast enough.

Not that this was just a Cosmos game. This had the added zip of international glamour. It was a doubleheader, part of the annual Transatlantic Challenge Cup series, which included the Cosmos and another NASL team (this year it was the Seattle Sounders) and two foreign clubs: Fiorentina of Florence, Italy, and São Paulo of Brazil. Portuguese and Italian were spoken, on the bus from Port Authority, on the concession lines, in the seats.

The Italians stood out more to me, not because they were Italian but because they had World Cup players on the roster. Not only a starter on the championship team, Giancarlo Antognoni—*Like the film director? No, different spelling*—who scored the winning goal for Europe in the FIFA World All-Star Game the year before, but also Francesco Graziani and the Argentines Daniel Passarella and Daniel Bertoni.

My scope was primarily limited to the World Cup, and especially to the players who took part in last year's, but also those who'd played in past World Cups (Eski, Bogie, Chinaglia, Carlos Alberto), and who might play in future World Cups (Ricky Davis, Jeff Durgan, Steve Moyers, Daryl Gee, one would hope). I still dipped into the FIFA All-Star Game program and learned most of the past greats: Bobby Charlton, Johan Cruyff, Alfredo Di Stefano, Eusébio, Just Fontaine, Garrincha, Gerd Müller, Ferenc Puskás, Lev Yashin, on and on.

There were no World Cup players on São Paulo, except the bald goalkeeper, Waldir Peres, and goalkeepers didn't seem very exciting to me, unless it was Yashin, long retired, a superhero dressed all in black. There was no Sócrates on São Paulo, no Éder, no Leandro, no Cerezo, no Paulo Isidoro. I loved how Toby Charles had said his name last summer in the replays of the World Cup games, almost as one name, like the other one-name, one-man carnivals: *Pauloisidoro*. He was one of the few Brazilians with two names, and Toby made it one. So no Brazilian national team members. Sergihno, the center forward, Paul Gardner wrote, was "utterly inadequate," had been with the club but left, as a young striker named Careca was emerging. And there was no Zico, Arthur Antunes Coimbra—I had memorized his real name, like I had with Edson Arantes do Nascimento.

These club teams, not just Fiorentina and São Paulo, but the others I'd come across, with these grand names—Nottingham Forest, Red Star Belgrade, Partizan Belgrade, Girondins Bordeaux, Boca Juniors, Sporting Cristal, Benfica, Santos, Ajax—were separate organisms, the rule rather than the exception. I'd have to learn more about club teams, the world over, on top of all of the World Cup history.

This game, or "friendly," as Seamus Malin described it on TV and radiocasts, seemed not only significant, but face-saving. Italy now had three World Cups, the same as Brazil, whose defeat to

Italy still seemed improbable. These were just two club teams, but virtually all the players on Fiorentina were Italian (Passarella and Bertoni the only exceptions) and the entire São Paulo roster was made of Brazilians.

The fans, and there were fifty-one thousand that afternoon, appeared to have more invested than the players. One got the sense that national pride trumped municipal pride in this game. How many of these fans, either expats or Italian Americans, were from, or of, the Renaissance epicenter? Weren't most of them from the south? How many New York Brazilians, in that massive country of theirs, whose corners I was still exploring through the atlas, were from São Paulo? How many Brazilians were there in New York? I'd never met or known any. And where did they live? Not the Bronx—I knew that. At the stadium, they were white, black, and brown.

My mother—born in Bushwick, Brooklyn, to parents from Flatbush, Brooklyn, to parents from Trapani and Marsala, Sicily—understood some Sicilian dialect, even less "pure Italian." But she knew the curses, not just the curse words, but expressions, which in dialect reached a baroqueness worthy of Sicily's own southeast. So when the cursing began in staccato spurts, and it didn't take long, she either laughed or grimaced or shook her head, depending. *Oh, god, I can't believe what they're saying.* Some of it, I gathered, had to do with sexual shortcomings or cheating spouses or cuckolded fathers, unfaithful mothers. Some was probably worse. *They take it a little too seriously, these people. Well, what are they saying?*

When a black, or brown, player touched the ball, we heard *bruta* this or *bruta* that. *Bruta* meant ugly—that much I knew from eighth-grade Italian class. The *this* and the *that* I didn't want to know. Was race an issue? I remembered being shocked when I read this from Brian Glanville, in that FIFA-UNICEF program, that was still close to my bedside: "Yet the Argentine style can never be that of the Brazilians—because the Argentines lack the key element of the Brazilian game, the black player. Rejected until well into the 1920s, black players have since then had a profound effect on the development of soccer in Brazil, with their sublime reflexes, their gymnastic ability, their ability to sprint almost from a standing start."

I circled it and put question marks in the margin, as if to say, huh? Was this allowed to be said? It was something that wasn't talked about in the U.S. Maybe it was thought, but never said. Did this game encourage uncomfortable stereotypes that American games didn't? I'd have to find out.

The Brazilian fans, meanwhile, seemed to give the players—their own, the Italians, the referee, this poor soul—hell. Only with Careca were they pleased; he had an undeniable sparkle to him and scored two goals. The Florentines absorbed kicks and elbows and Antognoni was the victim of a literal tackle, the American kind, from the Brazilian keeper. It all seemed very un-Brazilian. We didn't speak Portuguese, but cursing, its delivery, its irregular but melodic rhythm, is somehow understood, if not word for profane word, then by intonation. At Mets games you didn't hear, no matter how badly Craig Swan may have been struggling with his location, that he was the castrated son of a small-penised, cuckolded father and overweight mother who smelled of the Bay of Naples and orally serviced an entire precinct of corrupt *carabinieri*, and the local priest. At Shea, in the daytime, with little kids everywhere, you instead got "Take Me Out to the Ballgame." This was different.

July 17, 1983
Tulsa Roughnecks vs. Cosmos
WOR Radio

Even at a young age, even as a lover of sports, I never accepted the notion that athletes were artists, no matter how brilliant their performance. My parents drummed that into me: art was art, athletics was athletics, the former higher than the latter. For one, you could paint, sculpt, play or compose music, write, make films, well into old age, often getting better with age. *Lionel Hampton is the perfect example.* An athlete had a limited window of peak performance.

My father, who cherished baseball, even as he lost money on it, didn't think hitting a baseball was an art, as announcers would often reiterate, *the art of hitting*. He maintained that it was the single most difficult thing to do in sports, but that did not make it an art in his mind. Same with pitching, and did he love great pitchers, especially southpaws. But a physical act could be beautiful—a catch, a throw, a shot, a boxer skipping rope, or in this case a goal.

Home games for the Cosmos, like the Knicks and Rangers, weren't televised on Channel 9, only away games. Since there was nothing outside except trouble and my parents wanted me close, I may have been listening to it on radio. If I was, I don't remember Jim Karvellas's call of the goal, but then, how would you describe it? I saw it on the sports highlights of the eleven o'clock news, a couple of hours later. They showed it twice, maybe three times, and in slow motion, which was the only way to truly appreciate it.

A looping ball came from the right, toward the edge of the six-yard box, intended for Roberto Cabañas, the "Paraguayan international," even if the eleven o'clock sports guy didn't use these fabulous new terms I was learning through Seamus. But the ball was behind Cabañas, so he had to improvise—not unusual in sports, especially soccer, but he did so while he was already in midair, his body face down, perpendicular to the Giants Stadium turf. While levitating, and unable to see the ball, he swung the heel of his right foot and volleyed the ball out of the air and into the goal. When he landed, he kicked the ball in again, seemingly disoriented and confused. He hadn't even seen his own act of sublimity, of sheer beauty. The best goal I'd seen was Pelé's bicycle kick in *Victory*—a movie, of course—and West Germany's Klaus Fischer in the 1982 World Cup semifinal. This was something greater. It was more original, more athletic, more acrobatic, impossible to practice, and performed with utter abandon.

It had been seared into my brain, from gym teachers to these same eleven o'clock sportscasters, that basketball players were "the greatest athletes in the world." Were they? Why believe something that's said ad infinitum?

I got a chance to watch the goal again. There was a thirty-minute show on Channel 50, the New Jersey public channel, called *Cosmos Close-Up*, hosted by Jim Karvellas. We only had Channels 2–13, plus the UHF channels: 21 and 31, both public channels; 41 and 47, the Spanish channels; and 50. Reception for all of them was dependent on an antenna, and was spotty in both my and my parents' rooms. For whatever reason, Channel 50 was the clearest. *Cosmos Close-Up* was a joyous half hour, with player guests and usually the Brazilian coach, Professor Julio Mazzei, a larger-than-life personality. He was a gray-haired man, spectacled, full of hyperbole, warmth, and humor, given to Italianate hand gestures, professor of who knows what, but who cared? He was, like so many Brazilians—players, fans—impossible not to like.

Had the professor been a guest on *Cosmos Close-Up* after that goal? Can't say; don't remember. He would've been effusive, as ever, but still more. Maybe he'd said, "I never saw a goal like that. Worthy of, or better than, my friend Pelé."

August 6, 1983
China vs. Internacional of Brazil
Vancouver Whitecaps vs. Seattle Sounders
BC Place
Vancouver, British Columbia

In the summer of '83, my family managed a week in Canada, and since we'd seen Montreal and Quebec, we would try Western Canada. Vancouver.

Upon arrival, we bought newspapers and saw what events were in town. The first thing I checked for was the Vancouver Whitecaps of the NASL. Yes, they had a home game, great news, against their rival, the Seattle Sounders, but with an asterisk: *doubleheader with the Chinese national team and Internacional of Porto Alegre,

Brazil (a new place I'd have to find on the atlas when we got back home). Oh my god, this can't be. Impossible! If I'd only known about soccer, I could have seen games, not just at Giants Stadium, but in some of the great cities in the world. I could've seen AS Roma, the team of my new favorite player, Bruno Conti. I could've seen Real Madrid (instead we saw a bullfight) or Benfica or Tottenham Hotspur, where my program said Osvaldo Ardilias played, or Ajax of Amsterdam. The cabdriver who ripped us off upon landing at Amsterdam's Schiphol even pointed out a stadium, a large stadium. But we didn't know soccer; I didn't know soccer, didn't know it was all this. Only in Mexico City, but my father was bouncing checks to pay the hotels so money for a game was out of the question.

Now, though, he wouldn't get off the hook. I begged; he must take me to the doubleheader, and look here at the map: we were on Robson Street—like England's international Bryan!—and it was a straight line to the stadium. Maybe we could even walk. He hemmed and hawed and said he didn't especially want to go. My sister said, I'll go! And he and my mother said, Okay, just be careful.

And we did just that; we walked. It may have been a twenty-five-minute walk, but we did it in fifteen. We could hardly contain our euphoria. The Chinese national team—OH MY GOD! They hadn't been in the World Cup last year and none of their players were in the FIFA World All-Star Game, but it was a national team, the best of the best, which might well be in the next World Cup in Colombia. We would be seeing them in person and against a Brazilian team. Brazil! I didn't know this team; I only knew that Zico and Júnior played for Flamengo, Sócrates for Corinthians, and Falcão, surprisingly, in Italy for AS Roma. This couldn't be happening. The first thing we did was to buy the program, careful not to spill soda or mustard on it. Most of the Whitecaps and Sounders were originally from England or Scotland; the Brazilians looked cool with mini-Afros and gold chains; the Chinese with frowns and crooked haircuts.

47

The games were held at B C Place, a brand-new domed stadium that had just opened a few weeks before. We bought the cheapest seats and were surrounded by Chinese, who made up a large percentage of the crowd, and of Vancouver itself. And the Chinese, the thousands, tens of thousands, didn't make a sound.

The Brazilians, maybe fifty of them, down in the corner of the lower deck, in the red and white of Internacional, chanted, harmonized, played brass instruments, banged drums, though *bang* is not the right word. They performed, as much as the players did. Internacional won, the game and this mini-tournament. How could you not like them?

September 1983
Bronx, New York

I came back from Vancouver energized. I loved the city and saw what a miracle city life could be, a perfect, or near perfect, harmony of the urbane and the natural, bustle and serenity, of Europeans, Asians, North Americans (and fifty Brazilians).

Was any city perfect? Mexico City wasn't—it was quite imperfect—nor was New York City (or Co-op City). But Vancouver was, at least, an example of what a city could aspire to be. And there was the soccer, the first time I'd seen live soccer outside the metropolitan area. I'd never seen live baseball outside Shea or Yankee Stadiums, and already just a year into my new obsession, I'd seen soccer in a different city, a different country. The great Brazilians of Porto Alegre, "happy port," and the best that China had to offer. I brought this knowledge back with me along with two new magazines, *Match* and *Shoot*, both imported from England, both worthy of rote. A boyish-looking player, Ray Houghton, for a team I'd never heard of, Fulham Football Club, said his favorite food was "steak and lager." I loved that. I could read about all of these great teams: Notts Forest, Ipswich Town, Aston Villa, Leeds United, West Ham United, Manchester United, Newcastle United. Where were all these places and why wasn't there a London United? Or London Football Club? Where the hell was this place Fulham?

I was hungry for more knowledge and, again, to play. The new school year was soon to start and I was determined to have a better season than my first, in which I played little and not well. I hit the practice field of Truman High School, scaling the unwelcoming chain link or slipping under the hole to practice alone. It was still the best alternative, even if everything about the field said "keep out," even if the water fountains never worked, even if the grass was poorly kept, overgrown, dotted with dandelion clusters, or so uneven you risked turning an ankle. It was safer to kick or juggle on the running track and high-jump area. That or baseball infield dirt, cracked dry in August—at least it was flat. Most of the world probably played on dirt anyway, like that UNICEF picture of the kids in Rwanda. Why should I be any different?

Most of the "Greenway," our poor man's Great Lawn in the midst of Co-op City's maquette, was dug up in trenches, not unlike a war-movie set, to correct the failing pipes and waterworks, from the pressure of the settling buildings. If the rest of the Bronx was burning, we were sinking. If it wasn't dug up, this Greenway of ours, it was hardly used in these years, the bicycle path free of bikes, as so many were stolen, the walking path with a dearth of walkers. The Corbusian, tower-in-the-park urban dream was a place no one played in.

So here I was, again, at this field, to keep at it, to not give up. Amani was gone already, to his boarding school in Connecticut, and nothing had changed, no teams anywhere, no one to play with, no one to teach me anything. I had to learn from watching what I could on *Soccer Made in Germany*—now hosted by someone new, the great Toby Charles out of the picture without explanation—and the Italian game on WNYC and Club América on SIN. Once a month, maybe, a Jamaican or Trinidadian workman would see me kick the ball and call out to me, from fifty, a hundred yards away: *Yo mon, how do I get in here?* I'd run over and explain that all the gates were locked, that you either had to climb the fence or slip under the hole, behind Building 6, my building. If they had time, from their lunch hour or between jobs, they'd come in and kick with me. Those ten, fifteen minutes, made my day or week or month.

I got to enjoy practicing alone, the way Amani taught me—kicking against the bleacher seating, watching the ball slowly bounce down back to me, juggle with it, let off a hard shot, repeat—but getting to kick back and forth with someone was special. It was like playing catch, but with a soccer ball. One West Indian who joined me, never to be seen again in the vast monstrosity of Co-op City, called it "a kickabout." A kickabout, I liked that.

On one of these days mired in solitude and sun and soccer and my thoughts, out there in that lonely, massive field, someone called out for me: Hey boy! Hey!

It wasn't a West Indian worker wanting to kick with me, but a woman, a girl, more or less my age. A black girl.

I jogged over to the corner of the field, the one closer to where the high school met IS 180. On the other side of the chain link, the girl and her friend eyed me up and down. What could they want?

Yeah? I said.

Boy, you look fine.

I looked past myself. Huh? Who me?

Yeah, you, there's no one else in that big ol' field, is there?

I was stunned, even intimidated, by her approach, her boldness, and the fact that she was paying me such a compliment. No girl ever had before. It just didn't happen to me. Not in seventh and eighth grade, when I first liked a girl, the same girl, right over there, a hundred yards down, at IS 181, and not in ninth grade, with a different girl, at my tiny high school. I was nonexistent to them, visible only to my homeboys. *Yo, what up homie?* And now this?

He has those cute bowlegs, her friend said, looking at the twigs that were in navy Adidas short shorts.

Word, she said. Like a black boy.

I didn't know what to say. You serious? I said, or are you making fun of me?

She sucked her teeth, the way only a Bronx black girl could, and by the way she did it, I had my answer. She was serious. Stop, I ain't making no kinda fun of you.

Her friend agreed.

Sorry, I said.

How do we get in here? she said.

There's a hole in the ground you can go underneath, I said, or you have to climb over the fence.

Dag, she said. That's stupid.

Word, I said. That's Co-op.

Word. What building you live in? she asked.

Over there, Building 6.

I don't know anyone there, she said. She lived in one of the faraway buildings, 23, 24, 25, maybe.

She was cute, I remember thinking that, but black girls were off-limits. There were still some white people left in Co-op City, not nearly as many as ten, or five years before, but you never saw white boys with black girls. It would have been too dangerous and would likely get you taunted or beat up by blacks. White girls I had no idea how to talk to; black girls might get me beat up.

Awright, I said. I'll see you.

Yeah? she said.

Yeah, I said. I'm here a lot, practicing.

You kick that ball good. We were watching you.

I'm okay, I guess.

You like doin' those tricks.

Yeah, I guess.

No one plays soccer around here, she said. You need to find some Jamaicans.

Yeah, sometimes some West Indians pass by.

You play on some kind of team?

Yeah, in high school, I said.

Truman?

Nah, I said. They don't have soccer.

Where do you go?

I lied. New Rochelle Academy didn't sound cool enough. Uh, Mount, I said. I had no idea if Mount Saint Michael had a soccer team, but it's the first thing that came to mind. It was Catholic, but had street cred. My best friend, Calvin, who was black and an excellent athlete, went there for one year.

Oh, Catholic school, she said. I start Truman next month.

Word? I said. Some of my boys go to Truman. I went to 181.

I went to 180.

Awright, she said. So we'll look for you here.

Awright, I said, later.

Later.

I never saw her again.

May 30, 1984
Italy vs. United States
Giants Stadium
East Rutherford, New Jersey

My Africa poster stayed on the bedroom wall through high school, as did the postcards of Estadio Azteca. Now there was an addition: the poster of the 1982 World Cup-winning Italian national team. My family and I would make occasional forays into Little Italy, on Columbus Day and Good Fridays usually, with a requisite visit to Ferrara's and Di Palo's. On one of these outings, in one of the disheveled souvenir shops on Mott or Mulberry or maybe at the intersection of the two—with old-fashioned coffeepots and dusty vinyl records and the tricolor and kitsch—were posters: the most prominent was of eleven very serious-looking men in blue shirts and white shorts, six standing with their arms folded, and five crouched, like baseball catchers. Underneath, it read just the last names: Zoff, Antognoni, Scirea, Graziani, Collovati, Gentile; Rossi, Conti, Cabrini, Oriali, Tardelli.

Was I an Italy fan because they won the World Cup and I had gone with the winner?—one of the uglier features of human nature. I was never a front-runner. Or did roots—those vowels at the end of names, the reed-thin bodies, locks of gentle curlicues, the noses, of Roman or Neapolitan or Sicilian origin—lure me? If Brazil had beaten Italy and won the tournament, would I have been a Brazil fan? They did have Zico and Sócrates. What if the U.S. team was there? Would I have been the pied piper of American soccer from my corner of the Bronx, as I had been for American hockey and speed skating (thank you sister and brother, Beth and Eric Heiden) in 1980?

I was an Italian; if not a self-hating one, then merely a young person with a sense of rebellion on the one hand and on the other an anxious desire to assimilate with his peers, none of whom was Italian, most of whom were black. That I was largely accepted by blacks—and not all whites were, not by any means—made me feel special. The more accepted I felt, the more I wanted to learn about their lives, points of view, their music, their figures of speech. *Yo, what up blood?* But my interest wasn't for a planned essay to get into a prestigious college in a couple of years. It was out of a certain time and place, my corner of the Bronx in the '70s and early '80s, and comfort level in that place.

With the World Cup win, there was a shift. No longer was Italy grandmothers, smelly cheeses, and old ways. Now it was men, young men, who didn't look like the Italians I knew of, with Travolta haircuts, bad diction, and crude mannerisms. No, they ran like deer, were tough when they had to be, and graceful for the rest, even cavalier. Bruno Conti did tricks with the ball, and against these great Brazilians.

I was what I was, and that was an Italy fan. So when it was announced that the World Cup champions were to play the United States at Giants Stadium, I would go. No, we'll all go, my father said, like the previous summer to see Fiorentina–São Paulo, Cosmos-Seattle.

The U.S. team was billed not simply as the U.S. but as Team America, a carryover from the season before when the best American players were set up in their own franchise within the NASL and played out of RFK Stadium in Washington DC. The idea was to provide continuity for the American players, a chance to play and train together on an everyday basis, in preparation for 1986 World Cup qualification. Good idea, great uniform—red and white hoops, blue shorts—but it only lasted one year, 1983. Things were back to where they had been for the U.S. team, or rather Team America. I liked the players, but the team lacked an identity.

What to do? Who to back? Who knew this would be so complicated, choosing teams? But teams were more than teams. Teams were sides, and you had to pick one. Sides were often sides of town, or the town itself or a side of the social ladder or a region or a country. Sides had boundaries and sometimes boundaries are serrated. I'd be choosing one that wasn't my own (although it was), and choosing against the country of my birth, of my parents' birth, even my maternal grandparents' birth.

Was this allowed? Were there consequences? Maybe it wasn't even an issue? It wasn't war. When it was, my relatives all volunteered for the U.S. Armed Forces. So I'd go, backing Italy, my affection for Ricky Davis and the American Cosmos put aside for two hours.

I'd barely be cheering; not because of any loyalty issues but because of the rain. It poured nonstop the whole day and never let up. I'd already had a cold and a persistent cough but this was the Italian national team, perhaps a once-in-a-lifetime opportunity. The tickets, twelve dollars each, were already bought. My mother knew baseball, and knew of rainouts and rain checks, and thought this would be such an occasion. But no, soccer is played in rain, I told her. Nothing stops soccer.

We met my father for an early dinner at Toots Shor's, across the street from Madison Square Garden, the one-time haunt of

Ruyonesque figures. Make that a refurbished version of Toots Shor's, the original long gone, like the original Garden. Even if this was a chain version that Toots Shor, *may he rest in peace*, might not even recognize, it was completely incongruous with the forthcoming event, a game played by, on one side, mostly all-American, suburban white men, and on the other, by Italian Italians, who knew nothing of the American sporting icons—whether Italian American, Irish American, Jewish American, African American—that were pictured on the walls of this one-time institution.

The first thing my father did upon our arrival at Giants Stadium (by bus from Port Authority again) was buy me the program—anything to get my hands on something to read. It was slim, this program, not packed with history like the FIFA-UNICEF All-Star Game program, a primer on international soccer. There were no articles by Paul Gardner, Rob Hughes, or Juvenal. There were no think pieces on national styles of play and provocative ideas on national styles of play. There were the essentials, plus a little more, but I craved any and all information, and even in small details there was something telling. Look at this, the weights of the Italian players: Alessandro Altobelli, 6–0, 128; Bruno Giordano, 5–10, 136; Roberto Mancini, 5–10, 140; Paolo Rossi, 5–10, 132; Franco Baresi, 5–11, 140; Marco Tardelli, 5–11, 140; Antonio Sabato, 5–10, 132. Were these typos? Were the metric conversions miscalculated? Ricky Davis was 5–8, 155; Jeff Durgan, 6–1, 195; Steve Moyers, 5–10, 158; Mark Peterson, 6–0, 160; Chico Borja, 5–11, 155.

There was a profile of the U.S. team's Greek coach, Alkis Panagoulias, a naturalized American citizen, who went from the local, very local—managing a team called the New York Greek-Americans in the 1960s' German-American League, renamed the Cosmopolitan League—to the truly cosmopolitan, leading the Greek national team against Brazil in Rio's Maracanã Stadium, and these very Italians four times, from 1973 to 1983.

Six Olympic soccer games would be played in Annapolis, Maryland, an ad screamed—tickets available at select Sears stores.

SEE THE WORLD'S TOP TEAMS IN ACTION: FRANCE, QATAR, YUGOSLAVIA, CAMEROON, CHILE, CANADA, IRAQ. Were these really top teams? What was Olympic soccer? What did it mean, if anything? Was it redundant? Was it necessary? At least I learned a new country, Qatar, and where it was. *But how do you pronounce it?*

And this, something I'd never seen before, for an athletic outfitter named Kappa, which made, and sold, the full team uniform of Juventus—the club that so many Italian national team members played on, plus Platini and Boniek—socks, shorts, and jersey, with something called ARISTON, whatever that was, written across the front, all for sale. It was available at the Kappa store at Fifty-Third Street and Third Avenue. It didn't give a price, but it would probably be unaffordable. In the few games I'd attended, I'd never seen any fan wearing a team's jersey.

And this match? The fear for the U.S. was that it would be a repeat of the 6–1 loss to France three years ago. Really, you didn't miss much—or you missed a lot, perhaps the great turning point of American soccer. The game ended 0–0, the artificial turf now an amusement-park water ride. Section 128, row 3, seats 13, 14, 15, 16, weren't covered by the forgiving overhang of the mezzanine deck above. There was nowhere to hide, except under umbrellas and opaque ponchos that were handed out. Thirty-one thousand showed up, despite the deluge, busloads of Italians from Toronto. *Italians from Toronto?* I knew nothing about any Italian diaspora, beyond Philadelphia and Providence.

The Americans were happy with the result, which is how they referred to it—as a "result." The tie equal to a win for us—I mean, them—same as Pelé, Stallone, and the Allies in *Victory.* (The war always seemed to come up in soccer.) Jeff Durgan called it the "sweetest tie I've ever played in." Angelo DiBernardo, an Italian American with the Cosmos, said, "Maybe it's the start of a second boom. Who knows?"

"The Americans have a great future," said Marco Tardelli, the Italian captain famous for the "Tardelli scream," his celebration after scoring Italy's second goal in the '82 final. "In three, four years, they will be very good. There are a lot of good players."

In the downpour, something major happened for the U.S.: they tied the world champions, tied them at home, but were the away team, booed by fans, not during the national anthem, and not from me, but during the player introductions.

U.S. goalkeeper David Brcic, for one, wasn't pleased. "We expect it from a lot of foreign fans here. Those people are ignorant. They're in the U.S. now but they boo players representing the place where they live, make a living from, and take from."

Wow, so it's like that. Love it or leave it. And that was from a Brcic, not even a Bunker.

July 16, 1984
Paris, France

After the game, the 0–0 tie, I became the sickest I'd ever been. My illness lasted three weeks. I made repeated visits to my doctor on Burke Avenue in the Bronx with high fever; an ear infection that produced a foul, bloody discharge; nausea; strep throat; and overall torture, *all on account of that soccer game.*

When I became myself again, there was an unexpected gift, something I hadn't known about: the European Championships. SIN was televising the games live from France, the host country, and they would be on when I got home from school, those tantalizing last days of the semester. It was a mini-World Cup, eight nations divided into two groups. Italy, as hard as this was to believe, was not there. They hadn't qualified, which is why they had played the U.S. in New York. In one group it was France, the hard-luck story of the last World Cup; Denmark, a new team; Yugoslavia; and Belgium, with Erwin Vandenbergh. In the other, West Germany, Spain, and two more "new" teams, for me at least, Portugal and Romania.

Goals came from all angles, especially from France. Platini, with the Italian surname and Italian face and Italian curls, was the best creative force I'd seen, even better than Zico two years earlier. His tiny teammates, Jean Tigana and Alain Giresse, were nearly his equal. The ideas poured forth. No wonder Paul Gardner wrote in the World All-Star Game program that they were "the Brazilians of Europe."

The Danes were another bunch. I knew nothing about them. Where were they in the 1982 World Cup? They seemed as if they belonged. They played on the constant offensive, blonds in red-and-white waves, looking for goals and still more goals. And where did they get that uniform? It was better than Algeria's.

The France-Portugal semifinal was now one of the best games I'd ever seen, up there with West Germany–France and Italy-Brazil. I watched this match on my parents' bedroom carpet, with the bowtie antenna of their portable TV (a gift for opening a short-lived bank account somewhere) twisted in every conceivable angle and pattern, desperate as I was to get the best possible reception on SIN. If I could somehow procure a better quality of static, if the fuzz would stay consistent at least, and not veer in and out, the color along with it, then I could know the Portuguese, in all white, from the hosts, in their tricolor blue shirts, white shorts, red socks—Tigana's down around his ankles, sans shin guards.

Through the snowy reception, I could see the impossible: France lost its one-goal lead, the mustachioed Fernando Chalana assisting Rui Jordão, a black man, like Portugal's best player ever, Eusébio. In extra time, like France's semifinal two years ago, it happened again: Chalana to Jordão. I was only two years into my soccer education but I knew this wasn't supposed to happen. But France had the best player in the world, Platini. He created the tying goal and scored the winner from Tigana, in the 119th minute. They would win the final, in the grandly named Parc des Princes. That was June 27.

Eighteen days later, the day after Bastille Day, my mother, father, sister, and I landed at Orly Airport in Paris. We were there for a month-long trip around France. Why couldn't we have been here eighteen days earlier? And there would be no soccer to see live, like in Vancouver the year before; this was the off-season.

The newsstands all sold magazines, *Onze, Mondial, France Football,* in praise of the new European champions. I bought whatever material I could get my hands on—and whatever my father gave me money for—even if I couldn't read it.

September 1984
The Royal Mail
London, England

When we got back from France, depressed that we were back in the Bronx, I was determined to find a quality magazine that I could actually read. The French magazines looked incredible, full color, with long profiles of players like Fernando Chalana, who nearly ruined France's dream but was now headed to play for Girondins Bordeaux with Alain Giresse. *Onze,* which I bought each of the four weeks we were in France, had reviews and rosters from the European Championships and previews of the upcoming French season. It had a full feature with great photographs of Diego Maradona being welcomed by his new club, Napoli, in front of a packed stadium, Stadio San Paolo; and this wasn't even a game, just Maradona, in street clothes, waving to the crowd.

The only problem with the French magazines was that I didn't speak French. There had to be something like this in English. Where I heard about *World Soccer* magazine, I don't remember. Maybe I just sent my father on a mission and he came back with it. Or could it have been my coach last year, my sophomore year, who told me about it? He was young, his name was Doug, and he was our new gym teacher/soccer coach. He supposedly knew something about the game, since he also coached a swanky private school in Rye, I think it was. It was quite well known, for academics, as well as sports. He reminded us, from the first practice on, that that was his real job, his real team. He didn't even pretend to be diplomatic.

He made it clear that if games were scheduled at the same time, his team from Rye would be his priority, not us. When one of us asked if we might play them, he laughed and said that they were on a much higher level.

Maybe it was him, but maybe not. When I did try to engage him in talk about the 1982 World Cup or *Soccer Made in Germany* or the Italian game on Sunday morning—*there's an Italian game on Sunday morning?*—he didn't have much to say, except something like, You're really into it, aren't you? He didn't teach me anything I didn't already know about soccer, technically or historically. We, and I, were a waste of his time. About all he taught us was a practice exercise called "five v. two," where five players in a circle tried to keep the ball away from the two in the middle. *Yes, like monkey in the middle.* But that was it. He didn't improve us as a team; we still went winless and scoreless, we still played in the unschooled style known as "kick and run," and we still hoped to lose by less than six goals. He didn't want to be there; we were an embarrassment to him, a paycheck.

So let's give the credit of finding *World Soccer* to my father, who must have found it at the international newsstand in Times Square. When I got it, it was like a dream. Finally, something to read. I had the French magazines—*Onze, Mondial, France Football*—and *Shoot* and *Match* from England, though the more I flipped through them, they seemed like they were for younger kids. *Ray Houghton's favorite food: steak and lager.* I had the programs from the international games, the bible still being the FIFA-UNICEF World All-Star Game program. There was the Franz Beckenbauer World Cup book. There were a few copies of *Soccer Digest*, the hard-to-find *Soccer America*, and a local *New York Metro Soccer Report*, which was about twelve pages.

Now there would be something constant, and international, on a monthly basis—if, that is, my father would get me a subscription. It was expensive, but he was all about reading, and subscribing, and ordering: newspapers (the *New York Times*); magazines (*Daedalus*,

National Review, New York, Harper's, hoarding *the New York Times Sunday Magazine*); and books (which came from university presses by the day).

To get a U.S. subscription required an international money order. It wasn't the easiest thing to get. The Amalgamated Bank, across the street from us, founded by the Amalgamated Garment Workers Union, one of the founders of Co-op City itself, didn't have such emblems of worldliness. I don't think Chase Manhattan or Manufacturers Hanover Trust had them either.

My father finally got one from Barclays Bank, and the issues arrived in paper coverings marked Royal Mail. Royal Mail to the Bronx. So what if they were weeks late, and much of it was old news by the time it got to me? It was a new view onto the world, like a news digest, dispatches from all corners of the globe, some that I didn't see written about in the *New York Times*, which I was starting to read regularly now. The *Times* covered the conflicts in Central America, sure, but not Bolivian soccer. I could now see weekly results of The Strongest, and other great clubs from South America, Newell's Old Boys, Grêmio, Colo-Colo, U, and various Nacionals. It wasn't as glossy and colorful as the French magazines—only the front and back covers were in color—but I could read it. And it was written at a much higher level than either *Match* or *Shoot*.

It was about the now of soccer, but also told of its history, of the great stadiums, which they called "football grounds," and it would have a "club focus," which put a team in its century-long context. If it referenced one airline disaster, Manchester United in 1958, say, it inevitably alluded to Torino's in 1949.

And then there were the odd little surprises, like the classifieds with fans from unreal places—Salavat, Poccui, USSR; Aberdeen-shire, Scotland; Waremme, Belgium; Ploiesti Vest, Romania; Bogoso, Ghana; Hyogo, Japan; Cleveland, England (*there's a Cleveland in England?*); No. 6 Middle School, Wuxi, Jiangsu Province, China—looking to exchange team scarves and programs (or programmes, as it was written) and pennants and stadium postcards.

And pen pals, they were looking for pen pals—Milan fans from deepest Africa, looking for other Milan fans. Notts Forest from Jakarta, Indonesia. Notts Co. fans from Hong Kong. Who were Notts Forest—or Notts Co.? Were they the same team, from the same place? And where was Jiangsu Province?

I read the magazine until I fell asleep at night, with the hope that I'd dream about soccer.

May 29, 1985
European Cup Final
Heysel Stadium
Brussels, Belgium
Live (and tape delay) on SIN

In mid-spring, in the mid-Reagan-Thatcher eighties, there was a new hit song. Not just a hit in the U.S., but a worldwide sensation of goodwill and charity that had DEEP MEANING, caps intended. The song was "We Are the World." It was produced by Quincy Jones, whom I liked from his album *The Dude* and his production credit on Michael Jackson's *Off The Wall* from 1979. The more recent MJ/Q collaboration, 1983's *Thriller*, was given to me as a Christmas gift, on cassette, by my friend Calvin, but I found it overproduced, overplayed, overexposed, and overly marketed—pop made too perfect. I was no longer the audience. I was a jazz-head, more and more into early Miles and early seventies fusion-funk Miles, reggae, African, and world music.

God love Q; he turned "Ai No Corrida," a British song no one here was familiar with, into a disco classic, but "We Are the World" was Hollywood do-gooderism at its worst, patronizing and laden with white guilt. Who could argue with it? To help the starving of Ethiopia? The children? We, too, are the children, right? Who *can't* get onboard? What's *wrong* with you?

Sure, it was for a good cause—it was for the children!—but it was banal and out of touch. If anything could spread goodwill and charity to the third world, to any and all worlds, it was soccer. Had these recording stars been to the FIFA-UNICEF World All-Star Game? Could they find Cameroon on a map? Did they know Yaoundé? No. Soccer could heal, sustain, or help sustain, a village, a town, a culture, like the Rwanda photo. Soccer was everything "We Are the World" was supposed to represent. It could bring people together to make the loudest noise ever heard, like Danny Kaye told us.

I was right. And I was wrong. I was right about "We Are the World." It was a moment in time, a fad, a sentimental ditty, memorable for mideighties hairdos. But I was wrong about soccer. Soccer let me down.

It happened at Heysel Stadium in Brussels, Belgium, at the European Cup final, Juventus versus Liverpool. The match was shown live at 2:00 p.m. Since I didn't get home from school until 3:00 or 3:30, I would watch it on tape delay at 11:00 p.m.—as long as I didn't find out the score. But then who was going to tell me? There was no way to find out. It would be like watching it live. *Bless the Spanish channels.* Except this day was different; it was the day of death.

I don't know whether my mother heard about it on the radio, while cooking, or during the five o'clock Eyewitness News, or one of the Jennings/Rather/Brokaw telecasts, though we never watched those. Wherever, whoever, the news came through: 41 people dead, at least 250 injured, in a riot. A wall collapsed when Liverpool fans charged into a Juventus section. The consensus was that the English were the aggressors. In these last few months that I'd been receiving *World Soccer* there were steady reports of "hooliganism," a word I hadn't known. My first impression of the word *hooligan* was that it sounded like an Irish surname. *Houlihan.* The Millwall club seemed to have especially notorious fans. And a few weeks earlier, there was a fire at a game in Bradford, England, that killed fifty-three. That made the eleven o'clock news here. But a fire was different from a riot.

Brief clips were shown of Heysel, of the pandemonium, of rage, of extinguished lives. What I didn't understand was why the game was eventually played. This seemed impossible to me. How could the game go on as if nothing had happened? To lose one's life going to a game was not in a fathomable realm. It was supposed to be something to enjoy. It was a game, like at Shea, with souvenirs, programs, hats, hotdogs, and bad food. As bad as the South Bronx was, no one got killed in Yankee Stadium, not that I remember. This was unimaginable. It was a game, only a game.

It didn't matter that Juventus, the Italians, won, with players I had already seen in person—Platini, Boniek, Tardelli—on a penalty kick that was obviously gifted to them, a kind of sick consolation prize. The next day, there it was, in the *New York Times*. Soccer, for all the wrong reasons, on page 1, above the fold—RIOT IN BRUSSELS AT SOCCER GAME LEAVES 41 DEAD—and extended coverage inside, in the international section: EXPERT CALLS SPORTS VIOLENCE PART OF A CHAIN OF AGGRESSION; and THE MATCH GOES ON AND THE ITALIANS ARE VICTORIOUS.

And still more the next day: BRITISH SOCCER FAN: WHY SO WARLIKE?; A DISGUSTED THATCHER SAYS BRITAIN WILL AID THE BEREAVED; BRITISH SOCCER TEAMS BARRED BY BELGIUM; ITALIANS EXPRESS RAGE OVER DEATHS. Bettino Craxi, Italy's socialist prime minister, wondered how the game was allowed to go on. "Incomprehensible absurdity," he called it.

Two days later, the U.S. national team was set to play Costa Rica in a World Cup qualifying match, in Torrance, California. Apparently, there were Costa Ricans in or near Torrance. It was at a tiny stadium at El Camino College, with a capacity of 11,800 fans, most cheering either for Costa Rica or against the Americans.

The United States needed only a draw to progress to the final round of regional qualifying with Canada and Honduras. This was the same U.S. team that a year ago—a year and one day ago—tied Italy, the World Cup champions, at Giants Stadium, in the deluge, the start of something big. Instead, the U.S. lost, 1–0. The NASL was dead; financial mismanagement caught up to it. The U.S. national team was dead. Most shockingly, people, people who just wanted to watch a live game, were dead in Brussels, gone for no reason. The *New York Times Week in Review* on Sunday quoted *L'Équipe*, the French sports newspaper that gave birth to the European Cup in the 1950s: "If this is what soccer has become," they wrote, "let it die." Soccer—my new friend—was dead.

Summer and Fall 1985
Bronx and New Rochelle, New York

There was still the ball, striated with asphalt, in the corner of my room, and a long summer ahead with nothing to do. My closest friends, who had always been a couple of years older, had gone their separate ways, one to the Marine Corps, another to college, one within commuting distance but far beyond childhood comfort zones of playing ball on summer afternoons. My high school friends, there were only two, Lau and Jeff, since the school was so small, were not within commuting distance from my section of the Bronx. So it was me and the ball, without even Cosmos games on WOR Channel 9. And who knows when I'd see another live game, if ever.

Even Toby Charles, that knowing, friendly voice, was gone from *Soccer Made in Germany*. SIN still showed games but it was hard to know who exactly was playing or when or if the game was same-day tape delay or from the day before or the week before. Rarely was it *vivo en directo*. It was rarely if ever listed in the newspaper's *Sports on TV* box.

The Italian game was still broadcast. Like SIN, it was never advertised and you wouldn't know who was playing until you tuned in. Better still was the highlight show, *Novantesimo Minuto*. But the summer was the off-season, what should've been Cosmos season. International matches were promised, but never happened. So it was just me and the ball.

It would be my last season on the high school team, and I would be co-captain, with Lau from Tanzania. I'd do again, and I knew for the last time, all the training Amani had taught me, learning how to be alone, how to be productive alone, and how to demand more from myself.

The previous season we had a draw, and I managed to score twice. The first one came in the very first game, against the best team, a big, bullying rich-kid school that in the past would run up double-digit shutouts against us. This day they beat us but only 6–1, and my goal was from about forty yards out—lucky, mind you, as I kicked it perfectly on a bloop that caught the keeper off his line. Everyone was in shock, including me, but it won over my teammates. It was our first goal in years. The shutout seasons, I decided, would end, and it would be nice to score some goals and win at least one game. So I put in nonstop training sessions at the Truman High School field. The only break came when my family took a ten-day vacation to Switzerland, where I was able to buy a new copy of *Onze* magazine, this issue highlighting South American and African World Cup qualifiers.

Our season ended up being shortened to eight games, from ten, because of bad weather, but we actually won a game, for the first time in my four years, and tied another. I scored six goals, two from the spot. Our coach was the phys ed teacher, Mr. Barnum, a wonderful young guy, someone too good for such a low-paying job. When I graduated he gave me a copy of David Halberstam's *The Breaks of the Game*, about the Portland Trailblazers of 1979/80. He didn't know much about soccer, but at least he didn't make fun of the sport like a lot of people, and he whipped us into excellent condition. But when he and I met privately, I suggested we use the diamond defense that my tenth-grade coach—the blowhard—sort of taught us. Then it would be best, I said, if we played a simple four across midfield, one striker, and me, conceptually playing between midfield and the lone forward, but basically roaming to wherever I was needed—drifting left, right, and often as far back as our own penalty area. It was hard work, but I was ready for it.

I was dramatically underweight and managed to play many of these games without eating lunch. The high school I went to may have been "private" and may have been in Westchester—it was in New Rochelle, near the border of Pelham—but it had no cachet and was known as a place for white kids who couldn't get into, or afford, the truly exclusive private schools in Westchester or Riverdale (or were kicked out) and blacks and Latinos, whose parents wanted something better for them than the notorious public high schools of the northern Bronx and southern Westchester. Despite my color, I fell in with the latter group.

The school had a famously horrible cafeteria. While in public school, from kindergarten through eighth grade, I never ate the school food and came home for lunch or packed a sandwich. In high school, bringing lunch was strictly forbidden—why, I don't even know—as was leaving the bedraggled grounds. Which left me, Lau, and Jeff only one alternative: to sneak out and go to a deli for a proper sandwich. I tried on game days, but it was a risk and I often had to play on an empty stomach. Somehow I managed to play full games.

At the end of the season, I was invited to the all-star game. The league champions, a school from Rockland with impeccable facilities, were up against the all-stars from the other five or six teams. I started and was one of the three captains to come out for the coin toss. We won, 3–2, and on the winning goal, I made the outlet pass from deep in midfield that led to the pass that led to goal. It was so subtle, no one noticed. And that was the end of my playing career.

May 1986
Spanish International Network (SIN)
Paterson, New Jersey

After the various disasters of 1985, it seemed as if the World Cup would never arrive. When it did, I had to work through much of it. High school was over, and I'd be starting at New York University in September. Lau, who would be attending Howard University, got hired for the food service at Rye Playland, the old art deco amusement park up I-95 on the Long Island Sound. He asked if I wanted to join him—there was plenty of work—and now that he had a driver's license, he'd come pick me up with his father's old car. I said yes, sure, by all means. I would have loved to sit around the apartment and watch two or three World Cup games per day, like in '82, but my father was struggling financially, and I knew getting through NYU—even saving a few bucks on room and board by commuting—was going to be difficult for both of us. Making money was the priority, even if it was flipping burgers, which is exactly what it was, and frying fries and chicken and mopping floors.

Before the tournament started, one of the New York sports reporters wrote that if you sent a letter to SIN, the Spanish International Network, they would mail you a roster for each of the twenty-four teams. It seemed unlikely—what was in it for them?—but I did it anyway. Sure enough, to my delight a nine-by-eleven envelope arrived within a week with just that. And I hadn't even sent in a self-addressed stamped envelope. I was touched by this act of generosity and kindness. I didn't have a Spanish last name, nor did I write it in Spanish. They could've easily not responded. They had won my loyalty forever. And the sheets had everything you'd need: number, player's name, age, club team, and number of caps. I wrote back, basically saying *gracias* (*en español*), and let us hope for a good tournament. And it was, if only I'd seen more of it.

Almost upon my first day on the job at Rye Playland, I met a Jamaican coworker—not a kid, like the rest of us—but a grown man. I immediately introduced myself and asked him if he liked soccer. Of course, he said with a wide smile, and cricket, too, and he expressed the same dilemma I had: the beginning of amusement park season was colliding with the World Cup. And like me, he needed the money, perhaps even more, though he was too dignified to say. We made a deal that we'd trade information on the games that the other missed. He was a Brazil fan and was lucky enough to be off on the day Brazil played France, in the game of the tournament. I saw the Argentina-England match and told him that I didn't even notice Maradona's hand ball, that even when he cheated he did it with more skill and deftness than anyone else.

Vernon liked John Barnes, who was Jamaican born, and was torn about which team to support in that game, but agreed Maradona was now the finest player in the world. I told him I'd heard of this mythic goal Barnes scored against Brazil in the Maracanã. He claimed to have seen it—where I don't know—and assured me it was one of the best, a brilliant slalom solo run, not as grand as Maradona's and not in as important a match, but one of the very best he'd seen. Maybe someday I'd get to see it. Even after Maradona's great goal, I still rated the Roberto Cabañas goal higher, for sheer originality and gumption. Cabañas and another Cosmo, Julio Cesar Romero, were at the World Cup representing Paraguay, which was beautiful to see. Both scored two goals apiece. The Cosmos lived on in the greatest tournament and it proved that the best of the NASL could compete against the pedigreed. Canada's lineup was made up almost entirely of players from the defunct league. I watched them, holding my breath, hoping they wouldn't get embarrassed. They played eleven behind the ball and fought with all they had. It was as if the French, Hungarians, and Soviets had a ninety-minute power play against the Canadians. They lost all three games without scoring a goal, but maintained their pride. It was the last time I saw those NASL players, the Canadians or the Paraguayans. And when the summer job ended, I never saw Vernon again.

October 1986
Marshall Cavendish Books
58 Old Compton Street
London W1V 5PA

It was easy to forget that my first real soccer friend was my sister. Amani may have showed me how to play, and how to train, and it was my father who took me to my first game, but it was my sister who was with me, enthusiastically, watching the World Cup games in 1982, *Soccer Made in Germany*, and the Cosmos, and pouring over the FIFA-UNICEF Game program and the World Cup book edited by Franz Beckenbauer.

So when she reached her junior year of college and did a semester abroad in Segovia, Spain, I urged her to go to Madrid and see the Estadio Bernabéu and Michel, one of the best players in the world and maybe the most graceful. Plus, Real had Emilio Butragueño and Hugo Sánchez of Mexico, who we remembered from our FIFA-UNICEF program. But the señora of my sister's host family said that it wasn't advisable for a young woman to go to *futbol* alone. Things could get quite out of hand; not necessarily violent, but crude and boorish perhaps.

I wrote her letters, and it seems that, besides some polite talk of school and studies, the only thing we had in common at that stage in our lives was soccer. On October 6, I wrote: "Have you seen soccer on TV? In magazines? Last week, Channel 31 showed a Wednesday game, Torino vs. Nantes. I only caught the end, but it was exciting. It ended in a 1–1 tie."

On October 14: "Guess what, I have the order form to get "Mexico '86"!!! It costs $30. But I have a tough decision. They are also offering the books for the World Cups of 1978, 1982 (NOT the one we have!) and 1986 for a total of $78. I definitely would like ALL three, but the money is a problem. Either way, by the time you get home you'll have something to read."

And on October 28: "I heard there was a terrorist bombing in San Sebastián by the Basques, but that's all the way in the north, not near you. I just read in *Soccer Week*, that Real Madrid lost to Young Boys Berne of Switzerland in a European Cup match. Big upset, but they have to play again in Spain. They probably already have by now. I saw a game Wednesday night on Channel 31. Torino played a team from Hungary and won 4–0. The weekly game from Italy used to be on Sunday morning at 10:00 a.m. Now it's on 8:30 a.m., live. It's early for me, but they do show the best teams. Last time, they showed Juventus vs. Napoli."

When she returned home after the semester, I had bought those World Cup books, all three. I had a work-study job my freshman year—it was required—making minimum wage at the NYU book store, and with that I spent seventy-eight dollars to bolster my soccer bookshelf.

These new books—all imports from England, all written by Phil Soar, who, according to his bio, had also written histories of Arsenal and Tottenham—were more substantial, with better paper, better photography, and though they were mainly pictorials, better writing. The 1978 volume had photos of stamps from past World Cups and team photos in the back with headshots of each player. The '82 edition shamed Beckenbauer's with brilliant photographs, glossy paper, and box scores for each match and full team squads. Mexico '86 was better still and had summaries of each World Cup, the score of every World Cup finals match ever played, and each tournament's official poster. These, I knew then, were coming to the grave with me, which, even if I lived to a hundred, was only twenty more World Cups—a source already of real, profound despair.

Summer 1987
Soccer Learning Systems
Pleasanton, California

Trace Video Sports Club
Natchez, Mississippi

If soccer's future in the United States still seemed uncertain, its accessibility iffy and subject to change (and tape delay), well then why not live in the past, its deep, rich past, of which there was still more to sift through and revel in, through not only text and image but video cassette?

It may have been in *Soccer Weekly*, the tiny pamphlet on photocopied paper that was sold on newsstands, the same publication in which I saw the ad for the three World Cup pictorials. It may have been in the slim *Metropolitan Soccer Report*, of which there were a few copies sold in my local candy store. It may have been in *Soccer America* or *Soccer Digest*, the most professional of the publications, though neither was readily available in the Bronx.

But at some point, circa 1986, when my family finally bought our first VCR, there was an ad, a classified ad, from a guy in Atlanta—he had a long Greek name—who sold pirated soccer videos. He had a vast collection, including *G'olé!*, the official film of the 1982 World Cup. But could you trust sending a complete stranger a money order? The answer was, if you loved soccer, yes. A fellow soccer fan would never deceive.

I called him first, and he must have been my age, more or less, and though a morose fellow, sounded trustworthy. I ended up buying *G'olé!*, narrated, unforgettably, by Sean Connery. It was instantly my favorite documentary ever. I watched it over and over. The next year, I wrote to him again, and he copied *Hero*, the 1986 film, narrated by Michael Caine. He even had one on the career of Tostão, the little Brazilian genius I had only read about. I didn't ask where he got these, but I was surprised that such a fount of soccer knowledge lived in Atlanta. Who knew there were Greeks in Atlanta?

Soon after, there was another ad in another of these publications, not a classified, but one from an organization called, and I loved this, Soccer Learning Systems. It suggested that soccer was a learned pursuit, one with various systems and approaches to be studied and contextualized. You could send away for a catalogue in California, and so I did. Catalogue was a generous word; it was more like a brochure, with listings of its books and videos. Ordered straightaway was an oversized hardcover British volume called *The Soccer Tribe*. It was a pictorial matched with anthropological analysis. Next would be either *The Football Grounds of England* or *The Football Grounds of Europe* or, God willing, both, even if they were pricey.

The videos came by way of a company called Trace Video Sports Club, in the unlikely outpost of Natchez, Mississippi. They had "educational" videos, as in what drills to run in practice, coaching instructionals, and goalkeeping fundamentals. A few years before, these might have interested me, and could've helped me, when I was still a player. I did revel in the self-taught aspect of the game; what Amani's dreadlocked uncle said to me about juggling the ball stayed with me—that it was important, no matter what anyone said about it not being applicable in game situations, because it was all about controlling the ball and touch. I thought if I spent hours with the ball, even alone, I'd cultivate a relationship with it, I'd be able to maneuver with it, and then without it, and that would enable improvisation and creativity. So if I'd discovered these videos two, three, four years earlier, would I have bought them? Maybe. Could they have helped me? Probably. But my playing days appeared to be over, and perhaps it was more educational to watch the videos of great teams, the World Cups, the greatest goals.

This was mail-order paradise. If only they weren't thirty and forty dollars each. The ones I wanted, the Greek in Atlanta didn't have on his list, or if he did, I wanted fresh copies with the original cover, as I knew this was something I wanted to collect, along with soccer books.

The first video I bought was *Heading for Glory*, the official film of the 1974 World Cup. It didn't have the familiar "Scotto profundo" of 007, but instead was "spoken by" a daft English voice that belonged to Joss Ackland (an actor, I would learn), with text by Geoffrey Green (a football writer of some renown, I would also learn).

It began at the end, with the disconsolate Dutch. The saccharin was unrelenting and yet irresistible:

Johan Cruyff, the natural heir to Pelé, lonely as a mounted wind. He has tilted at windmills—and lost. It is etched on his face.

Winner take all; the loser is jilted. Holland are yesterday's men, with a great future behind it.

The flying Dutchmen head for home in their big white bird. Cruyff and his wife; he flicks a speck from his eye. Or is it a tear? Others fondle their medals, not gold but silver in the stars. . . . They've pricked our pretty balloon and our moon has been taken away. Where did we go wrong?

Then it circles back to the beginning of the tournament:

Now the football story begins. Sixteen nations playing in nine German towns come to the starting line. The establishment is here, minus England. But in the field are outsiders: East Germany, blood brothers of the host from over the wall; Australia, jolly swagmen; Haiti, from the land of Papa Doc and voodoo; Zaire, leopards from the steaming Congo basin.

It was $39.95 but the pricelessness continued. *Meanwhile, back at the ranch, West Germany, reigning European champions open their account against Chile, men from the high Andes in a royal hunt of the sun.*

The elements take a hand as West Germany face Poland to Wagnerian overtones. Crashing thunder and lightning fork the black heavens. This is the twilight of the gods.

Brazil, "the ebony champions," eliminated by Holland, are hardly portrayed as saints, nor for that matter are the Dutch. With a groovy soundtrack of organ and electric bass that might as well be out of the funky oeuvre of Deodato, or a porn movie, we learn the following:

Brazil, their crown toppling, now unsheathe the broadswords. . . . Rivelino, twice bodily obstructed, plays Henry Irving, the outraged actor. . . . But the Dutch themselves are not all light and innocence. Rep supplies an eyeful of elbow to a dark face.

We arrive back at the final, in its lead-up, with Henry Kissinger, Prince Rainier and Grace Kelly, and Willy Brandt all making cameos.

It is the dawn of the final. Munich's Olympic Stadium is silent under its strange roof, a mosquito net where soon the gnats of fate will sting.

Paul Breitner has an "Afro hairstyle and left-wing opinion." The Dutch players' wives are "viragos on springs." Beckenbauer is "the fingerpost pointing the way, unhurried as a man strolling down the boulevard for an aperitif." And being this is a British production, there's a lot of screen time—too much—for Jack Taylor, the English referee.

We see the perfect illustration of Total Football, in fact its apotheosis: the first sixty seconds of the match, when Holland string together, like the love beads around Ruud Krol's neck, nineteen uninterrupted passes in a seamless interchange of positions, an intellective exercise that appears perfectly organic, that led to the first goal, started by the lithe Cruyff, pointing this way and that, a nonstop talk machine, as the last man on defense. It was a minute for the ages.

And then this final bit:

J. B. Priestley once wrote, "To say that people pay money to see twenty-two hirelings kick a ball is merely to say that a violin is made of wood and catgut." In contrast, George Orwell wrote that "sport at the international level is frankly mimic warfare." Whoever was right, that's what the World Cup is all about.

August 21, 1988
Sporting Cristal vs. Barcelona
Benfica vs. Atlético Nacional
Giants Stadium
East Rutherford, New Jersey

Fast forward one more summer and as if by magic—or was it magic realism?—soccer returned to Giants Stadium for two doubleheaders. Sporting Cristal of Lima, Peru; Nacional of Medellin, Colombia; Barcelona of Guayaquil, Ecuador; and Benfica of Lisbon. They called it the Marlboro Cup. As before, I took the bus from the Port Authority, still as decadent as it was in 1982. I had wanted company, naturally, but my only hope—a full-timer in the NYU bookstore from St. Thomas—didn't want to spend the money.

These were the darkest days for soccer in the U.S., but a recent, improbable announcement, made for a whiff of hope: the U.S. was selected as host of the 1994 World Cup. I was happy, of course, but with some doubts. Colombia had been scheduled to host in 1986 before it had to withdraw. The United States didn't have the internal and financial issues Colombia had grappled with, but could we overcome the lack of widespread fan interest and artificial turf stadiums, something FIFA would never sanction? Even Giants Stadium—formerly "Cosmos Country," where we were on this summer night, and not 76,891 in attendance, not even half that—wasn't selected as a World Cup venue. So I'd wait and see, cautiously optimistic, and enjoy these two games in front of me. It opened with the players entering the field single file to the familiar, rousing theme music of Marlboro cigarettes, originally from *The Magnificent Seven*, which sounded as if it could've been the work of Ennio Morricone (a loyal Roma fan), but wasn't. The crowd erupted, relieved perhaps, that we'd lived to see another live game. For a while, this wasn't a given.

The spectators were almost entirely Latino or Portuguese. I sat, by chance, next to a Portuguese family. We began chatting immediately after the Nacional goalkeeper—whom I'd never heard of but had hair like Rick James and was nicknamed "El Loco"—did something so bold it veered into the taboo: he dribbled the ball all the way to midfield stripe. His name was René Higuita. The audience seemed confused. Some appeared to curse him, as if he wasn't taking this exhibition game, and by extension us, very seriously. How could a goalkeeper commit such a heinous and disreputable act? Others, maybe those familiar with him and this team, laughed a knowing laugh.

Higuita, as if to confirm to those of us not in the know, did it again and again. This is who I am, he seemed determined to announce.

I remembered a T-shirt that Carlos Santana wore in a photo in *Down Beat*, the jazz magazine. It was an image of John Coltrane and it read, "Damn the rules, it's the feeling that counts." Higuita seemed to embody that quote, and I was immediately drawn to him. He was an iconoclast, but was he an iconoclast merely for the sake of iconoclasm? Was he a precocious child craving attention—or a lucrative contract from a bigger club? But if so, from where? The days of the Cosmos writing big checks were gone.

Was Higuita flouting orthodoxy an inchoate movement in the New World that Eurocentric soccer observers were unaware of? Were other goalkeepers in Colombia and South America freelancing as sweepers, otherwise known as *liberos*? (It's the continent of the Copa Libertadores.) Or was Medellin to soccer what Zurich was to the Dadaists, a place to upend reason and embrace the irrational, the intuitive, the nonsensical, to veer into the surreal? Was his a reaction to a European game that was becoming more and more inhibited and stifling? Or was he soccer's Puck, a mischievous merrymaker.

One thing was clear—he had good technique, so that alone told me that there was something life-affirming, or *futbol*-affirming, about him. When, though, would it all go horribly wrong, in this meaningless game or in one with far more import?

At half time, I spoke more with the Portuguese family seated next to me. They lived in Newark's Ironbound section, where so many Portuguese migrated in the '70s and '80s. Today, they were there to see Benfica. The patriarch of the family was originally from Mozambique, he told me, and when Benfica's former great, Eusébio, thick and paunchy now, was announced to the crowd and waved, the man beside me began to cry. But he turned toward me, hand over his eyes, so his family wouldn't see. A grown man weeping at the mere sight, all these rows back, of the player known as the "Black Pearl," himself from Mozambique. This, I knew, was something Proustian for the man next to me, or more traumatic, in a colonial way that I'd never be able to understand—maybe about betrayal, maybe benevolence, maybe both. I didn't know what to do, how to save him from embarrassment. So I kept talking: "He was something, Eusébio," I said. "I've read about him, nine goals in the '66 World Cup." He nodded, as if to say, keep talking, just keep talking, a few more seconds, then I'll gather myself. So I did, recalling every factoid from the FIFA-UNICEF, Paul Gardner-edited program with profiles of past greats. "Four against North Korea, the European Cup win over Real, one of the greatest players of all time." Then he smiled and said to me quietly, "Yes, yes, you know, you know. But how do you know?"

October 8, 1988
NYU vs. University of Rochester
Asphalt Green
555 East Ninetieth Street
New York, New York

I'd been at NYU for two years and hadn't yet declared a major. Now, as I entered my junior year, I had to declare something. And so it was journalism. One of the two journalism professors who actually knew my name, who encouraged me, Jon Katz, told me it was vital to get some experience, and soon. He urged me to write for the school newspaper. I found this terrifying somehow, and wasn't ashamed to say so. He was a journalism professional, had been for some time, in newspapers and TV, but empathized. He said this: "Write what you know."

I knew this was a rule in publishing, and I already distrusted it. It seemed to me that rules should be broken, *damn the rules*. So maybe I should write about what I didn't know, school government, say. Did NYU even have a school government? If they, or we, did, two years went by without me knowing. But then I wouldn't enjoy writing about school government. And how square: school government at NYU. Maybe we should overthrow this student government, if it did exist.

I told Professor Katz that I knew soccer. He seemed intrigued and asked if NYU had a team. Yes, I said, but it's Division III. Doesn't matter, he said. The rules are still the same, right? A journalist would prepare for and write a story no matter what the level. Find out if you can cover the team. (And speaking of square: NYU athletics? The Violets?)

But was sports writing considered journalism? Did it have integrity? Was it frivolous? Was it second class? I asked. To the contrary, he said, sports departments, whether in print, TV, or radio, were the most innovative. And his best student, by far, at NYU was a sportswriter, whose name I recognized from the back page of the student paper, and who was accepted into the prestigious internship program for *New York Newsday,* a paper that was approaching the *Times* in its quality and breadth of coverage. It was a tabloid in format only. He asked if there were any reputable soccer publications I could intern for. Yes, I said, *Soccer America,* but they weren't in New York, and I had written to them the previous year and hadn't heard back. Well, then, focus on the student paper.

Jon was right, and I had to fight back my fear and approach the paper, the *Washington Square News.* So I did. I went to the ninth floor of the Loeb Student Center on University Place, just south of Washington Square Park, and asked if they needed writers, sportswriters. They couldn't refuse anyone and said I was welcome to try. Just don't expect to cover basketball. Everyone wanted to cover basketball but you had to work your way up to that.

I understood, that made perfect sense, and besides, I told them, I loved soccer and knew quite a lot about it. Great, they said, we need someone for soccer, no one liked soccer. But first (kiddo), we need someone to cover women's volleyball. You're up for that, right?

Sure, I said.

After a couple of early-season women's volleyball events, I finally had my first soccer game assignment, NYU vs. the University of Rochester. NYU was in a relatively new sports conference of respected academic schools, the University Athletic Association, the UAA: its member schools were NYU, Carnegie Mellon, Case Western Reserve, Rochester, Brandeis, Emory, University of Chicago, and Washington University of St. Louis.

With the lack of open space downtown—an ongoing problem for the athletic department—the NYU soccer team was essentially homeless. Home games, at least this season, would be played at Asphalt Green, a narrow, artificial-turf field wedged between Ninetieth and Ninety-First Streets and York Avenue and the FDR Drive. I knew this was called Yorkville, not the Upper East Side, and knew it was once Germantown. My father, a New York-ologist, had educated me about all the city's neighborhoods, but I had no idea there was an athletic field there.

The game was on a rainy Saturday, and I felt that it was the most important day in my life. It was a test, I knew, of my ability. If I failed, I might not be welcomed back to the newspaper, certainly not encouraged, and I might fail at my new major before I'd even started.

I took the subway down from the Bronx—I was a commuter student—got off at Eighty-Sixth Street, walked east to First Avenue, and up to Ninetieth Street. I left early, so that I could stop at Doss Soccer Sport Supply. It was a small store, truly mom and pop, and they sold shoes, balls, and cheap knock-off jerseys, which were disappointing. Still, I could've spent hours there, mainly for the memorabilia they had on display: stadium postcards from around the world, old brown leather balls, high-top cleated boots.

At the game, there were few if any spectators, mainly parents and friends of players who sat in the spare bleacher seating or lined the field, which was a shiny pea green. I scribbled notes under the foldout scorer's table, where I sat. I got home and began writing the game report on a pad. Come Monday, I'd go into the *Washington Square News* office and type it into the computer, a brand new Apple Macintosh desktop, the kind that had just replaced manual typewriters in the NYU journalism labs.

In my game report, I was tempted to liken the conditions to the West Germany-Poland game in the 1974 World Cup, but thought better of it. Instead I worked in all sorts of soccer jargon—inside baseball stuff—that would drive our faculty adviser, a copyeditor from the *Daily News*, insane throughout the semester. *Who's this Michael Agovino? Hey, what's a "through ball"? Who "caresses" a pass?*

The NYU coach seemed both surprised and impressed when the story appeared on Wednesday, and recognized, I think—through the words—that he had a partner in crime, which is what soccer sometimes felt like. His name was Gus Constantine, an NYU graduate and former referee in the NASL and CONCACAF, the emphatically unmelodic acronym for the Confederation of North, Central American and Caribbean Association Football. He was a kind man, large, with a dark brow and imposing mustache. He was in his fifties and was determined to turn NYU's moribund program around. With him on the sidelines—and I covered virtually every game that season—was Asher, an Israeli, as not so much his assistant coach but what would you call him? Technical Director, as they had in Europe? (Though this was hardly Europe.) Adviser? Emissary? Sidekick?

It was unclear if Asher was paid; I don't think so, at least not officially. He often had outside commitments, though what they were, and what he did with the rest of his days outside of NYU soccer games, was never clear. He was early- or midthirties with a blond mullet, the sport's de rigueur hairstyle. He wore slick suits or the trendiest sweats if he was going to warm up with the team. He was wildly popular with the players and whenever he was around, he became the life of the party, if you would characterize an NYU soccer game against CCNY as a party. He was more of a distraction than counsel. The only advice I remember him imparting to the players during a game was to chip the ball. *"Cheeep the ball! Cheeep it! Cheeep it over the defense!* It appeared to be a fancier way of saying "kick and run"—something Coach Constantine, which he liked to be called, whether by player or budding journalist, insisted he would never promote.

Asher and I would talk before and after games, not about the NYU game so much but about the recent European Championships, the last World Cup, and the upcoming World Cup in less than two years. I can't wait, I'd tell Asher. Neither could he, he'd say. Besides Louis, a Haitian from southeast Queens, and Vasilios—he went by Billy—a Greek from Jersey City, few of the players seemed to follow the European leagues, nor did they seem interested in the sudden intensive coverage their team was receiving. Many were freshmen—maybe they thought it had always been like this—but some, usually the out-of towners, were just unapproachable, which was just as well. My editors let me know at the outset that it was better not to be friendly with the players.

So I talked most with Coach Constantine and Asher, who spoke about his days as a player for the grand Belgian club Mechelen, which he'd say with the wildest of inflections. No way, Asher, I'd say, you didn't play for Mechelen. He assured me he had and that he was still good friends with one of its star players, the Israeli international Eli Ohana. *Why would I lie?*

One thing I learned from watching all those games up close was that college soccer was never going to produce world-class players. The player I was most impressed with in the summer's European Championships—televised live on Channel 41, now called Univision—was the angelic left back Paolo Maldini, who was still only nineteen during the tournament. He was younger than some of the NYU players and was playing professionally not only for AC Milan but as a starter for Italy, which could only be stopped in the semifinal by Valeri Lobanovsky's indefatigable Soviets, who, in turn, could only be stopped by the goal of goals by Marco van Basten and the Dutch. Van Basten was only twenty-three but had been a regular on epic teams like Ajax and Holland since his late teens.

By age eighteen or twenty, or certainly twenty-two, it seemed to my still-developing soccer sensibility that a serious player who wanted to achieve greatness should be at it professionally virtually year-round, not just fifteen games from September through early November. As good as NYU was (it went 10–4–2) and even as competitive as it was against the occasional Division I opponent like St. Peter's, St. John's, and Manhattan (1–1–1), if you wanted to be among the best in the world, you had to compete against the best—and the most savvy and cynical, too, from a young age, not against the wholesome, honest, hardworking players of Case Western and Emory.

October 29, 1988
Legends Game
Giants Stadium
East Rutherford, New Jersey

On one of the last NYU game days, there was a special event at Giants Stadium—an old-timers game, billed as a legends game, between former greats of the Americas versus those from the Rest of the World. The NYU game was in the early afternoon at Asphalt Green against Manhattanville College and the Legends Game was at 4:00 p.m. at the Meadowlands. Gus Constantine was excited to go and invited me to go along with the team. Remarkably few went: maybe his son, who was on the team, and maybe Louis and Billy.

On this legends day, Gus would see an old friend of his, one from his refereeing days—perhaps I'd heard of him? David Socha.

The David Socha, I asked?

You actually do know who David Socha is?

Are you kidding me? He was the first American to referee a World Cup game, Scotland–New Zealand. He was the linesman in the Italy–Poland semifinal in the 1982 World Cup. He reffed the Italy–South Korea game in the last World Cup and was a linesman in the USSR-Belgium match, one of the best games ever. How could I *not* know David Socha?! Doesn't everyone know David Socha?!

Gus laughed. *You're funny, Michael Agovino.*

The just-retired Michel Platini would be there—his farewell match. The Michel Platini Jubilee was broadcast on one of the Spanish channels and I was sure to record it. Roberto Rivelino, Paolo Rossi, Johnny Rep, Zbigniew Boniek, Pat Jennings, Ruud Krol, Johan Neeskens, Ricky Davis, Hubert Birkenmeier, and Andranik Eskandarian would also be there. And there would be David Socha, and, Gus said, I was welcome to have dinner with them after the game.

I'd grown to like Constantine a great deal, and in addition to the game stories, to which my editors gave ample space, I included him in various sidebars and features. Earlier in the month, I wrote a column titled "World Cup Comes to U.S.: But Soccer's Future Is Still in Doubt," about whether the United States being awarded the 1994 World Cup on July 4 was indeed the seismic shift many of us had hoped for. The immediate goal, and Constantine agreed with me, was to qualify for the 1990 tournament. I wrote:

> If the U.S. does land a spot as one of the 24 finalists in 1990, it will probably take the same road as the Canadians in '86: playing in its own zone, with little attack, and even less creativity. But why should such drab, stout soccer be tolerated? Especially with the successful arrival of Algeria, Morocco, South Korea, and Cameroon on the international scene. . . . And what about the reports that soccer is the most popular sport among our youth? Why can't the U.S. develop talent or build a successful national team?

"It's coaching," Constantine said. "Coaching has worked two ways. Because the sport is relatively young in the U.S., you don't have many qualified coaches. As a result there's been some suffering. On the other hand you have those who over-coach. To them everything is a set play. It's programmed like basketball. If a kid is not in the right position a coach is going to yell and scream. Forwards are especially over-coached."

About the lack of a professional league, the coach said, "I don't think you're going to see it for a while. A true professional league, unless you have a television contract, can't survive." But he was optimistic. "A lot of things are changing now. I think the leadership in the federation, the new leadership, is very progressive. They know what has to be done and I think they will be successful."

We took the team van to Giants Stadium. Gus drove and got there in time. Traffic wasn't a problem as there weren't many fans.

The next day, the *New York Times* said there were 20,731 "soccer-hungry spectators," which was what we were. I was ravenous myself. It was surprising there weren't more since the *Times* had written about the game the previous month. And the previous day, Alex Yannis, who along with George Vecsey tried desperately to keep soccer coverage alive in the paper, wrote on how the U.S. Soccer Federation signed contracts with fourteen players to keep the nucleus of the national team together by paying them basic living expenses and encouraging them to supplement this while playing on clubs in the regional American Soccer League and the Western Soccer Alliance. Quoted was Sunil Gulati, the chairman of the federation's International Games Committee, a name that was coming up with more frequency in these tiny soccer dispatches. The goal was qualification for the 1990 World Cup and to prep, already, for 1994. This announcement was made at a luncheon for the legends game, so I was surprised more didn't turn out.

The match ended 2–2, Rivelino and Carlos Caszely of Chile cancelling out Platini and Rossi. I wondered what the former Juve teammates thought of the small crowd, compared to the 1982 All-Star Game, which they had both played in. It must have seemed that soccer had regressed in this country, so why then were we awarded the World Cup? Or maybe that's why? Anyway, no one asked them, or if they did it wasn't reported anywhere. The *Times* wrote less than two hundred words on it the next day.

For dinner, Gus choose a steak place in SoHo, perhaps the loudest single spot on Manhattan Island, a restaurant that either aspired to be a nightclub or a restaurant that turned into a nightclub at a certain hour, an hour, apparently, that was upon us. It was impossible to hear soccer war stories from someone who was on the field at the last two World Cups. He brought two friends of his down from Massachusetts—nice guys, not in soccer; I think they were state troopers. Socha seemed shocked that anyone outside the fraternal order of referees would know who he was. He was flattered on the one hand, puzzled that anyone would care so much on the other. Problem was it was too loud to have any kind of meaningful conversation.

I earnestly shouted questions that he could barely hear, but he tried to answer as best he could over all the noise. That was how the rest of the night went, but it was my first brush with an international soccer legend, if anyone considered referees legendary.

December 4, 1989
The *Washington Square News*
NYU's Loeb Student Center
566 LaGuardia Place
New York, New York

After my initial hesitation to approach the student newspaper, I couldn't get enough of the place, sometimes at the expense of my actual classes. After that first semester of assiduously covering the soccer team, I was offered—and gladly accepted—a promotion to associate sports editor. Even better, it came with a small stipend, which would count toward the required work-study job that I needed to retain my scholarship and financial aid.

Throughout the semester and beyond, I had an ongoing conversation about international soccer—its history, its issues, its philosophies, its future—with Louis, a reserve player on the NYU team. Like me, he watched it on TV and was an addict. Like me, he had a long commute, in his case from southeast Queens, but we'd spend hours on the phone, long-distance from the Bronx to Queens, often on weekends, and never once was NYU soccer or school ever brought up. He seemed to take pleasure in reminding me, in literally every conversation we had, that Haiti scored a World Cup goal against Italy in 1974. And a fine goal, I'd say, a well-deserved goal. When it came to soccer, I always looked for something admirable in a team that wasn't my own, while not being obnoxious about any team I supported. I always looked for the weakness in my team(s) and expected disaster to strike, and accentuated the positive on other teams, especially if they were of underdog stature. But sometimes enough was enough. So yes, I told him, I knew the story of the 1974 World Cup. I had the official film. I watched it over and over and over, and I may have even let Louis borrow it. It was a good goal, a great achievement for a small nation making its first appearance in the tournament, really it was, but okay, I get it: yes, Haiti scored against Italy . . . and Italy won the game 3–1.

Despite that minor cold war, we remained friends, even made a joke of it, Haiti-Italy 1974. During one conversation, Louis came up with a great idea. Why don't we try to start a group called something like the International Soccer Club and rent an office in Loeb Student Center? Hmm, I thought, I'm in Loeb all the time, so it would kind of make sense. He went on: In the office, we'd have couches, subscriptions to *World Soccer* and other international magazines, and a TV and VCR. We'd charge members dues and with them buy videos and have screenings. And on Wednesday afternoons we could watch the European Cup, UEFA Cup, and Cup Winners' Cup games on WNYC, which would show them if any Italian clubs were playing and inevitably they were. *Oh, this will be awesome!* Yeah, and we could get guest speakers to give lectures on soccer history and on various soccer philosophies. I interviewed the former Cosmo and U.S. national team player Boris Bandov after NYU played Manhattan College, where he was now an assistant coach, and he seemed like a nice guy; maybe he'd give a lecture. *Oh, that would be incredible, a real Cosmos and U.S. international!*

We weren't sure who our members would be. NYU players? Billy, yeah, Billy would join, but probably not the other players. Louis knew a few other Haitians; they would join. Cool, but who else? I could get someone at the newspaper. He doesn't really like it, but he doesn't hate it. Great, we'll get him. *Awesome!* I had connections in the student life office since I worked for them one summer. This could work, and it could be awesome and we always talked about it and talked about it some more. But with our long commutes, the upper reaches of the Bronx and the outer ones of Queens, classes, his time with the team, and mine with the newspaper, it remained just that, talk. But good talk it was.

In the spring semester of 1989, I had to devote my time to all NYU sports, but I didn't abandon soccer. Every May, in the last issue of the academic year, the editors of the paper would include a picture of themselves with a clever caption. I was camera shy, so I decided to pose in the newsroom with my face inside an issue of *World Soccer* with the caption: "Leave me alone. I'm doing my reserve reading." Which was more or less true. (On the front cover is a Bayern Munich player; on the back, a Toffee.)

Just a few days after that, the *New York Times Magazine* ran an incredible piece of long-form journalism on soccer violence, by Lesley Hazleton, from her upcoming book *England, Bloody England*. Its focus was the latest soccer tragedy: the death of ninety-six Liverpool fans, crushed to death in an FA Cup semifinal at Hillsborough Stadium in Sheffield. Like Heysel, it just became known as Hillsborough.

Since Heysel, the *Times* had devoted more coverage to the scourge of hooliganism. The year before, during the European Championships, it ran a story on page 1, entitled "British Government Devising Plan to Curb Violence by Soccer Fans," by Howell Raines. But Hazleton's was the longest and best piece I'd read yet on hooliganism, *World Soccer* included. And could she write; that's how I wanted to write, but after I'd reread my college newspaper articles, I realized I wasn't close. She wrote of an Arsenal–Manchester United match at Highbury:

> There was something about their enthusiasm that attracted me, despite the violence with which they expressed it. Their vigorous language was free of the repression that's so characteristic of England. They were 18 or 19, they were uneducated, they were already stuck in dead-end jobs or living on the dole, but for the space of a Saturday afternoon, they could forget all that and openly, loudly, and raucously enjoy themselves. There was no holding back. This was mainly a working-class crowd, uninterested in the stifling niceties of upper- and middle-class life. This was another England—the England ignored or conveniently forgotten by Anglophiles, who find it hard to reconcile their upper-class fantasies with lower-class reality. There was no masking here. No embarrassment. That was the pleasure of it, and that's why the stadium was crammed. Football—soccer to my American

ear—is where the emotional restrictiveness of being English breaks down. This is where you can let go.

This:

Visitors and home team had been carefully separated from the start. At one end were the Arsenal fans, cheering and jeering. At the other, Manchester United fans jeering and cheering to match. Chanted insults were traded back and forth the length of the pitch, as though medieval armies were trumpeting their calls to arms across the field of battle. A huge inflatable banana got big play in the Arsenal terrace. It was raised high and jiggled up and down whenever Manchester's star player neared the goal. A chorus of monkey noises went up, and the fans started jumping up and down and scratching under their arms. The player was black.

And this:

The list of weapons found on football fans in the last few years includes the following: sharpened coins, bottles, bricks, catapults, lumps of concrete, razor blades, sheath knives, spring-loaded spikes, flares, plastic lemons filled with ammonia, stones, cans, smoke bombs, tear-gas grenades, hammers, machetes, blackjacks, surgical scalpels, knuckle-dusters, firecrackers, iron bars, studded maces, spiked balls and chains, and darts. . . .

In a sense, football violence is a huge, obscene gesture directed at the ruling classes, at the rigid structure of English society. It is a working-class howl and, like most howls of the powerless, it ends up hurting them more than anyone else.

Wow! To her powers of observation, to how her mind worked, to her writing. But also a wow, holy shit, I can't believe this goes on. Darts?! Monkey chants?! And then later in the piece—Hazelton has an empathic ear, too—she quotes a police officer: "I'm so ashamed you should see football this way. They're morons, the lot of them—complete morons. They say you have to go to South America to see good football nowadays. It seems they really know about crowd control there."

South America? So he thought. So I thought. But soccer confirmed, and confounded, stereotypes. Later in the year, there was a killing, not ninety-six, just one, and not a fan, but a Colombian referee named Alvaro Ortega. On December 4, with my first full year at the *Washington Square News* just about complete, and my first decade as a soccer fan, I wrote a column. I had introduced two concepts after my small promotion: that the sports editors take turns writing an opinion piece, and that we could occasionally write about non-NYU and professional sports. On this day, I wrote "Medellin, Soccer, and the Yen: The Politics Behind It All." It was on the murder of Ortega and how the upcoming Toyota Cup final in Tokyo between AC Milan and Nacional, whom I had seen live the previous year, should be cancelled, just as the remainder of the Colombian season had been—that money, in this case, the sought-after yen of Japan, like the United States an underdeveloped soccer frontier, should not have the final word over the integrity of the game. Still, I loved this Colombian club and its players; I described the Nacional defender Andrés Escobar as elegant, a word I'd used not for the first time, and not for the first time describing defenders. I valued defending; I always thought it was half of the game and needed to be stressed and paid attention to, but thought defenders should be, well, just that, elegant. But in the future, I'd have to find new words.

So all this. Fan violence (still), the surreality of it, referees murdered, drug money, avant-garde goalkeepers, fans—with just a few, like Louis, obsessed in, mostly, the best of ways, who could be touched to tears. There was menace, the inexplicable, and then this: hope. The United States made the World Cup on its own merit, a 1–0 win in Port of Spain, Trinidad, when a draw would do them no good. It was the first time I remember an entire crowd dressed in its team color, red in this case. As happy as I was for us, the U.S., I couldn't help feel Trinidad's deep disappointment. I met Trinidadians in the Bronx. I liked them. Sometimes when I assumed someone who would stop and kick the ball with me for five minutes in Co-op City was Jamaican, I was wrong; they were from Trinidad, and god, did they love soccer. I was happy (maybe the U.S. would save soccer from itself, *take me out to the ball game)*, and I was sad (maybe the Trinidadians could have, too). Was that okay, that ambivalence? Or was there one side, and one side only, in wars, however simulated?

June 4, 1990
The *New York Times*
229 West Forty-Third Street
New York, New York

In 1990 I was still full of questions, as always, but full of hope and frustration, too. Hope in that, for the third time now, a World Cup was imminent. The excitement, particularly this year, was unbearable. Everyone, it seemed, was in agreement: This tournament could well be the best ever. For one, it was being held in Italy, which had the best league in the world, Serie A, and a passionate fan base. Then there were the extraordinary teams and individual talents: Giannini, Vialli, and the Italians; Maradona, Caniggia, and the Argentines; Careca, Bebeto, and the Brazilians; Zavarov, Aleinikov, and the Soviets; Gullit, Van Basten, and the Dutch; Michel, Butragueno, and the Spanish; Higuita, Valderrama, and the Colombians; and always the Germans.

I bought one three-pack of Fuji VHS tapes after the other to record every single game from Univision. I knew I'd want to relive many of these games again and again, for years to come, and now with the VCR, I'd be ready. I did this the previous summer for Copa América. That, too, was in a great soccer country, maybe the greatest, Brazil, but ended up being a major disappointment, the stadiums three-quarters empty, the games dreary. I taped every game, but the minute the tournament ended, I began taping over them, and would continue to for the upcoming games.

But waiting in anticipation wasn't enough. I had to write about it. I used my bullyish pulpit at the *Washington Square News*—I had been promoted again to sports editor—to write a lengthy World Cup preview. Fortunately, it was one of the last issues of the semester—a slow time for NYU sports—so I was unlikely to hear any grief from fellow staffers, our soccer-suspicious faculty adviser, or the student body at large.

I wrote this: "As long as violence doesn't ruin it, this could very well be the best World Cup since 1970 and maybe of all time."

I wrote that Maradona was still the world's best, but that with the exception of Caniggia, he didn't have much support. That the U.S. team could only hope for 0–0 draws. That this Brazil team, although the favorite, was functional and not as pleasing to the eye. That the Colombians would be one of the most exciting teams, though Higuita's "stunts against the Germans could cost his highly skilled team dearly." That Köln's "pint-sized midfielder," Thomas Hassler, could claim superstar status after the tournament.

Then there was the frustration. On June 4, I opened our front door to scoop up the *New York Times*, faithfully delivered every day in front of our twenty-second-floor apartment. I anticipated a World Cup preview in *Sports Monday*—I still kept the *Times*'s preview from 1986 and a file of most soccer articles since then—and there it was, bigger this time. But then I started reading.

It was sloppy, second-class treatment, I felt. I had to do something. The next day, I wrote a letter to the *New York Times* sports editors.

There was one mistake after the next: Maradona played for AC Milan (not Napoli); Austria, it was said, qualified for the second round in the 1986 tournament (they weren't even in the tournament); Spain, we were told, had "lightweight" competition in Group D, but Uruguay, also in D, were in a "difficult" group. There were several names misspelled (Sebastiao Lazaroni was suddenly Sebastiano; Gianluca Vialli was Gianlucca; Van Basten was Van Baston). For

Scotland's flag icon the *Times* used the Union Jack, not the Saltire. I was on a roll. I then cited an article from the day before, Sunday, June 3, that claimed that Liverpool was the scene of the 1989 tragedy in which ninety-six fans were crushed to death. "Wrong again!!!" I wrote. (I used an embarrassing number of exclamation points in this two-and-half-page letter.) "The city, gentlemen and ladies, if you care, was Sheffield—Hillsborough Stadium in Sheffield, to be exact, in a FA Cup semifinal between Liverpool and Nottingham Forest." And then I told them they'd misspelled Gary Lineker's last name in another column on the same page. And Argentina didn't defeat host country Belgium 1–0 in the opening match of the 1982 World Cup. It was the other way around—and Belgium wasn't the host, Spain was.

Then I pulled out the file I kept of soccer articles. I kept going. I informed the *Times* that they had misspelled John Harkes's name in a caption back on February 4 and misspelled (again) Brazilian coach Sebastiao Lazaroni's name on February 1 and João Havelange's name in a front-page story on July 5, 1988. I told them that in a June 10, 1988, article about the Heysel disaster that they had said the teams were from Liverpool and Milan. "Juventus," I wrote, "is a club team from Turin, NOT Milan."

I concluded with this: "I bet the *Times* thinks soccer in this country is for a bunch of illegals and blue collar ethnics who don't read English or even if they do, don't read the *New York Times*. Well, if that's what you think, you're very wrong. . . . It's about time this sloppy soccer coverage is put to an end. It is, as they say, an insult to my intelligence."

Touché!

The tournament? Best since 1970? Best ever? I was wrong. It was the most disappointing World Cup ever. There was a spitting incident, one low-scoring game after the next (followed, it seemed, by penalties), and that number: 2.21, the average goals per game, the lowest ever. And the *Times* never ran my letter.

December 1990
Esquire Magazine
1790 Broadway
New York, New York

During my last semester at NYU, I got an internship at *Esquire Magazine* as a fact checker. I went in once or twice a week and researched short front-of-the-book pieces, the first one being on head cheese by Verlyn Klinkenborg. I had no idea what head cheese was, and after I read it, I still had no interest in it, even if it was clear that this was "manly food." I was beginning to think the research chief, not much older than me, had little faith in me since he'd just give me one short item after the next.

But as the months went on, more and more of the magazine began to make sense. By November, the editor's letter was head-lined "American Potlatch," and there was debate between the copy and research desks about whether the word was used correctly. In fact, it was. I had taken a Native Art of the Americas course my sophomore year. It was difficult, but I learned the concept of the potlatch, a massive giveaway that would bolster one's status. That same month, the research editor gave me a feature—just to read; he claimed he wanted my feedback—on a book editor named Erroll McDonald, a black man from Brooklyn, who was an unlikely new star in the cloistered, lily-white world of New York publishing. I loved the piece, I told him, and loved this guy McDonald even more. Then he gave me an excerpt from an upcoming Don DeLillo novel. I knew of DeLillo, but, embarrassingly, I told the editor I hadn't read him. The excerpt was called "Shooting Bill Gray," a wonderfully inscrutable scene between a reclusive writer and a photographer attempting to take his picture. The novel, out next year, would be called *Mao II*. What a title, I thought.

I don't know how he knew, but my editor got wind that I was a soccer fan, and *Esquire* would be running a feature-length excerpt from another forthcoming book, this one nonfiction and, of all things, on soccer. It would be called *Among the Thugs*, by Bill Buford. *Would you like to check the facts on it?*

Would I?!

As repulsive as it was—reportage of mayhem and destruction—it was exhilarating to read. The excerpt was the section that detailed the 1984 second-leg Cup Winners' Cup Juventus-Manchester United match, specifically on the terraces just out of camera range and outside the Stadio Comunale after the match. My head was spinning after I read it; I had to walk about the block in the cool air. The writing levitated off the page:

I felt weightless. I felt nothing would happen to me. I felt that anything might happen to me. I was looking straight ahead, running, trying to keep up, and things were occurring along the dark peripheries of my vision: there would be a bright light and then darkness again and the sound, constantly, of something else breaking, and of movement, of objects being thrown and of people falling. . . .

Again we moved on. A bin was thrown through a car showroom window, and there was another loud crashing sound. A shop: its door was smashed. A clothing shop: its window was smashed, and one or two English supporters lingered to loot from the display.

I looked behind me and I saw that a large vehicle had been overturned, and that further down the street flames were issuing from a building. I hadn't seen any of that happen: I realized that there had been more than I had been able to take in. There was now the sound of sirens, many sirens, different kinds, coming from several directions.

The city is ours, Sammy said, and he repeated the possessive, each time with greater intensity: It is *ours, ours, ours.*

First, the Lesley Hazleton in the *Times Magazine* last year, now this, wowed again. I couldn't wait to read the rest of the book. I couldn't help but be revolted by the fans of Manchester United, a team I always had some affection for, reading about the old days of George Best. Now everything about the club repulsed me. I was struck by the timing of when this took place: April of 1984. Heysel, I'd read in some versions of the events, was retaliation for the abuse Liverpool supporters endured in Rome, during the previous year's European Cup final, which would have been May 1984. But after reading Buford's account, it seemed likely to me that the English destruction of Turin a few weeks before may have been the real source. Maybe the *romani* thought, "It could happen in Turin, but not in our town." I told my supervising editor of my theory. He didn't know soccer—to him a rivalry was Texas vs. Texas A&M—but he listened closely and seemed impressed.

I gained new confidence working within this material. From a bleary-eyed intern who wore the same pair of jeans the entire semester, I had become an authority on something and could keep up in conversation with these very smart young editors. I even spotted mistakes—a couple that were essential to correct.

It was another language, soccer, one spoken by this editor of *Granta*, the British literary magazine, and I spoke it, too. Soccer had been an aid for me in intangible ways; this was the first time it was tangible.

It was my last assignment for the internship—the semester, and my NYU life, was about to come to an end—but it was a test, I was certain, that I had aced. (And I didn't ace many tests.) I hoped I left a good impression.

May 18, 1991
FA Cup Final
The Sporting Club
99 Hudson Street
New York, New York

It was hard to stay away from NYU. Just when it got good, it ended. The school newspaper, my life for two-and-a-half years—was hardest to keep away from. So come the next semester, I'd go back, say hi, hang around. There was a war and a recession and few jobs so I had time on my hands. I found some part-time copyediting work at Scholastic on the nearly desolate Lafayette Street, just a few blocks from NYU.

On one of my visits, I heard a British accent. Someone either introduced us or I introduced myself, I forget. His name was Tom, and my first question for Tom was this: What's your club? Without hesitation he said, Fulham. The conversation went something like this:

The same Fulham in the Third Division?

Don Mackay's black-and-white army, he said proudly, pronouncing the last name Mac-eye. And then he asked: How do you know Fulham?

Ray Houghton played for them, didn't he?

Fuckin' hell, mate, how'd you know that?

I had kept the copies of *Shoot* and *Match* from a few years ago and the back-page interview one of them had with him. His favorite food is steak and lager, I told Tom.

He burst out laughing. *Steak and lager. Fuckin' hell.* A friendship was born.

Tom was doing a semester at NYU while his father was transferred to New York by his British company.

The conversations went on for hours.

Why Fulham, if you're from Wimbledon?

Why Roma?

I asked him if he'd heard anything about a new book about soccer violence called *Among the Thugs.* No, he hadn't but if you're interested in hooligan culture you must read *Steaming In* by Colin Ward. Brilliant, he said, fucking brilliant.

We talked over and over about last year's World Cup. It was disappointing for me and everyone, I thought, but not for Tom and England fans. It was their best showing since they'd won in 1966. I hadn't thought of that. He told a story of watching, with a few mates, England's tragi-heroic semifinal against West Germany. After Chris Waddle missed his penalty, and the Germans celebrated, they paused for a moment, took it all in, and began to sing, slowly at first, then picking up the tempo, to the melody of "Auld Lang Syne": "We're proud of you / we're proud of you / we're proud of you, we are / we're proud of you / we're proud of you / we're proud of you, we are . . ."

He said he hated the Germans, and that during the game, he and his friends had put their thumbs and forefingers together in an O shape over their eyes and made a buzzing sound, pretending they were the Royal Air Force dog-fighting the Luftwaffe.

He told of road trips on Brit Rail to see Fulham away matches against Third Division opponents that all seemed to begin with the letter B: Bury, Bristol Rovers, Bristol City, Bolton, Brentford, Blackpool, Birmingham City.

Then there were the away matches against Swansea and Cardiff in Wales. I told him I'd always wanted to go to Wales. I imagined Swansea to be all dramatic cliffs and crashing waves. Mikey, he said, you've gone mad, mate. It's nothing like that. It's absolute *shite*. Complete, fucking *shite*! And the Taffies, besides Tom Jones, are a bunch of incestuous tossers. Like your West Virginia.

He could not be stopped. "This is what we sing when they come to the Cottage," and then he, again, broke into song: "Harry Secombe fucks his brother, Johnny Toshack fucks his mother, all the Taffies fuck each other, fuck off back to Wales!"

This one was funny, most of his stories were funny, hilarious, but then there were some about England that were hard to believe, but apparently true. That when Tottenham Hotspur, known as "the Jewish club," played away, the opposing supporters would make hissing sounds to mimic the gas chambers.

No, I said, that can't be. That's sick; who could do something like that? Did you actually see it and hear it? I asked. No, he said, he never saw the Spurs in action—they were in the First Division and North London *shite*—but it was well-documented.

Then there was the stuff he did see and hear. His second team was the Rangers in Glasgow. I knew well the sectarian rivalry the club had with its cross-town rival Celtic. He'd periodically take the train up to Ibrox Stadium and hear things like "Fuck the Pope and the Vatican" and worse.

At the end of the semester, we decided we had to see a game together, not that there was much to choose from. While I was still at the student newspaper, I wrote a story on the Sporting Club, at 99 Hudson Street in TriBeCa, which claimed to be the first-ever sports bar, and probably was. The manager I interviewed said the best-attended event was the FA Cup Final.

So we went, in the morning, since the bar showed the game live, to see Nottingham Forest vs. Tottenham Hotspur. I invited two other friends: Louis, the Haitian-American who was on the NYU team (we never did launch the NYU International Soccer Club), and one of my former colleagues at the newspaper, who was from New Jersey, but knew little about soccer. He kept saying the names of the two teams incorrectly and loudly—"Mike, who are you rooting for Totting-HAM or Notting-HAM?"—so loudly that the British expats who were putting away pints and screwdrivers at ten in the morning kept giving us cold stares. Tom whispered in my ear: Would you get your mate to shut up with that Totting-HAM, Notting-HAM *shite*. Some of these lads are hard men and they'll twat him.

And I didn't know who to root for—or did I now have to change my vocabulary and say "support"? I, too, liked the England team from the previous year. I wanted them to beat West Germany, and I liked the sportsmanship they showed after losing to my Azzurri in the game for third place, dancing around arm in arm with one another after the match. Forest had the smooth Des Walker in defense, whom I was a big fan of, and the more fearsome Stuart Pearce, whose nickname was Psycho, Tom told me. The coach was the charismatic figure Brian Clough, who *World Soccer* wrote about regularly as some kind of maverick.

Spurs had Paul Gascoigne, an ongoing drama, and Gary Lineker, one of my favorite players since the '86 World Cup when he scored one ugly clutch goal after another with a wrist cast.

It didn't matter who won, or that Des Walker, bless his heart, scored an own goal in extra time. It only mattered that I was watching the FA Cup live from the pristine Wembley, among friends and strangers, maybe a few hard men like Tom said, but we all shared the bond.

July 21, 1991
Cosmos Reunion Match
Giants Stadium
East Rutherford, New Jersey

In May of 1991 I was hired at *Esquire* full time, not in research but in the copy department. The relationship I had built up during the internship was the step in the door. There were many young people there, and they all had photographs and such tacked and pinned onto their cubicle walls.

It took a few weeks, but I finally clipped some photographs from *World Soccer* and other soccer magazines—one was of the Estádio do Maracanã with the rolling hills in the background—and put them up. The magazine was on two floors, a kind of upstairs-downstairs arrangement, with the top editors above and the grunts—the fact checkers, copyeditors, art, and production—below. We were connected via a spiral staircase with many of the magazine's illustrious George Lois covers on the wall in between. Of course, it was routine for the senior-level editors to walk down and confer on layouts, research findings, and copyedit queries.

One afternoon, an editor whom I knew was second or third from the top, a man with an indelible mustache and neurotic gait, who walked by midlevel staffers more senior than me, stopped dead in his tracks when he saw the pictures in my exposed cubicle.

He appeared in shock. The photos were from a fan who really knew the game. One was from an Italian magazine, another from a

French one. He finally spoke, and asked the question I'd heard again and again, sometimes even when it wasn't spoken, but only asked through a look or a glance or a smile: "What? You like soccer?"

His name was David Hirshey, the articles editor, and although I'd known of him for months, that was the day I met him. He was, then and there, effusive and friendly, and colleagues in neighboring cubicles looked on in stunned silence. David didn't talk to young staffers unless he had to, or if they were a somebody.

Knowing soccer, in this case, made me a somebody. He asked me if I'd been to Maracanã. I said no, but that it was a dream. How, why, since when, did I like soccer? I said, 1982. He said he was at the Italy-Brazil game with his father. I didn't know whether to believe him. He told me he covered the Cosmos. We talked about the Cosmos. Like Tom, the conversation was uncontainable. It jumped from one topic in soccer to the next.

Within weeks came the news that a soccer game would return to Giants Stadium. Former Cosmos would play a doubleheader against Italians from the 1982 team and Brazilian legends. David couldn't control himself. He would get tickets, he said. He lived up to it, but went one better: he got press passes for both of us—with locker-room access. We could meet the players. Now I couldn't control myself.

It was my first professional soccer game since the two excursions to Giants Stadium in 1988 for the exhibitions. None other, to my knowledge, was played in the New York area. Over thirty-one thousand turned up. We kicked balls in the parking lot.

Paolo Rossi, Claudio Gentile, and Alessandro Altobelli from Italy played and still looked as they had at their fighting weight, which, seeing them up close, didn't look like much, maybe 150 or 160 pounds. Carlos Alberto, Johan Neeskens, and Wim Rijsbergen were there. So were Vladislav Bogicevic, Ricky Davis, Hubert Berkenmeier, and David Brcic.

David talked to colleagues from the old Cosmos days, which already seemed like a lifetime ago. What a shame it ended that way, we all agreed. Bogicevic told Filip Bondy of the *New York Times*, "I could really tell the boat was going under the hill by the last year. It was problems at the top with Warner Communications. Atari was having trouble. Nobody was buying video games. If Nintendo starts sooner, there would still be a Cosmos."

We all knew the NASL and the Cosmos weren't coming back. We had the World Cup to look forward to, but beyond that, who knew?

As we headed to the locker room, I recognized someone. It was my soccer coach from tenth grade, the one who had also coached the much more prestigious school in Rye. I never particularly liked him—he always reminded my teammates and me of our inferiority—but since the atmosphere was collegial this afternoon, I went up and said hello. He didn't remember me, but I wasn't especially bothered; he was always a blowhard. Sure enough, he started bragging, if that's the word.

Mike you said your name was, right?

Right, I said, Michael.

Mike, look at me now. I'm not coaching high school anymore. I'm with *the Cosmos!* The Cosmos, Mike. Look at me!

March 23, 1992
The Waldorf-Astoria
301 Park Avenue
New York, New York

I remained convinced that holding the 1994 World Cup in the United States would somehow fall through. I always looked for precedent in soccer, and I remembered Colombia 1986 going to Mexico. There was still a stadium problem in the U.S.—and not merely the question of whether anyone would show up? There was the artificial turf issue and beyond that the question of field width.

Would Giants Stadium, as close as we had to hallowed soccer ground in this country, even be selected as one of the venues? It was a few feet too narrow, and when the U.S. was first awarded the competition, there was wild talk of constructing a platform above the field and the big blue wall and building a field above that, in effect eliminating the first few rows of seating. It seemed farfetched. But could there be a World Cup in the United States and not in its most cosmopolitan city? The Yale Bowl in New Haven, which hosted international games in the 1970s, was a proposed site, too. It would also be a venue for this summer's U.S. Cup along with RFK Stadium, Soldier Field, and Foxboro Stadium. There had been another press conference for that, at the Plaza Hotel, just a few weeks before. That I didn't attend; I don't remember why—perhaps because it was on my birthday—but the shadow of the Yale Bowl hovered disconcertingly.

My fears were allayed finally at a press conference at the Waldorf for the announcement of the host cities and stadiums. FIFA showed it could adapt by voting earlier in the month that exceptions could be made so that Giants Stadium's eighty-yard width, two yards shorter than FIFA regulation, would work. Ah, relief.

I got a credential—even if it wasn't a coverable event for *Esquire*—and the afternoon off. For the first time, the World Cup felt as if it was going to happen. They gave out goodie bags, including a large Nike duffel bag—black with an aqua-green trimming—that seemed unusually generous and practical. I put on a tie under my leather jacket and my shiniest shoes. This was the Waldorf, although the conference room they put us in, perhaps like all hotel conference rooms, seemed unremarkable, in a pigs-in-the-blanket kind of way. Was the Plaza conference more glamorous? Prominent sportswriters were here, and I said hello to George Vecsey of the *New York Times*. I told him I kept a of file of his articles and thanked him for keeping alive the memory of soccer, especially of the 1982 World Cup, which he seemed to invoke lovingly any chance he could. He was gracious and thanked me for reading.

Giants Stadium would have to be converted to natural grass, which I still couldn't picture, but so would the iconic fortresses of the great American gridiron: the Cotton Bowl, Soldier Field, and the Pontiac Silverdome. Again, I thought, seeing would be believing.

July 14, 1992
Ultrà
The Public Theater
425 Lafayette Street
New York, New York

If sports had little intellectual or cultural ballast among my peers at *Esquire*, books and music did. But perhaps even more relevant were movies, especially foreign and independent ones.

One of my fellow copyeditors went to film school and spoke lovingly and engagingly about cinema. Listening to her was like auditing a graduate course on film. She would talk about her weekends huddled in places like Film Forum, Theater 80, Angelika, Cinema Village, and the Quad. She spoke reverentially of John Cassavetes, John Sayles, and Jim Jarmusch; Kurosawa, Fellini, and Godard. Her tone wasn't superior, but, rather, infectious. As learned as she was, she didn't lecture; she beamed. She was open-minded, her tastes egalitarian. If she'd been a sports fan, soccer, I'm certain, would've been her game.

I liked movies, sure, but didn't go regularly. My parents were big film buffs, especially in the 1960s and '70s, so I was familiar with the great directors, especially from Europe. So to have something to talk about come Monday mornings—besides sports, which, with the exception of soccer, I was watching less and less of—I began going to movies soon after I started the job in the spring of 1991.

I became a sponge. I'd see almost anything, with the exception of big blockbusters. Like my colleague, I began leaning more and more to the small American independents, classics, and foreign, which included Italian.

The Joseph Papp Public Theater, it was announced, would host a summer Italian film festival that organizers hoped would be an annual event. The theme was to match an old classic with a more contemporary offering since recent Italian cinema fell into near obscurity.

A couple of nights after my first Antonioni film, *Le Amiche*, one I had problems with—the pace, some of the wooden dialogue, a scene at the end that seemed easy to parody today—but one that still left me wanting more, I had a treat. Not only would the first of the double bill feature a Visconti adaptation of Dostoevesky—both favorites of my father—but the second film was about soccer. It was called *Ultrà* and was directed by Ricky Tognazzi, son of the late actor-director Ugo Tognazzi, who, to be honest, I'd never heard of.

The Public Theater, probably because it wasn't a movie theater per se, was an exciting venue for film. The steep incline, the vantage point of looking down at the screen but without that suburban multiplex contrivance of "stadium seating," combined with an eclectic crowd, gave the screening an immediacy, as if this was the most important place to be on a sultry July night.

Ultrà, a story of a road trip with the hardest-core fans—*ultras*—of AS Roma, had come out in Italy the previous year and also won Tognazzi a Best Director award along with Jonathan Demme at the 1991 Berlin Film Festival. Why, I wasn't sure at the end. As devastating as *White Nights* was, in the best of ways, *Ultrà* was disappointing. And not because it wasn't whitewashed or may have made my team look bad. I didn't care about that. The last thing I was interested in was PR for Roma or Italian soccer. I wanted realism and an attempt at truth in all of its elusiveness.

I knew Roma had *ultra* groups that crossed into violence, as did Juventus, who are also depicted in the film. I had read *World Soccer* cover to cover for almost ten years. I knew from the Heysel reporting that the hardcore Juve supporters were at the other end of the stadium during the day of the dead, the 1985 European Cup final, and that the fans set upon by Liverpool supporters were merely *tifosi*, fans, not *ultras*. I knew, from Brian Glanville's column, that Roma fans had attacked Liverpool fans after the 1984 final. He wrote that Lazio fans attempted to help the Liverpudlians—to spite their hated rival. It was hard to forget, as Glanville would often repeat what he wrote.

So if hooliganism was known as "the English disease," I knew it existed, especially domestically, in Germany, Holland, Greece, and many other places, Italy included. What threw me in this movie was its opening scene, what appears to be a gang rape but isn't. Then there's a love triangle and an intrusive soundtrack. And there are mullets. There's no glimpse of soccer, just the stadium's strobe lights as the bus approaches the Stadio Comunale, as in *Among the Thugs*. That I liked. Hooliganism is never about the soccer. The final scene, excruciating and brutal, was also well done. But it didn't seem like enough. Maybe *Among the Thugs* spoiled me. Or maybe this material would best be handled as documentary.

What I did know was that I never wanted to be in the midst of crowds like this. *Romanisti* or not.

August 12, 1992
Cup Final
Film Forum
West Houston Street
New York, New York

Every day on the way to work on the West Side, I bought the *Times* and the *Post*. I'd read the *Post* back to front, as most city guys did, and lead with sports. My first section of the *Times* had always been page 1 and International, but now was Arts and especially the movie reviews. I read each one, and it seemed that I saw every American independent and foreign film that played in New York. I thought I'd like to, one day and one day soon, either go to film school, as my colleague on the copy desk had, or write on film for a living—that's how intense, seemingly overnight, my relationship became with celluloid. Most films came out on Friday but Wednesday usually had one or two worthy releases. This day, when I read a review of a new Israeli movie, I was stunned, pleasantly so.

It was called *Cup Final* and took place in the summer of 1982 after Israel's intervention into Lebanon, which had been mired in a civil war. It concerned an Israeli POW who bonds with his Palestinian captor, not only over soccer and the concurrent World Cup in Spain but over their mutual love of the Italian national team. If ever a movie was made for me it was this: foreign; war, or, rather, antiwar; soccer; Spain '82; and the Italy team, not as divider but as uniter. After work, I was the first on line at Film Forum, which, besides the rare screening at the Public, was fast becoming my favorite theater in town.

Any murmuring or glimpse of soccer, even with the World Cup approaching, was still rare and had something of a nurturing quality to it. It felt like teaspoons of ginger ale after having the life sucked out of you by a stomach virus. The European Championships earlier in the summer weren't televised, not even on the Spanish channels. Euro '84 and '88 brought me as many great memories as the World Cups in '82, '86, and '90. Not having access to it felt like a regression. Even the 1978 World Cup final, I had heard, was shown on closed-circuit at Madison Square Garden—or maybe it was the poor, unkempt Felt Forum, where my father took me to see Sugar Ray Leonard and Roberto Duran on CCTV in the summer of 1980.

Denmark, so fresh and bold in France '84, when I first saw them on TV, became champions of Europe. Denmark had a similarly adverse relationship to Germany as did Holland, and one that was more than the rivalry of neighbors. It went back, like everything else in Europe, to the war. So for the Danes to beat Germany—and the new, unified Germany that many observers believed would be virtually unbeatable for years to come—seemed impossible and exhilarating. To win it in Sweden, among their Scandinavian cousins, who lob jokes at them from across the Øresund, was the equivalent of a soccer exacta, something like Holland accomplished four years before in West Germany. Or maybe a trifecta, since Denmark hadn't even qualified for the tournament and was only admitted after UEFA disqualified Yugoslavia on account of the war, or wars, when the country broke up.

So while it might have been nice to see the Danish Dynamite win its first major trophy, maybe it was a blessing. When I would finish the movie reviews and get back to that front page of the *Times*, the news from the Balkans was sobering. Should a pan-European tournament even be played while atrocities were, again, being committed in Europe? At what point is it frivolous?

Speaking of war, here was a new Israeli film that looked back to an ugly period from ten years before, one that was only on the periphery of my fourteen-year-old radar at the time. As the world celebrated soccer in Spain that summer, the summer I fell in love, life carried on in all its brutality.

In *Cup Final*, Ziad, a dashing Palestinian with a faraway gaze, only wants, we find out later, to study pharmacology and be with his Italian wife and son. He's especially tender with a younger Palestinian, a diabetic, who resembles more a mama's boy than a soldier. And poor Cohen, the Israeli. He was all set to spend part of his summer vacation away from his clothing store in Holon to go to the World Cup. He shows anyone who cares his game tickets—good seats, too—and his hotel reservations. But, as he puts it, "That asshole starts a war." To which his fellow Israeli retorts, "I told you not to vote for Likud."

Cohen and Ziad aren't fighters. Some of their comrades are diabolical, but not them. If they had gone to a New York City high school, they surely would have been friends. They are, these two characters, like you and me: smart (or so we'd like to think), funny (on occasion), and lovers of soccer. They just want to watch the games. But duty (and blood and tribe and country and land and honor and grievances and slights) calls, and these two perfectly decent men have little or no choice. They can't run away. There's no Canada in the Mideast. They'll be changed, at least part of them ruined, for the rest of their days on earth, however long or short that may be.

Which team do you like? Cohen is asked early in his captivity. "Italia," he says. "Italy."

Says the laconic Ziad, "Good team. Very, very good."

Cohen at one point shows his tickets for Italy-Scotland and Italy–North Korea. When the BBC World Service, after news from Lebanon, announces that Italy beat Scotland 2–0 and West Germany loses to "Algiers" 2–1, there's a moment of contentment between Ziad and Cohen. But, frivolity aside, for someone who came to soccer because of the 1982 World Cup and who could still break down each first-round (and second-round) group and could remember virtually every result, it was hard for me to tolerate two very odd mistakes. Italy–North Korea? That was in 1966. And Italy-Scotland? Horrendous. Especially since the filmmakers made sure the faux BBC World Service reported it, too. Why get the West Germany–Algeria score right (though why "Algiers"?) and not the opponents of Italy, the team the two protagonists profess to support? Even if Americans wouldn't know—or care—Israelis would, so would Palestinians, Europeans, Africans, South Americans, and virtually everyone on the burgeoning film-festival circuit.

The movie kind of stopped for me at that point. Was there a good reason for it? Did the allusion to North Korea–Italy's most famous loss—have some kind of hidden meaning? Then what would it be? And Italy-Scotland? They never played in the '82 World Cup. Then I realized it was just an oversight, a moment or two of laziness. But, I wondered, what else was inaccurate?

By the time I was able to refocus on the movie, I had to question the sanity of the otherwise endearing Cohen. When he and Ziad go position by position and name their preferred Italy starting eleven (though they only name nine players, if you listen carefully), Cohen says he would prefer Marco Tardelli to be on the bench. Ziad, and he's right here, says, no, Tardelli is a great player. Bruno Conti, my guy, the guts, heart, and skill of that team, isn't mentioned by either. Shame!

Finally, something made sense. As they march toward their destination, Beirut, Ziad announces on the long walk that they're going to watch the game. One of his men asks, What game? Italy-Brazil. But we can't find food, one says. Man doesn't live off bread alone, Ziad responds.

They break into an empty, well-appointed house, relax, and watch the game. It's Italy-Brazil, how can you not? As the game reaches its crescendo, where's Cohen? Napping in the lavish bathtub.

The night of the final, they approach a checkpoint outside Beirut. There's more inaccuracies at the end of the movie, all easily avoidable. You hear the British announcer talking about the third goal by Altobelli, but as Ziad looks through his binoculars at a T V screen in the checkpoint booth, he sees Tardelli celebrating with his famous "scream" celebration—which was the second goal. Then all hell breaks loose and the film ends.

All that said, it was impossible not to like *Cup Final*. I just would've preferred if it had ended ten or so minutes earlier, in a last minute of calm just before the final between Italy and West Germany, with this scene between Ziad and Cohen, both of whom are certain Italy will win: Cohen, in a beautiful act, digs into his wallet, where he keeps his unused tickets, some of which he used earlier to wipe his ass. He takes out his ticket to the final and gives it Ziad.

"Do you think I'll make it?" Ziad asks?

"Maybe for the second half," says Cohen.

September 14, 1992
The Terrace Room
Plaza Hotel
New York, New York

Soccer films at art house theaters were nice—no, they were great—but did this count as World Cup buildup? Certainly not. Movies like this went largely unnoticed, even in New York. What was needed to hype the tournament was marketing, the kind that could get Americans to buy into virtually anything.

In late May, early June, there was something called the U.S. Cup, a four-team, six-game tournament played in Chicago; Washington DC; Foxborough, Massachusetts; and New Haven, Connecticut. The teams were predictable—the United States, Italy, Ireland, Portugal—as were attendances, ten thousand to about forty thousand. The winner, the United States, was the only surprise. But there were often international friendlies in the United States and they didn't enhance the perception, reputation, or coverage of soccer in America.

What this upcoming tournament needed was sparkle outside of soccer. What it needed was a mascot, and no one did mascots better than Americans. If Roberto Baggio, Luis Figo, and Ray Houghton couldn't bring out the masses, then a cartoon character surely could. And so one would be announced, not in the final slow news days of August, but after Labor Day, when the new cultural and sports calendars began to blossom.

For this major announcement, of course, there was a press conference, and for the second time this year it was at the Plaza Hotel. If anyone was keeping score of press conferences, it was Plaza 2–Waldorf 1. I missed the first one at this illustrious establishment in March; this one, then, was essential. It was, after all, where my parents got married, in the Edwardian Room. When I told my mother that the Plaza, where she would still go every once in a while for tea, hosted a soccer event, she couldn't believe such a thing. *What? Soccer in the Plaza?*

When I explained that it was just a morning press conference with snacks, she asked what they served, whether those exquisite tea sandwiches were offered. No, I said, but pedestrian old mini-Danish and muffins. Then she lost interest.

And there was nothing much to report, except that the new mascot would be named Striker and was a cute dog. I was a junky for World Cup trivia and weird facts, and besides the mascot from 1966, World Cup Willie, a lion in a Union Jack, and Ciao, a Rubik's cube-like stick figure with a disembodied head from 1990, I didn't know of any mascots. Posters yes, I loved the World Cup posters, and one of my books had them all, with the official logos, too, my favorite being Mexico 1986. (My goal was to find a T-shirt with the two hemisphere globes and the red-and-white ball.) But mascots? Who was the '86 mascot? Or '82, a World Cup I knew everything about? Joan Miró did the poster, so why didn't I know the mascot?

Judging Striker against Ciao and Willie, it seemed rather simple. Willie pranced, arms out, with confidence in his step; Ciao, hello and goodbye, was more enigmatic, and appears to be juggling a ball off his (or her?) thigh, like a true Italian *fantasia*. Striker, on the other hand, simply looks straight at us and smiles. It's a warm smile but there's no mission there, or mystery. Now, though, the World Cup seemed official. It wouldn't get moved to Mexico like it did in '86. There were still dark days ahead; the following year would be as bleak as any in the mideighties for us American soccer fans. But the World Cup was going to happen. It was coming. There was light. This being America, the mascot made it official.

Part 2

THE RENAISSANCE, 1994–2003

After literature and eros, football
is one of life's great pleasures.

PIER PAOLO PASOLINI

June 25, 1994
Argentina vs. Nigeria
Foxboro Stadium
Foxborough, Massachusetts

So it arrived. Nothing happened to the tournament or to me. I lived to see it. The Knicks made the NBA finals; the Rangers, my team when I still cared about hockey, ended its curse and won the Stanley Cup; and the Juice had a gun to his head in the back of Al Cowlings's white Bronco. I didn't care; the World Cup was here. There were events surrounding the tournament: a photo exhibit of Pelé's American years at the South Street Seaport; an English soccer collector's memorabilia at Sotheby's; Symphony Space on the Upper West Side would show the movies *Cup Final* and *Ultrà*, both of which I'd seen, as part of a summer film festival; and there would be international music, dance, and food festivals.

And there were the games. I saved up what money I could and would go to as many as I could afford.

The obvious choice was the opening game at Giants Stadium—Italy, my team, against Ireland. Tickets didn't present themselves, for one, but I had a bad feeling about this match. Italy were known to be slow starters (even if the facts didn't always support this), but more to the point, the Irish had a good team. I watched them beat England in the 1988 European Championships and saw them give Italy a tough game in the quarterfinal of the last World Cup. In fact, the Irish were one of the few teams that came out with its reputation not only intact after Italia '90 but bolstered.

Even at the draw for host cities at the Waldorf, all the talk was of how Italy wanted to be centered in New York. Careful what you wish for. And there's a lot of Irish love in New York. Just compare parades: St. Patrick's vs. Columbus. Where all these Italian supporters were on that day was anyone's guess. The stadium was a sea of red, white, and orange (though my English friend Tom told me that the Irish referred to that band in their flag as gold, not orange—and by the way, that you should call the city of Londonderry just Derry). The story, apocryphal maybe, went that the Italians, assured of victory, sold their tickets to the Irish at a steep markup.

What happened didn't surprise me, nor did the fact that Ray Houghton, who tallied against England in Ireland's Euro '88 opener, scored the goal against Italy. *Steak and lager.*

My first game was not at my "home field," Giants Stadium, but outside of Boston, at Foxboro Stadium in Foxborough, Massachusetts. (I didn't get why exactly the town and the stadium were spelled differently, yet I sort of did; something akin, I guessed, to the Throgs Neck Bridge and the Throggs Neck section of the Bronx. Some things were best left unexplained.) It was a stadium I was familiar with from NFL telecasts, along with the Orange Bowl and Mile High Stadium, for no other reason than "it looked great on TV." In reality, I'd always heard it was a dive or a dump. And, in fact, it was. There were no backs to the seats, something I'd never experienced. Not that it mattered; it was Argentina-Nigeria. The Super Eagles of Nigeria were first-timers, but one of the hot picks to go far. It was an edge-of-your-seat kind of game—just as well we sat on benches, then. The vantage point was good—I went with David, who got hold of the tickets, and he always scored good seats, a talent he seemed born with—and the fans created a delirious atmosphere. The Nigerians jumped up and down nearly the entire ninety minutes; so did the Argentines, but more in a kind of choreographed unison, like I'd seen on TV. They also dusted the now converted grass with ticker tape, just like back home. Foxboro/borough as if it were Rosario or Mendoza.

And of course, we would see, both of us for the first time, Diego Maradona. This was not the Maradona of 1986 or even 1990. We realized that. He was thirty-three—old in soccer years—and had already served a year-long drug suspension. But still. He even scored in Argentina's first game, a win against Greece. After he scored, he ran to the sidelines and screamed into the camera lens. The eleven o'clock news programs loved that one. What else to call Maradona at this point? A genius? Tortured genius? The best of his generation? The best ever?

In the Nigerians, he would face a blend of skill, speed, brute force, and swagger—and Taribo West's hair style, inventive even by soccer standards. When Rashidi Yekini, the massive striker, scored Nigeria's first World Cup goal ever in the previous game, he ran into the net, grabbed the twine with both hands, and howled, a howl of joy, of arrival, of sorrow perhaps that it took so long. And then he put his arms through the webbing and clenched his fists toward the crowd. It was a T-shirt waiting to happen. This was a team no one wanted to play. And after just six minutes against Argentina, Samson Siasia scored a goal, a beautiful, self-assured goal, chipped from the edge of the area.

But Argentina had its own rock star, Claudio Caniggia. After leaping over one scathing tackle after the next against Cameroon in 1990—a famous win for the Indomitable Lions—Caniggia appeared to be ready for this afternoon. He wore a thin headband, more a woman's beret really, to keep his blond hair out of his eyes—the kind that in a few years would become routine. But had substance in addition to style.

Against Nigeria, Caniggia was there to put in a rebound after a low, unruly free kick from Gabriel Batistuta. And seven minutes later, Maradona, as he did so many times—the winning goal in the 1986 final, the tying goal of the 1990 semifinal—acted as enabler. This time with a quick free kick, seamlessly placed in the path of Caniggia, who curled it, inch perfect, past Peter Rufai.

This was the sport at its highest level. Maradona, Caniggia, and the Nigerians gave us a gift. We didn't know it when we left the stadium—emotionally spent—but Maradona would test positive for amphetamines and would be banned from the tournament. He would never play for Argentina again. My first World Cup game was his last World Cup game.

June 28, 1994
Italy vs. Mexico
RFK Stadium
Washington DC

For my first Italy World Cup game, I overslept. I scored tickets from an editorial assistant at *New York* magazine. It was on a Tuesday afternoon—in Washington—so a day off from work was needed. David was only too happy to play hooky.

The plan was for us to meet at 8:00 a.m. for the Metroliner at Penn Station and have plenty of time to get from Union Station in DC to RFK Stadium for the 12:30 kickoff. David was to bring a stack of newspapers—not just the local papers but *USA Today*, the *Washington Post*, and any he could get his hands on—and he and I would criticize all the World Cup coverage and laugh up a storm. Ha, these NFL or NBA guys trying to cover soccer. *Only George Vecsey knows what he's talking about.*

That was the plan, anyway. Let's just say I've never been a morning person. But if anything could get me out of bed, it was soccer. For whatever reason, the alarm didn't go off on this Tuesday morning. Maybe I had it set for 7:00 p.m., maybe I didn't actually slide the switch to "on." Instead, I woke up feeling oddly well-rested but with that terrible feeling that something was wrong. When I looked at the clock—almost 8:30—my face morphed into Edvard Munch's *The Scream.*

I put on clothes—no way would there be a shower—and frantically called David at home, knowing he was already waiting for me at Penn Station, but telling his wife that if David called to check in, to let him know that I would be there, that he should just wait, and we'd get a later train.

When I got to the station, he was still waiting with his pile of newspapers. Instead of chastising me, which he could've (I deserved it) we ran—we didn't jog, we ran—in unison to the track. The nine o'clock train, barring delays, would get us to Union Station by a little after noon. After that, we'd have to hope the Metro was all that it was cracked up to be. During the trip, we went through the papers and had a few laughs at the coverage. Only the British papers got it right. And Vecsey, don't forget.

Before we pulled into Union Station, we waited by the doors, as if it were a subway, assuming a sprinter's starting position. The doors opened and we ran, not exactly sure where we were going, just looking for signs to the Metro. The soccer gods were with us: we zigged when we were supposed to zig, zagged when we were supposed to zag, and jumped into a Metro just as the doors closed. We had to transfer, but didn't have to wait. When we got to RFK, there was still a modest walk ahead of us. Again, we ran. We had played soccer together, and even basketball on Friday afternoons on West Fifty-Fifth Street, an *Esquire* tradition, and were in decent shape. We sprinted toward the stadium, and then up the ramps to the upper deck (remember, David didn't score these tickets, I did), and just as we got to our seats, Mexico's captain, Marcos Ambriz, stood over the ball at the center circle, made the sign of the cross, and rolled the ball to Alberto García Aspe.

We made it—and for kickoff.

We shook hands—it was an achievement, given the circumstances—and sat down to enjoy the game. An enjoyable game it wasn't. It should've been. It was the last game in the group, and Italy, after losing to the Irish and barely squeezing by Norway 1–0, needed a win to guarantee progression to the second round. Mexico, too, also had a win and a loss and everything to play for. This was not Argentina-Nigeria—few were, I suppose—but Italy played as if they had a slate of games remaining, not merely one. They lacked the urgency they had had against Norway, when they played with ten men and had the audacity to take off Roberto Baggio.

Mexico, in white shirts and red shorts, were better for large stretches. It ended 1–1; all four teams ended with a win and a draw with four points. As we left the stadium, it was still unclear if Italy would advance. Its fate was now in the hands of Russia, who needed to beat Cameroon, which it did, 6–1, thanks to Oleg Salenko's five goals.

Would I have gone to the next day's game at RFK—Saudi Arabia vs. Belgium—if tickets had come up? Maybe, maybe not. No, probably not. But I would've missed a gift, the gift of the tournament.

Saudi Arabia's Saeed al-Owairan's goal was likened to Maradona's goal against England in the 1986 quarterfinal, four minutes after his sublime act of deception.

But al-Owairan's goal was more beautiful. There, I said it. I had never heard of him. In a preview article I did for *New York* magazine, I touted a Saudi named Majed Mohammed, "the Desert Pelé." Now, twelve seconds, three-quarters the length of the field, and a slalom through six Belgian players later—including one Michel Georges Jean Ghislain Preud'Homme, winner of the Yashin Award for best goalkeeper—there was a "Desert Maradona." It was the only goal of the match and enough to get Saudi Arabia through to the next round.

Where Maradona was round and thick, with the proportions of a meatball, al-Owairan was lithe, balletic. Where Maradona's stride was short, the ball proverbially "attached to his boot with a shoestring," al-Owairan's was like that of a gazelle. Where Maradona thrived in close quarters and seemed to welcome contact, even enjoy it, al-Owairan effortlessly eschewed it. Beauty, and from the most unexpected of sources. If only I'd been there a day later.

July 10, 1994
Germany vs. Bulgaria
Giants Stadium
East Rutherford, New Jersey

Thanks to my first published freelance articles, I had extra funding for more game tickets. One was for the *New York Times* Style section on the history of the World Cup poster. Peter Max did the latest version, but Joan Miró and Antoni Tàpies had done posters for España '82 and Annie Leibovitz for Mexico '86. To my surprise, Eric Asimov of the *Times* answered my query letter with a phone call and a green light and there it appeared on Sunday, June 12.

The very next day, I shared a byline in *New York* magazine, the feature-well, no less, on a World Cup preview. Not your regular preview, but one distinctly out of the mind of my former colleague Michael, who had recently moved there to be the deputy to legendary editor Kurt Andersen.

Michael was my first encounter with a Harvard graduate. If they were all like him, I could see why the school had the reputation it did. He simply knew everything. When a few of us once talked about Carl Schurz Park on the Upper East Side, someone asked, "Who was Carl Schurz anyway?" and Michael responded, "Wasn't he an educator?" The fact that he phrased it as a question, made me secretly admire him more. He wasn't a know-it-all, like so many Ivy Leaguers I had already met, but he did know it all. And if he didn't know it, he wasn't afraid to admit it—for me a real sign of security. While one person, if asked if they had seen Fellini's *Amarcord*, might respond, "Yes, but a long time ago" (read: so I don't remember anything about it), Michael wouldn't. In fact, he did see *Amarcord* and, when it came up once, he recalled the scene with the fat prostitute.

But one thing he didn't know was soccer. Clearly he was intrigued, enough to defer to someone else in a lower position—someone like me. So when he called me about doing something for *New York* magazine, I was shocked—pleasantly so—and flattered.

His concept was thoroughly irreverent and original. "A Nasty and Brutish Sport: Why This Month's World Cup Is More American Than You Think," he titled it. One of his staffers did the main essay while I did four of five sidebars, including "Reason No. 3: It Inhabits a Moral Universe All Its Own" and "Reason No. 4: You Can Cheat." Their bulldog investigative reporter John Connolly did "Reason No. 5: It's a Chance for a Few Rich White Guys to Get Even Richer." It began this way:

> Imagine this scenario: George Steinbrenner is chosen to put on the World Series. He rounds up sponsors and cuts a deal with the networks. Since all the people who run baseball are friends of his, they agree to give him 30 percent of all profits from the World Series. And because he's such a swell guy, he gets to own the entire league as well.
>
> Preposterous? It would seem so. But that's the type of cushy deal Alan Rothenberg, president of the United States Soccer Federation, managed to wrangle for himself as the organizer of World Cup '94.

It detailed a variety of conflicts of interest and questionable ethics. I thought for certain it would kick up a storm. It didn't. The corridors of power are impenetrable, I thought, even in sports.

I was proud to be a part of the package. David feared that purists, including friends of his, would think it was the usual American put-down of the game. I didn't think so. In my mind, we were celebrating soccer, warts and all, sure, while giving it a good send-up. There *was* the Soccer War, it *was* xenophobic, and players *did* try to cheat. Soccer reflected life, to me, more than any other sport.

As for Michael, he didn't say it—he wasn't demonstrative or forthcoming necessarily—but I think he was falling in love. It was the first time I encountered someone falling under the spell of soccer before my eyes.

I had been similarly afflicted twelve years earlier. I fell in love with the spectacle (the opening match in 1982); the ritual (the national team uniforms that mimicked the flags, the exchanging of crests, the team photo, the goal celebrations, such as Erwin Vandenbergh dropping to his knees; a player (Bruno Conti); a team (Italy); the upsets (Algeria over West Germany); the cheating (West Germany—Austria); the weirdness (Kuwait walking off the field); the subtexts (the Solidarnosc banners taken down during Poland-USSR)—or were they just texts? And the players, the ball, what could be done with it, on finesse over power, on ball trickery. Beneath it all was fandom.

With Michael, it was hard to tell what was beneath the burgeoning love. Something was different. Not in a bad way, but it seemed as if he would possess the game in a different way than I had.

I knew people who had grown up playing the game or grew up watching the game, or both, who came to it through a parent or a culture. I was none of these, but came to soccer through serendipity, endless curiosity, and a sense of an underground, populist international brotherhood. Not opportunism. Michael wasn't entering this obsession opportunistically; it's not as if he had his eye on the editorship of *Soccer America*. I just didn't know.

Why didn't I just ask him? He was always friendly to me—maybe because I was from the Bronx and seemed different somehow—but you never wanted to seem foolish in front of him, ask an obvious question. He was intimidating.

My last chance to ask was probably on the day Germany played Bulgaria in the quarterfinal, a certain win for the current titleholders. David had two tickets and brought me, and Michael had two of his own and brought an *Esquire* writer who was working on a book on Germany—the country, not the team, though the two were inextricably linked. Michael gave us a ride to Giants Stadium in an old beat-up convertible that, whatever the model was—cars never registered with me—had an unmistakable cool.

But it never seemed appropriate to ask: Hey, why do you like soccer anyway? Besides, who cared? Everyone was welcome, even Harvard grads who may have been conversant in crew.

Then we got to the stadium and sat in our separate seats. David's were upper deck, but only four rows up and at midfield. We watched Jürgen Klinsmann get fouled in the box, and to make sure the referee, a Colombian, saw him, he embellished—something he was good at. He thrust his head out, his hair followed, and down he went down, like Frazier at the ferocious hands of Foreman. Lothar Matthäus, the stoic captain, converted. Germany led 1–0, as expected. The win seemed only a formality.

I didn't like Germany, but I can't say I was displeased. I had already bought a ticket for the semifinal at Giants Stadium, with Italy securing a spot against the winner of this game. Even if Germany appeared in good form, I knew they never beat Italy in a World Cup or European Championships match, and I liked Azzurri's chances. Who wouldn't want to see Italy-Germany in a semifinal?

Then, with fifteen minutes remaining, Bulgaria's Hristo Stoichkov decided to make an appearance. The wily FC Barcelona great had an indifferent match. Then Andreas Moeller breathed on him and he went down. Whereas Klinsmann truly was fouled earlier, his embellishment only for the referee's sake, Stoichkov was not fouled at all. But he knew how to work a ref, especially one who spoke Spanish, and was waiting for this the whole match. He got the whistle and took the awarded free kick himself, as he was wont to do. Was there any doubt?

A photo shows the Germans in a perfect six-man wall, with each of them airborne—Klinsmann is highest—arms to the sides or in some cases linked, eyes all squinty. Keeper Bodo Illgner is in the background, protecting his half of the goalmouth. Stoichkov has his right foot firmly planted at a forty-five-degree angle, both arms have careened to his left side, and his left leg, obstructed by his torso, has swung high like a dancer's. The ball appears headed for the thirteen on the front of Rudi Voller's jersey. Instead, it went over the wall just so and plopped into the back netting. As soon as he struck the ball, Stoichkov began his celebration run toward the crowd. Germany's coach, Berti Vogts, blamed the wall.

Three minutes later, Yordan Letchkov thrust his forehead, one that recalled Saint Anthony's, into a cross: 2–1. For a moment, our mouths remained open in shock, and then we started the chant, a chant that emanated from the lower deck, where the red, white, and green horizontal bands predominated—a chant that was new to us: Bul-gar-ie, Bul-gar-ie, Bul-gar-ie.

This wasn't supposed to happen. If Michael hadn't been convinced before, I imagine he was now. I didn't need to ask.

July 13, 1994
Italy vs. Bulgaria
Giants Stadium
East Rutherford, New Jersey

The day before Germany-Bulgaria, I watched the Italy-Spain quarterfinal on West Broadway in SoHo at a large Italian restaurant called I Tre Merli. At the half, when Italy led 1–0, I figured the game was over, and went downstairs to the men's room, where there was a pay phone. I called Ticketmaster to see if there were any seats for the semifinal on the thirteenth. To my surprise, there were seats, and I pulled out my credit card and bought one on the spot: two hundred bucks for the upper deck, section 327, row 12, seat 23.

I went back upstairs. The place was packed on this Saturday, even if Italian fans didn't usually pack the bars the way the Brits and Irish did—confident the game would finish 1–0. Italy had been without Franco Baresi since the Norway game, but still had his three Milan teammates in defense: Alessandro Costacurta, Paolo Maldini, Mauro Tassotti—the former two, along with Baresi, first-ballot hall-of-famers, if there was such a thing in this sport. Joining them after the Baresi injury was the impossibly tiny, not even 5-6, 150-pound Antonio Benarrivo. No way would they blow the lead. Wrong again.

After José Luis Caminero tied it in the fifty-eighth minute, I began to sweat. I'd just spent two hundred dollars, a lot for me, to see Italy most likely play Germany. Now it could be Spain playing

Germany. Not a bad thing, but given Spain's ongoing underachievement at World Cups, that would almost certainly mean a German win and another trip to the finals and possibly a second consecutive World Cup.

But just as he did on the same Foxboro turf against Nigeria, Roberto Baggio saved the day for Italy. Against Spain, the winning goal had come two minutes from time, the same as the tying goal against Nigeria, a vintage Italian counterattack that began virtually at their own touchline and nearly traveled the full length of the pitch. The finish, from a delicate man, was exquisite.

Italy, like everyone else, was light and dark, sun and shadow, *paradiso* and inferno. Inferno appeared in the form of a Tassotti elbow to the face of Luis Enrique. It was ugly and should have been a red card and penalty for Spain. The Hungarian referee missed it, one of several that escaped him this match. He could've sent off Spain's Abelardo in the third minute for a reckless foul—even *World Soccer* said so—but he didn't; he only showed yellow. Italy were unlucky when Gianfranco Zola, gentleman and genius, was sent off for nothing—for kicking the turf—against Nigeria; on this day Tassotti wasn't sent off.

But when the whistle blew and Italy won, the restaurant erupted and they played the Gipsy Kings' "Bamboleo" as loud as possible, either sarcastically or because they genuinely liked the song.

So Italy was in the semifinal against, not Germany, but Bulgaria. One thing was certain: the final would be Italy against Brazil. For me, it felt like a minor victory. After the *New York* magazine piece came out, ABC's *World News Now*, a program that aired from 2:00 a.m. to 4:00 a.m., invited me on a few days into the tournament. Italy had already lost to Ireland. The host knew nothing about soccer and had me identify some players in highlights. Then she asked me who would be in the final. I said Italy and Brazil. This seemed to antagonize her, for some reason. Italy lost already, she said. This isn't unprecedented, I assured her. The segment was never broadcast, but the producer sent me a tape.

No one at ABC's *World News Now*, I was certain, remembered my prediction, but Italy would play Brazil in the final; not a spectacular Brazil but an efficient one, with two great goal scorers—Romario and Bebeto.

Of course, the semis still needed to be played. I went alone this time, by my old route from the Port Authority. I hadn't been to the Port Authority in years, probably since 1988 for that trip to Giants Stadium. It was a place I only went to for two reasons: to get the bus to Giants Stadium or to accompany my sister, where she would get a bus to Worcester, Massachusetts, and head back to her university. She graduated in 1987 and the Cosmos were no more—if only in the mind of my former high school coach—so, thankfully, there had been no occasions to go to the Port Authority.

But 1994 was not only a new year, it was the beginning of a new era. Rudy Giuliani had only been mayor since the beginning of the year, but if you were in the city for any substantial period of time before that, you could feel a difference. Less of the things New York was known for would be tolerated: disorder, crime, and the illicit. It would all be a windfall for big business and real estate—and those who could afford real estate—not so much for the rest of us. But the Port Authority appeared purged. Even the area around it felt less frenetic, less rancid, less scary. It was Travis Bickle's dream come true.

So it was back on the bus, almost twelve years to the day after my first game. That game meant nothing, but changed everything; this game meant (almost) everything, but changed nothing.

Italy wouldn't lose this game. Where the blue oval rings of Giants Stadium had been covered in the Irish tricolour for Italy-Eire, today they were red, white, and green—and not because Bulgaria had the same tricolors as Italy, only in horizontal. No, it was because the *tifosi* turned out this time.

Baggio scored two goals within the first half hour. They were not of his 1990-versus-Czechoslovakia vintage—a top-ten World Cup goal of all time—but were of impeccable technique that required balance, touch, and placement.

That would be the game. Italy may blow one-goal leads but not two-goal leads. Arrigo Sacchi, who had been hired at AC Milan from Serie B's Parma by Silvio Berlusconi in 1987, led a revolution for the Rossoneri, as Milan was nicknamed. For Italy, it was never quite the same, even with a Milan-centric lineup. But he got them to the final. His dress sense was appalling. A powder-blue polo shirt with lime-green pants that looked more like hospital scrubs, pulled high up to his midsection. As an Italian, and one who spent a significant amount of time in Milan, he should've been ashamed of himself.

Baggio limped off the field with an injury and you knew immediately that Italy would have no chance against Brazil—technically, Brazil or Sweden, but at these stages, soccer got very predictable. Baggio would provide a puncher's chance; without him, or with him at less than 100 percent, there would be no chance.

So enjoy the moment now, I thought. And I tried, really I did. But there was no one to hug or celebrate with. Weren't you supposed to hug strangers? Even Bill Buford, from Louisiana, hugged strangers at a Cambridge United game, and his was a book about violence. There were *tifosi*, not in jerseys but blue T-shirts with Italy's FIGC crest and Baggio written across the back, and they were all happy but they were not huggable strangers. I'm not sure why. I asked one group where they bought these blue Diadora shirts. I don't remember what they said. They were Italians from Boston and came down for the game. They were nice, but then what? Sing? Neither they nor I spoke Italian. Dance? To what? Chant? Even at I Tre Merli, no one uttered the slogan *Forza Italia*, which was adopted for political purposes by Silvio Berlusconi, the new prime minister, but instead said *Forza Ragazzi*. So what did we do? We high-fived maybe, and wished each other luck for the final. Then I got back on the bus to the Port Authority. It was rush hour now, and no one seemed to care, or was aware, that a World Cup semifinal had just been completed. It felt hollow. I realized there, amid the burnished bustle of Eighth Avenue, that it wasn't other fans that I wanted to be around nor was it "atmosphere" that I craved. I wished my father could be with me.

August 24, 1994
East Eighty-Third Street
New York, New York

The World Cup was over. Six years of interminable waiting and that was that. It would only be memories that would change consistency as the years wore on. That and VHS. I was ambivalent now that it was done. Despite moments of emptiness and disappointment, there had been great rewards. I saw Maradona play in person. I saw Baggio score two goals. I attended a World Cup semifinal. I saw one of the great upsets. I had a party for the final, and people came, only seven or eight, but that's about all my small apartment would hold. Still, when it was over I was mentally drained. I needed a break. In fact, after the final, when I walked through Central Park, I thought I'd need another four years to recoup.

But addiction is addiction, and it comes calling, whether you want it to or not. By August the withdrawal symptoms needed to be addressed. So I talked to David. Since the party had gone so well, even without David, who was at the final in Pasadena, I thought it might be time to pull out one or more of my VHS tapes from Soccer Learning Systems and have a viewing at my apartment.

I'd heard from an *Esquire* writer that the legendary New York journalist Jack Newfield had invited friends over occasionally to watch the fights, past and present, another love of mine, so I thought this could be the start of a kind of salon, not of Pynchon or the Mongoose, but of soccer. (In my daily planner earlier that year, I marked off March 5 with this scribbled in: "'66 final" but have no recollection of watching it, at my place or elsewhere. And on July 22, just five days after the final, my calendar reads "soccer movie," but what movie?) David thought it was a great idea and volunteered to bring the beer.

For the inaugural screening, I selected *Heading for Glory*, the official film of the 1974 World Cup. There were seven or eight of us, all familiar faces, with the exception of Parker, the husband of a co-worker. Parker would visit his wife on occasion in the office but I didn't know him nor had I been introduced. One afternoon, I went to the men's room and pushed the door open a little too hard as Parker, with his two-year-old son in his arms, was on the other side. The door hit the kid in the head and he began to cry—and cry and cry. I felt horrible, the kid may have even had a blemish on his forehead, and I apologized profusely. Parker and his wife were nice about it, but I still felt bad and went out to a nearby sporting goods store to find something for him. What to choose? A kids' Mets or Yankees jersey, but then what if the father was a fan of one and not the other? Same with Giants and Jets; Knicks, Nets; Rangers, Islanders, Devils. So I decided, instead, on a spongy soccer ball, not to proselytize—I loved soccer but wasn't evangelical about it—but thought the kid could actually play with it and I remember enjoying spongy toys when I was very young, even if I ended up chewing on them.

When I presented the mother with the ball, Parker and the son had left by then, she was touched and said something like, How did you know? Know what? I asked. Parker absolutely loves soccer, she said.

A day or two later, Parker was back with his son and he came to my desk to personally thank me. Turns out, he was a big fan of the Holland teams of the 1970s. In fact, he could've passed for a retired member of those teams. He was tall, skinny, had longish hair, and was literally a rock star—he had his own band, eponymously named. There was plenty to talk about: Total Football, Cruyff, Neeskens, Rep, Resenbrink, 1974, 1978, 1988, Gullit, van Basten, and this past summer, Bergkamp, Aaron Winter, and my favorite, Mark Overmars, the fastest player I'd ever seen. It seemed, sometimes, that everyone liked soccer, that it was the silent majority of sports.

For the screening night, perhaps I was influenced by the fact that he was coming all the way to the easternmost Upper East

Side, Yorkville, formerly Germantown, and I wanted him to feel welcomed into our fold, informal, inchoate though it was. That, and it was a good tape.

After the film, even though we already knew the famous outcome, we were all sad. Holland and Total Football lost. Their beautiful blond wives cried on the plane ride home. *They've pricked our pretty balloon and our moon has been taken away. Where did we go wrong?* But then we were exhilarated. We all decided we would do this again, back here at my place for *101 Great Goals* or *Boys from Brazil* or *G'olé!* or *Hero.* Or *Liverpool: The Mighty Reds, Road to Munich,* or *Ten Faces of Platini.* My collection had grown. And two months later, on October 29, my date book says, we went to see Parker's band play live.

October 17, 1995
The Palladium
126 East Fourteenth Street
New York, New York

As promising and (mostly) fulfilling as the World Cup was, when it ended you couldn't help but wonder if it was another piece of cultural ephemera, an NASL in miniature. A league was promised to follow, but it would've helped to have it debut just months later in September, or, if it were going to keep the same calendar as the NASL and be a spring-summer-fall league—fair enough considering our brutal winters—then April 1995 would have made sense. But soccer never could make sense of America and America could never make sense of soccer. So the league would wait until spring of 1996. After all that, it appeared as if the momentum was lost, that the Dark Ages had returned. What a shame.

Especially since the U.S. national team had built upon its good performance in the World Cup with an even better display in the Copa América—the South American Championships—in July 1995. The American and Mexican teams were special invitees, and the U.S.

beat Chile and, impossibly, Argentina, 3–0 in the first round, then Mexico in penalties in the quarters and lost to Brazil, again by 1–0, in the semis. And it wasn't on TV, not even the Spanish channels, which had spoiled us for so long. No *vivo en directo de Uruguay.*

Two weeks later, the emboldened U.S. team was at Giants Stadium for another midsummer international exhibition—for so long the soccer fan's hemoglobin. This one was called the Parmalat Cup and also featured Parma, Boca Juniors, and Benfica. I got a freakish summer flu and didn't go.

By the end of the month, there were English games—the First Division now transformed into the more readily accommodating Premier League—being televised in bars and, always a few weeks later, the Italian game of the week on WYNC followed, after a cooking show and the RAI news, by *Novantesimo Minuto,* the highlight show with the gargantuan host Giampiero Galeazzi, known as "Il Bisteccone," the big beef steak. So it was kind of like before, in the 1980s.

In October there was another press conference, although officially, it was an unveiling of the planned Major League Soccer, or MLS. And not at any place as stodgy as the Waldorf. This would be at the Palladium, the famed dance club on East Fourteenth Street, formerly the Academy of Music, which hosted the Band's 1971 New Year's Eve concert and the Clash and Springsteen and Frank Zappa and the Ramones. It became the Palladium in the midseventies and a dance club in the mideighties, when Ian Schrager and Steve Rubell of Studio 54 bought it. Studio 54, legend had it—I was too young to go when it mattered—was an effervescent mix of decadence, exclusivity, and fun. Star athletes would go—New York Yankees, Rangers, tennis players, and Cosmos. David told me a story of when he was with Pelé in Studio 54, hanging out with him while cowriting his biography. Pelé had a blonde and a brunette on each arm (or was it two blondes?) and disappeared into a back room. He looked back at David and said, "Not for the book, my friend, not for the book."

That was then. "Fun City" was no more; this was "Giuliani Time." I went to the Palladium a year or so before for a work party. *Esquire* had something there, maybe something fashion related, and it was okay. It was fun, but not Fun.

MLS hosted this unveiling, with the hope of regaining some of the the World Cup buzz and momentum. So what did they do? They held it at one in the afternoon on a weekday. The league unveiled sponsors and TV contracts—ESPN and ABC would show games without commercial interruption, something that was still thought of as ground-breaking in the United States—players, the ball, logos, and the uniforms, some quite hideous, like the LA Galaxy's "black, chili red, Kenyan gold and juniper."

Hockey still looked back at its fabled Original Six. Major League Soccer, if it ever did get under way and if it would last, would have its Original Ten: the Columbus Crew, DC United, the New England Revolution, the New York/New Jersey MetroStars, the Tampa Bay Mutiny, the Colorado Rapids, the Dallas Burn, the Kansas City Wiz, the Los Angeles Galaxy, and the San Jose Clash. A good trivia question one day, if this league survived.

Less than two years later, the Palladium closed. It became an NYU dormitory.

November 5, 1995
Roma-Padova
Stadio Olimpico
Rome, Italy

In the first days of November, it rained in Rome, rained and rained. I liked inverted clichés, especially during travel—*Parisians rude?*—but not when it came to weather. Where was all of this famous, gentle Roman light? The kind the *New York Times* wrote about over the summer. "The Rainbow That Is Rome," it was titled: "The city changes colors from moment to moment, ranging from pinks and purples to yellows, golds and silvers."

I was a tourist for just five days, having saved some money over the past year to afford a round-trip ticket on TWA, the grandest of all airlines that was now on life support, and a two-star hotel in Ottaviano. I stayed dry by ducking into the major and minor masterpieces on every other corner: a baroque treasure here, a Romanesque gem catty-corner, a Caravaggio nestled in the fifteenth-century Santa Maria del Popolo at the edge of that epic piazza, and everywhere Bernini. I was jet-lagged, sleepwalking, wet, and lost, but happy to be there.

On my last full day in the unholiest of cities, a Sunday, the sun came out just when I needed it to. Henry James, as the *Times* cited, once wrote about a similar day on his own trip to Rome in 1872: "The weather is perfect, the sky as blue as the most exploded tradition fames it, the whole air glowing and throbbing with lovely color." He could have been talking about this day. And this was game day.

I walked direction northwest. What began as a ramble around the placid Villa Borghese slowly turned into a determined march as I fell in with a legion of fans trimmed in red and yellow-orange. Not in jerseys, mind you. It was unseasonably chilly, and anyway these fans seemed far too fashionable to be seen in a sports jersey. They usually wore a scarf wrapped round some sort of stylish, slim-fitting jacket. I did the same.

I was finally going to see AS Roma, the team I had called my own ever since I watched Bruno Conti in the 1982 World Cup. This would be in person, not *vivo en directo* from the old Estadi de Sarrià in Barcelona, when Conti and Italy beat one of the greatest teams ever, and not on WNYC Channel 31 in New York City via the bow-tie antenna that had too often turned my Giallorossi into various shades of gray and appropriated shadow.

Conti had retired and Roma was in a post-Giannini moment. A couple of days before, a young guy who sold me my ticket and a T-shirt at the Roma team shop said I must remember this name: Totti. He wouldn't be playing Sunday because of injury, but he was a local, only nineteen, and could well be the new Conti.

Now the team's emblem was Aldair, the Brazilian center back who'd won the World Cup the previous year. The opponent, Padova, wasn't glamorous, but had Alexi Lalas, the American who'd also played in the World Cup and last season scored at the San Siro in his first season in Serie A.

As I got closer to the stadium, I met a family—a husband and wife and their teenage son. I asked if I was headed in the right direction—to the Olimpico. I knew it was a stupid question, but as my excitement began to build, I needed someone to talk to. *Si,* they said together, *dritto,* straight, just follow everyone else. I showed them my ticket and asked if I would be sitting near them. No, they told me, but it's a good seat, away from the *ultras,* the hardest-core fans in the Curva Sud, the section behind the goal.

The Curva fascinated me—from a distance. Secretly, after all I'd read about European soccer for more than ten years, I also feared it. For so long, news of soccer back home had been about riots, hooligan gangs, and death: Heysel; *Among the Thugs*; the Hillsborough disaster, a photo of which was used in Don DeLillo's novel *Mao II.* Soccer violence may have been known as "the English disease," but I had seen the movie *Ultrà,* and that was Italian and about Roma fans.

After I parted with this kind family, I became disoriented as I approached the monstrous stadium. I either misread my ticket stub—how many *tribune* are there?—or misread a sign or misunderstand the answer to a mistakenly asked question. I joined a line that would take me inside. We inched forward until the line became a roiling mass of humanity, with me in the middle. By the time I realized I was in the wrong line, there was nowhere to go but forward—forward, I now saw, into what must've been the Curva.

It closed in on me from all sides, this surge. Within seconds, this wasn't cool or colorful in an off-the-beaten-path way; this was just getting scary. Then the pushing started, first from the back, then, in reply, from the front. I was part of this wave, at times losing control of where I could plant my feet. I was afraid for my 35mm camera, the one I'd used to photograph the Borghese Park that morning. As we approached the turnstiles, I began to make out what was happening: *ultras* without tickets were trying to push their way in without paying, and the stewards, the few that there stationed here, were pushing us back. Anyone who lost their balance and fell to the ground could easily have been trampled.

I yelled out in English—something like, "Calm the fuck down"—and suddenly became the focal point of this socioeconomic scrum. As I closed in on the turnstile, I began to hear the word *Americano*. Maybe they were telling the stewards that the American had their tickets, something like, "We're with the American." When I showed my ticket, the steward pantomimed that I was at the wrong gate. He let me in—he had no choice really, there was no way to push back through the crowd—while the *ultras* shouted at me, at each other, at the stewards, *Americano!* They were having fun with it—an experience that nearly confirmed my every fear of international soccer, but that seemed rather routine for these characters.

After the chaos at the gates, there was this: nothingness. I was shown to another door and found myself in an area with no ushers or stewards, no amenities, no game programs, and, though I was too wired to eat, no food stands or beer vendors in sight. I settled upon a section of empty seats and sat to catch my breath and snap some pictures, content, for the moment, to be away from the masses. Maybe I was supposed to be in this section, deep in the corner, maybe not; it didn't appear to matter. So I stayed, with one of the least desirable vantage points, far from the field. About the only thing I saw was Alexi Lalas's hair, unwieldy and orange.

No more than fifteen minutes into the game, a cluster of fans not far away began to wave frantically for the paramedics. I hadn't seen a fight or heard a commotion. The medics carried someone out on a stretcher. A hooligan incident? A heart attack? Should I ask? No, I decided, no more questions. I just stayed in my seat, which may or may not have been mine, and watched the rest of the game. I watched Balbo, the Argentine, and Fonseca, the Uruguayan, score for Roma. I told myself to keep the ticket stub.

April 20, 1996
New York/New Jersey MetroStars vs. New England Revolution
Giants Stadium
East Rutherford, New Jersey

Could you call this Opening Day—cap O, cap D—that reverential word coupling loaded with metaphor and usually reserved for hopeful April afternoons? This was April, after all, but it wasn't the National Pastime (cap N, cap P) or our real pastime, football.

This was soccer, the kind of anti-pastime, the butt of jokes from sportscasters on local TV stations to insecure commentators on the political right (soccer is communist, un-American) to those not quite comfortable with their own sexuality who put down the sport as unmasculine.

And here it was, opening before us again, this time reimagined for the 1990s. And what gall on these newcomers, Major League Soccer, eleven days after a real Opening Day among Major Leaguers at Yankee Stadium. But was this Opening Day or opening day? Was it Grand Opening Day? Or Re-opening Day? Or Debut Day? Or Welcome Back Day? Those Cosmos reunions and visiting foreign clubs may have quenched our midsummer thirsts every now and again, and they may have been fun, but they could feel like a sporting version of Memorial Day.

Of course, today's game didn't really open anything. Our new team, the unfortunately named New York/New Jersey MetroStars (one word or two, we all wondered), had opened the season the week before at the Rose Bowl. For the home opener, forty-six thousand of us showed up.

In the parking lot, that endless parking lot of Giants Stadium, balls ponged back and forth, trickery was displayed, scrimmages—three against three, four against four, six against six that soon grew into nine against eight—were hastily arranged. Kickoff was approaching. And when we settled in, and scanned the crowd, this very respectable crowd, more than half full, even if the *New York Times* wrote that the team expected sixty thousand, you heard this: "It's like old times." Meaning, it was like the Cosmos. This was meant as a positive.

The New York/New Jersey coach was Eddie Firmani, the South African Italian, who'd had two tours as Cosmos manager. The team appeared to be well-constructed, with local players Tony Meola and Tabaré Ramos, who grew up playing for Thistle FC in Kearny, New Jersey—as fertile a soccer landscape as any in the country—and former Rutgers and U.S. international member Peter Vermes. Miles Joseph was a promising young American chosen from Clemson in the inaugural draft.

Then there was the coup, Roberto Donadoni, who had played ten years with AC Milan, the greatest team of the era with three European Cup titles—now rebranded as the Champions League—and over sixty caps for Italy. He'd logged some city miles on his thirty-three-year-old legs in Serie A, but he was in impeccable condition and still had a few top-flight years in him. People in the stands even asked, Why the red-and-black vertical stripes? Are the uniforms in his honor? Another Italian, Nicola Caricola, was also on the team, though in all my years watching Serie A, I didn't know of him.

Donadoni hadn't yet joined the team, nor had Tab Ramos or Colombia's Rubén Darío Hernández, but a strong nucleus appeared to be in place: past, present, future; foreign, American, and even local talent. How could you not have a top team in the New York area? (Then again, why should that be guaranteed?)

But, the ball remaining round, Caricola, in a golden age of Italian defending, put in an own goal with just a few seconds left. Would it be an omen? Eddie Firmani lasted eight games, Hernández ten, and our Metros finished the season tied for the sixth-best record in the ten-team league—the same as saying fourth from bottom.

July 24, 1996
Aldershot Town—Fulham FC
The Recreation Ground
Aldershot, Hampshire, England

Later in the year, I was fortunate enough to be able to afford to go to Europe again, this time to London.

I had been writing a fair bit on the side for my friend Jay, first at the *New York Observer* and now at *Spin*. After the 1994 World Cup there was little opportunity to write about soccer, even with the debut of MLS. As nice as that would have been, I still had my other interests: books, music, and film. I wrote another Style article for the *New York Times* on Romare Bearden, the artist and my father's old friend from the New York City Department of Welfare, and another *Times* profile of Italian director Gianni Amelio. When Jay left *Esquire*, he assigned me a two-thousand-word profile of the Harlem writer and thinker Albert Murray, and when he went to *Spin* he had me profile my favorite singer-songwriter Gil Scott-Heron, who was releasing a comeback album. There were also pieces on Tobias Wolff's Vietnam memoir, a young director named Todd Solondz, and, since Jay knew I'd read Nick Hornby's *Fever Pitch*, he had me do a review of *High Fidelity*.

One hundred here, two hundred there, five hundred dollars for a longer piece, I was developing a second income, and I knew I wanted to spend one of my two weeks of vacation overseas. The choice was obvious. Tom had moved back to the UK a few years before to attend the University of Leeds. We stayed in touch by letters—mainly about Fulham and how it was faring in the Third Division—the occasional phone call, and when he visited his family in New York for holidays. When he graduated, he moved to London to attend law school and rented an apartment in Dalston with Martin, one of his college friends (and a Bury supporter). I had an open invitation, so long as I didn't mind Tom's messiness.

The ideal would have been to go during the European Championships, but I couldn't get away from work during that time and instead arrived soon after the tournament ended. When I landed at Heathrow, Tom was with one of his boyhood friends, Dave, whom I had already met in New York. Dave spoke in a deep baritone and more often than not about Fulham. What I most remembered about Dave was a story Tom shared with me, one of those that should remain between best friends, but was too good to keep in, especially after a night of drinking and darts at Bleecker Street Bar. When Dave was engaged in amorous copulation with a charming West London lass, Jewish preferably, and felt himself reaching what could only be rivaled by Fulham scoring a goal, he would, he told Tom, who would tell me, recite as many football clubs as possible to distract himself and keep from, shall we say, finishing too soon. "Tom, Tom," Tom would say, impersonating Dave, who always started a sentence by saying "Tom" twice, "I do it alphabetically, starting with Arsenal, then Aston Villa, Barnsley, Birmingham City, Blackburn Rovers, Blackpool, Bolton, Brighton, Bristol. I once managed to get to Cardiff City."

When Tom and Dave met me, I was terribly jet-lagged; it was hot for London, but they piled me into the car, and the first place they took me was not for a bite to eat or to the apartment for a shower and a nap, but to Craven Cottage. There was no game—it was a weekday morning in the summer—but to Tom, there was no more important place in London. Not Wembley, not the British Museum, not Buckingham Palace.

You're here, Mikey, finally. Cameras were whisked out, including mine, arms were flung around one another, and shutters were clicked. Tom's friend Jed, of Irish parentage from Manchester, said I must come north and stay with his family for a United match. They had season tickets and there was nothing like Old Trafford, he said. Next time, Mikey, next time.

There was another stop nearby: Stamford Bridge, which no one seemed at all excited about. It was merely on the way and they knew I loved soccer.

Dalston appeared to be a working-class white neighborhood, now with an influx of immigrants. There were satellite dishes positioned on the window sills and Turkish and Portuguese and Croatian flags flown outside many balconies and windows, remnants of the European Championships that had just ended—with a German win, recalling the Gary Lineker quote from the 1990 World Cup: "Football is a simple game. Twenty-two men chase a ball for ninety minutes and at the end the Germans always win."

The next big thing was to see Fulham play. The season was still weeks away, but training had started, and Fulham had a friendly away to Aldershot, the military town just outside London. It was a must road trip. Neither Tom nor his roommate Martin would accompany me to Maryon Park in Woolwich, across the Thames Barrier, a park I'd been obsessed with since seeing Antonioni's film *Blow-Up*. It wasn't easy to find this park where so many pivotal scenes played out—the metaphysical crux of the film—but when I finally found out where it was, I had to make a pilgrimage. Not only wouldn't they come with me, they suggested I shouldn't bother.

You're bloody mad, Mikey, they argued. It's fucking awful down there. It's near the Valley, where Charlton play. And they're bloody nutters.

They were right. I took an overground train, then a ferry, and walked and walked and walked. It was as depressing a part of any city that I'd been in. And I was from the Bronx.

But Aldershot, now that was essential. The town appeared down on its luck and the club had gone bankrupt. It was now below even Fourth Division and was in the semiprofessional zone. In other words, this game would be a cracker, one that couldn't be missed. Tom, Dave, Dave's two younger brothers, an eccentric former high school teacher of theirs named Swain, and I piled into two cars and headed southwest on the M3. Two of them wore black Fulham away jerseys, even if the players were in their home whites; I wore my 35mm around my neck. Such an epic occasion had to be documented. I may have missed the first-ever MLS all-star game two weeks earlier at Giants

Stadium—combined with a FIFA legends match and sold out—but I wouldn't miss Fulham. I wouldn't be allowed.

Even if we were just sixty kilometers outside London, we clearly stood out. We looked like city folk. The away Fulham shirts didn't help, nor did my Minolta. Ridiculously, we stood in the away terrace behind the goal. We were the entire "away" section. So should we have been surprised that midway through the first half, we were pelted with golf balls? Two or three, from where we couldn't be sure. From behind, I thought, but crazy Swain thought it came from the front and ricocheted back toward the field. Or did it come from the side? Dave seemed to think so. Or was it a coordinated effort from all directions? Tom wondered aloud if there was a grassy knoll in Aldershot.

It was a funny line, but we weren't really laughing. Maybe there would be more later and maybe it wouldn't be only golf balls. No one was hurt but it left enough of an impression that we couldn't enjoy the game. If a game like that could ever be enjoyable. Fulham won, maybe on a goal by Robbie Herrera, whom we all declared "man of the match," even if we had a horrible view and weren't really concentrating. We left the ground and got to the cars without incident. On the way back, we still talked about the golf balls—one of which we kept, as a souvenir I suppose—but eventually of Fulham's promising preseason. *Black army! White army! Black army! White army!*

July 25, 1996
Tate Gallery
Millbank
London

For almost my entire stay at Tom's apartment in Dalston, there was virtually no hot water. Tom was sorry but, he said, this happened from time to time. The showers I took were more like sponge baths and happened every other day. I found partial relief in museums.

The first, and best, was the Wallace Collection, since it was virtually empty. I had visited England in 1979 with my family and we had stayed a few steps away from the small, pristine Marylebone museum. Since we were close, we took it for granted and kept putting it off for the next day. When we finally decided to go in, it was closed. So I made myself a promise that this time I would visit the Wallace Collection. And I was glad I did. There may have been Rubens, Velázquez, and Rembrandt, but there was also hot water and empty bathrooms. I didn't disrobe exactly, but I felt reborn.

The day after Aldershot, I went to the Tate, and my first stop was the men's room. But the Tate was the Tate, and was well-trafficked, unlike the Wallace Collection. I couldn't take my shirt off and take a sponge bath in the stall. Instead, I had to settle for dousing my face—and neck, and arms, and while no one was looking, my arm pits—with hot water and liquid soap. It felt great. I could now comfortably enjoy the Leon Kossoff retrospective, a real London painter in the most London of institutions.

My last stop was, and I wish I could be more original, the gift shop. I picked up a copy of the Tate magazine for £2.95. To my astonishment, delight, and disbelief, the magazine had a great soccer-related article by Robert Garnett titled "A Frame of Two Halves." This was better than a Tate T-shirt. It was a think piece and review of a show called Offside! Contemporary Artists and Football—not at the Tate, but at Manchester City Art Galleries, occasioned by the European Championships. It set out to review "the current state of play between art and the 'beautiful game,'" and specifically the relationship between English soccer and the English art scene.

I'd noticed how the crowd at a few of the Euro matches I watched at Kinsale Tavern in New York weeks earlier had seemed somehow more—what was the word?—posh, as Tom would say. I remember thinking that when I walked in for France vs. Spain. The crowd was the opposite of Euro trash. I felt somehow underdressed—*are my sneakers cool enough?*—even if it was a late spring Saturday afternoon. I knew, too, that writing about soccer could be smart;

I'd read *Fever Pitch* and *Among the Thugs*. One was a literary, personal story, the other was reportage of the highest order, both of which I responded to. But could soccer—and the word "soccer" was used in the piece, even if it was a British publication—inform a piece of criticism? It was enlightening and revealing in ways I never expected. It began this way:

> British soccer isn't the funny old game it used to be, and neither is British art. Both have undergone radical transformations in the 1990s, and the siege mentality of British football of old, with its gung-ho, long-ball tactics, looks as dated and irrelevant as the dull provincialism of its art counterpoint, the School of London. Art and soccer are now fashionable spectacles, popular beyond their once exclusive constituencies. Soccer, on and off the pitch, has changed almost beyond recognition . . . the tabloidesque buffoonery of Saint and Greavesie and the platitudes of Jimmy Hill have been replaced by the deconstructionist analysis of Alan Hansen, Andy Gray, and *Observer* writer Gary Lineker that is as incisive, in its own way, as much art writing.

Tom's way of consuming the game was becoming passé. Five or six away fans to Aldershot. The writer even took a shot at Jimmy Hill, the former Fulham chairman. It went on:

> Soccer has become bourgeoisified; its fans can no longer be caricatured as Neanderthal members of the Soccer Tribe, to quote the title of Desmond Morris's misrepresentative study of soccer fanatics. Confounding the views of *Among the Thugs* writer Bill Buford, and a number of sociologists whose function it is to perpetuate the myth of the soccer fan as a dysfunctional moron, soccer is now the mainstream mass-cultural phenomenon that it has been for a long time in a continental Europe. . . . Soccer, despite the tabloids' best efforts, was suddenly respectable. Since then countless mainstream celebrity soccer fans, including Tate Gallery trustees such as Lord Attenborough, have come out of the closet.

Wait. Hold up. Time out. There was so much going on there: notions that I had always been certain of (that the English game had been unsophisticated, provincial, and for the working classes), some that I had began to suspect (that it was becoming "bourgeoisi-fied," though I didn't think of it with that term, but, rather, whether my sneakers were cool enough), and some that I disagreed with (that Bill Buford perpetuated a myth, that *The Soccer Tribe* was misrepresentative).

Buford, I wanted to point out, reported what he saw, sometimes, as he admitted, while he was, shall we say, impaired (meaning dead drunk), but it was truthful—maybe a partial truth but weren't all or most truths partial? It ends with England fans rioting after the semifinal loss in Italia '90. That was true, but so was Tom's hap-pier story of him and his mates singing "We're proud of you . . ." to the melody of "Auld Lang Syne," as Gazza, Lineker, and Waddle walked off the field. And *The Soccer Tribe*: I admit that I had a sen-timental attachment to it, being it was the first real soccer book I purchased (after the Franz Beckenbauer 1982 World Cup review). It may have the look of a time capsule now, but Desmond Morris was an anthropologist and zoologist of some note; and while it can be enjoyed on a variety of levels, including the purely pictorial, which is how I appreciated it when I first bought it from Soccer Learning Systems, the book's wit shouldn't be taken as frivolity. And what it "misrepresented," this piece didn't say.

Still, I was loving the whole concept of the article—in fact it was an entire package—and I devoured it. Garnett's piece tells of Louis Althusser and Jacques Derrida, "two of the biggest heavy-weight thinkers of recent decades, having delighted in [soccer's] pleasures." The larger-than-life deconstructionist, Garnett writes, often went to see Paris St. Germain with Jean Genet in the late 1960s and early 1970s.

He writes about one of the works in the Manchester exhibit, Mark Wallinger's *They Think It's All Over . . . It Is Now*, the title taken from a quote that, at some point, becomes part of every soccer fan's vernacular. "Wallinger's work," Garnett writes, "reacts against previous notions of artistic personae, confronts the contradictions of identity and experience and rejects the assumption that you can't like West Ham and W. H. Auden at the same time."

And there were sidebars: one on a piece called *The Last Supper Arranged According to the Sweeper Formation (Jesus Christ in Goal)*, another on a former player, Pat Nevin, who was a closeted art enthusiast. There was something on Eric Cantona's artwork that "he refuses to sell . . . refuses to exhibit and refuses to talk about" and one more on a collective known as Leeds United, not the famous club, but "a group of artists challenging the elitism of the clandestine circles of high art."

I went to the Tate to see some paintings, to bathe my face in hot water, maybe buy a T-shirt. Instead, I received an unexpected souvenir of soccer-informed literary criticism.

My last day in London was a Sunday, the twenty-eighth. The night before, we went to a dance club. Jed from Manchester bought me pint after pint. I'd take two sips of one and he was already handing me another. He stayed over with us that night, as Martin was back up north for the weekend. Jed woke me up, earlier then I would have expected. My flight wasn't until later in the afternoon. I was hung over, my mouth dry, my head splitting. Jed, normally cheerful, said, completely sober and grave, "Michael"—not Mikey or Mickey as he had been calling me—"Atlanta has been bombed." I thought, of course, it was a joke, that Tom put him up to it, that they wanted to get me up or wanted to put a scare in me the day of my flight. Jed, I mumbled, just let me sleep.

It's true, Michael, Tom confirmed. It's on the telly now. Come have a look. It happened a couple of hours ago in the Olympic Park.

I called the airline and my flight was still on as scheduled. We had an awful brunch down the road—though Tom and Jed inhaled it—and then they drove me to Heathrow. We hugged. We said things like see you back in New York, see you up in Manchester, see you at the Cottage.

April 20, 1997
United States vs. Mexico
New England Revolution vs. Tampa Bay Mutiny
Foxboro Stadium
Foxborough, Massachusetts

My first U.S. national team game since 1984 required a road trip, back to Foxboro/Foxborough. It was a group of four: David; our coworker at *Esquire*, John, a native of Kearny, New Jersey, who was raised on soccer from Scotch-Irish parents; and Steve, an old friend of David's. Steve was at the wheel, as he had been on my first trip to Foxborough for the Argentina-Nigeria match in 1994.

Steve had also covered the Cosmos in the 1970s, which is where he met David, but had since changed careers and become the college admissions adviser for one of New York City's most prestigious private schools. He was one of the people David thought would hate my off-the-wall World Cup preview in *New York* magazine a few years earlier. On the contrary, Steve genuinely seemed to enjoy it, thought it was smart and funny. This was the first time I'd seen him since 1994.

As we headed northeast on I-95, we told stories—John about his playing days growing up in Kearny and later at the college level at Carnegie Mellon. He spoke affectionately about his father, *my old man*, his father's team, Kilmarnock, and how he would watch them whenever he could, which wasn't easy. John last saw the national team at the 1990 World Cup, when the United States played Czechoslovakia in Florence, and we all groaned, *ugh, Skuhravy*, in unison, though each pronounced it a different way. Steve was at the Italy-Argentina semifinal a few weeks later in Naples. He punctured the notion, one that had gained currency as the years passed, that the Neapolitans, forever Italy's underdogs, were supporting Argentina at the urging of Maradona, who played his club soccer there and brought them two *scudetti* (winning the Italian Serie A Championship title), which had been unthinkable before his arrival. Nonsense,

Steve said, the crowd was pro-Italy—and crestfallen when they lost. Being in education, he enjoyed his summers off, for his beloved Yankees and soccer tournaments. He planned to go to France the following summer for the World Cup, whether the United States qualified or not.

Today, though, the United States was playing Mexico, now coached by the deracinated Serb Bora Milutinovic, who had coached the United States in '94, Costa Rica in '90, and Mexico, for the first time, in 1986. If there was a Larry Brown of international soccer, he was it, and he got results: Mexico, as host, made it to the quarterfinals; Costa Rica, a debutante in '90, made it to the second round; and so, too, did the United States.

Mexico, the traditional power in the region, was leading in the qualification standings, but the U.S. was second and was slowly gaining ground, not in the table necessarily, but in the larger picture of overall performance and results. Besides the success of '94, there was renewed interest at home and a new league, though all four of us in the car admitted to not following it as much as we could (or was the word "should"?).

But what if, after 1994, the new Year Zero for American soccer, the U.S. national team continued to improve? Soccer was the one thing of import that our southern neighbors did better than us, and I can't say that was a status quo that needed to be upended.

Sure, I liked the American players from the early 1980s, especially the ones I had access to from the Cosmos—Ricky Davis, Steve Moyers, Jeff Durgan, Boris Bandov, Angelo DiBernardo, Darryl Gee, Erhardt Kapp—and thought it was a real tragedy that they didn't have a chance to play in a World Cup, '86 specifically. But when they disappeared, it was hard to sustain any interest.

It was nice to see the smaller national teams of CONCACAF qualify for the World Cup finals. It meant everything to them, nothing to Americans, or nothing to most Americans. The United States had everything—money, power, military might often used at the expense of those in our hemisphere, and sporting success in everything *except* soccer. So was it bleeding-heart liberal of me to want to see Mexico succeed or Honduras or El Salvador, who we put through hell in the name of proxy war? Was it un-American of me? Treasonous? Was I expected to be on the jingo train that had begun to gain momentum since '94?

Sam's Army—a dedicated fan group devoted to the U.S. national team—was born, appropriately, in this stadium two years before. And they were out in huge numbers today. Of the 57, 000-plus—sorry, the 57,407, the largest crowd for a World Cup qualifier in the United States—most were for the U.S., including the four of us. It was nice. There had always been the complaint from American play-ers, coaches, and fans that even when the U.S. played at home, it was as if it was a road game. I heard this after the 1984 friendly at Giants Stadium vs. Italy and many, many times after that, especially when the opponents were from CONCACAF. I could understand. And on the road, in Central America, the U.S. team had to endure an unusual amount of abuse from fans, the very Latin form of protest—the banging of pots and pans, and while the players were sleeping or trying to, the least of it. They were unloved. They did deserve better. Sam's Army was there to fill a void. But the in-your-face patriotism made me uneasy.

One thing I knew, was that I liked the new U.S. coach, Steve Sampson, as American as could be, but also fluent, or close to it, in Spanish. It showed an openness, especially to Latins, that Americans rarely showed. And he had this team playing well. There was that startling fourth-place showing at the 1995 Copa América, which, since it wasn't televised, recalled the question: If a tree falls in a forest and no one is there to hear, does it make a sound?

Just look at today's lineup. Would this, one day, be considered a U.S. national team murderers' row? Keller—Pope, Balboa, Lalas, Agoos—Harkes, Sorber, Dooley, Stewart—Reyna, Wynalda. The two substitutes were Michael Mason and David Wagner, both twenty-five-year-olds born, like Thomas Dooley, in Germany, which had the potential for an entire new talent pool.

They may have been second to Mexico in qualifying at the moment, even after this 2–2 draw, but this team would only get better and better, of that I was certain.

The Mexican team? I knew the keeper Jorge Campos, of course, a more contrived Higuita, and he didn't even start today; Carlos Hermosillo; and Luis Hernández. If we were all being honest, we would admit to knowing more English players, more German players, more French players, more Italian players, more Dutch players, more Irish players, more Nigerian players. There was no excuse. Mexican soccer, even in the darkest days of the Dark Ages, was on TV. It was on SIN and then Univision and Telemundo.

I watched it, but in fits and starts. If I had a complaint, it was that it was always Club América that was televised from Azteca. But I had a little game I played with myself: I'd tune in to a Mexican game, watch the clock, and within two minutes there would be a shot toward goal, sometimes a goal or a save. It was quality, attacking soccer, if haphazard tactically. Those two minutes were more than most American fans paid attention to Mexican soccer. So why couldn't I stay with it, pick a team, be a fan? I could never answer that question, to myself or to others, and others would ask it to themselves, but with a tone of derision, as if it were not worth their while.

I didn't feel that way. It was more exciting than Serie A, that was obvious to me. I had real feeling for the CONCACAF region—Davids to the Goliaths of the South—and no, it wasn't just my bleeding-heart—*Meathead!*—liberalism, though that may have been part of it. Was it the language barrier? No, since I loved watching the international tournaments—the World Cup, European Cup, Copa América—in Spanish *y hablo futbol español, no?* I respected Mexico and its fans—they cared, they rejoiced after a win, mourned a loss—but I couldn't name more than five or six Mexican players. Was it about Mexico? Or the Mexican league? Was it my own (soccer) immaturity? Or was this the exact opposite, the expression of a mature soccer fan? Was bias, even prejudice, natural? If there was prejudice against the Mexican league, would we see it against the fledgling MLS? Would we, the four of us, be those people? Would I? After the U.S.-Mexico game there was an MLS match, New England's home opener against Tampa Bay. We didn't stay.

July 3, 1998
Café Sicilia
Steinway Street
Astoria, Queens

At *Esquire*, we often used freelance fact checkers. A new researcher, it turned out, was from Sofia, Bulgaria. His name was George, Gueorgui, and we struck up an immediate friendship that began with, who else, Hristo Stoichkov. George's teams were Arsenal and Inter Milan. His real team had been Slavia Sofia, one of the four teams in the capital. But he had left Bulgaria in 1993 to study in New York and hadn't been back—nor did he want to return. His country, he told anyone who would listen, was now in the hands of the Russian mob and their Bulgarian apparatchiks.

That emphatically established, he still regretted missing Bulgaria's run in the 1994 World Cup. While I was proud to say I was at the quarterfinal at Giants Stadium, he was still new enough to New York that he had to work any job possible to pay the bills, including one for a moving company that scheduled him during the quarterfinal and the semi against Italy.

He had been a keeper back home and played on weekends with his former Queens College buddies in Cunningham Park in Bayside. They were an international bunch: Spaniards from Galicia who were Deportivo La Coruña fans, I remember him telling me, and two Sicilian brothers whose parents were from Messina. As is common in Sicily (and Queens and Brooklyn and throughout the Italian diaspora), they were for Juventus and the Azzurri, especially this iteration of the team with Alessandro Del Piero as the expected breakout star. Italy still had Roberto Baggio, Paolo Maldini, and prolific striker Christian Vieri. They were stacked at every position and hopes were high. For the second-round match, I went with George to their home in Jackson Heights, Queens, and watched the 1–0 win over Norway. The next match would be against host France and we pledged to watch it together, among *tifosi*, which, even in New York, was always a difficult thing.

There was a place appropriately (and punningly) named L'Angolo—the corner—on Thompson and Houston whose owner was an Inter fan, but it was tiny, filled up quickly for big matches, often with nonsoccer fans who wanted to see the game with ethnics or foreigners to absorb "atmosphere." For that, I had a problem. Often these types would root against the partisans, whoever they may be for, just to get a rise out of the crowd. It may be funny to cheer on the Red Sox in a New York bar, but not in soccer, and not even in New York. Sure this was a free country, and an Open City, but it still felt rude to go to, say, Heidelberg, one of the only surviving German joints left in my nook of the Upper East Side, Yorkville, and cheer against Germany. I also thought it was, depending what ethnic group you were observing, either patronizing or gawking at the natives like zoo animals.

The Irish and English bars in the city were never attended in big numbers by Italians—or Spanish or Portuguese or Greeks or even French. (You might, though, run into someone famous. For an Ireland World Cup qualifier, I went with George to Fiona's on First Avenue between Eighty-Sixth and Eighty-Seventh Streets, where we saw Richard Harris, in ecstasy, just one of the Boys in Green.)

But for Italy games, it was always a problem. You often had to watch qualifiers at a bar on pay-per-view or satellite and usually ended up at a pub and had to hope no one made a nasty remark, and if they did you'd have to hold your tongue or expect to get into some kind of back and forth or who knows what else.

This time, for the quarterfinal against France, there was an option, and a good one. George's Italian friends assured us they knew a place, nearby in Astoria. It would be all *tifosi*. It was called Café

Sicilia. As soon as we approached, we saw the mass of blue shirts; even from a distance it was clear to a fan this was the blue of Italy and not that of France. Unlike four years before, soccer jerseys were now readily available through a catalog supplier called Eurosport, in of all places Hillsborough, North Carolina. There were also, with the rise of the Internet, stores in England that were happy to customize them and send via airmail.

David had bought me one for my birthday the previous year, just after I was promoted—a kind of sideways promotion—to become his assistant. The official Nike jersey came weeks after a rigorous magazine piece I closed for him, so with the jersey he included a note: "Happy birthday and congratulations on your first editing cap," it read. He knew Roberto Baggio was my favorite player and was sorry he couldn't get a number 10 and name on the back. There was no need to be sorry—there really wasn't—I loved the jersey regardless. I went to Gerry Cosby, the famous sporting goods store in the lobby of Madison Square Garden, which customized jerseys. At the last minute, I decided to be counterintuitive. Make it D. Baggio, as in Dino Baggio, I said (not that they knew the difference). With the ubiquity of jerseys now, everyone would have Roberto Baggio for this World Cup, and, as much as I loved him, I always liked to be different.

Sure enough, in that haze of Azzurri jerseys, most were of the Roberto Baggio or Del Piero variety. The place was, as promised, partisan. It was not a café at all; nothing was served, though there were older men who appeared to sip espresso. There was no cover charge, even though they could've charged. It looked to be what was known in ethnic neighborhoods as a "social club": just card tables, foldout chairs, the one TV, and, this being of Italian congregants, an espresso maker. We squeezed in, somehow. All the Baggios and Del Pieros couldn't change the result, although Baggio—Roberto, not Dino—almost scored a golden goal in extra time. He held out his fingers about six inches apart to signal how much he'd missed it by. I knew then that Italy would lose.

When it went to penalties, and Luigi Di Biagio missed, the younger brother of George's friend—Dino was his nickname—yelled NOOOOOOOOOO!!!!!!!!! so loud that Café Sicilia, already filled with pedestrian cursing in English, Italian, and Italian dialect, went as quiet as a funeral parlor. I put my arm around the kid. He was a teenager still; I remembered 1990 and knew how cruel this game was. It was only the second or third time we had met, but from that moment on, I knew we would be friends.

October 4, 1998
Sampdoria vs. Roma
Stadio Luigi Ferraris
Genoa, Italy

Lovely Foxborough was one of the only trips I made out of the five boroughs in 1997 and there were no trips overseas. No Rome, no London. So in 1998, I did the unheard of in corporate America: I combined two weeks of vacation time. Things had soured at the magazine. A new editorial team had taken over and many of my longtime colleagues, some of whom had become both mentors and friends, were asked to leave. One of those was David. There would be no sneaking into the conference room or McGee's pub next door on Wednesday afternoons, dodging the managing editor, for World Cup qualifiers or UEFA Cup or Cup Winners' Cup.

My days were clearly numbered, so I asked for back-to-back weeks. They granted me my wish. I had the money. So why not? I was still writing on the side and bringing in a modest little second income. I had plenty of ideas and was getting published. Earlier in the year, ESPN had launched a magazine and a former co-worker asked me for a World Cup contribution. I suggested a chart, similar to what I did for *New York* magazine in 1994. I didn't have the chance to make predictions. If I had, my boldest one would have been that Brazil, no matter how indomitable they had appeared in the run-up, would somehow fall short. That indomitability was extravagantly embodied in one play: the Roberto Carlos free kick in Le Tournoi, the previous summer. He took it from thirty-five meters out, farfetched from that distance; but it was not that unusual for a player to think big, especially a Brazilian, even a defender. The French put only four men in the wall, not the usual five, and Roberto Carlos took a running start that suggested a revved-up college place-kicker teeing off a football game. He kicked it with great power, but it appeared as if it would sail harmlessly wide into the advertisements. Instead, the ball took an odd, almost mystical turn, the kind no one, no matter how long they had watched this game, had ever seen, and curled just inside the post.

It was physics, of course, a law of such-and-such, and something Roberto Carlos practiced apparently, but it appeared as if the soccer gods had decided to intervene, as they do now and again, and, as if before a birthday cake, had leaned down, pursed their lips together, and blew.

Despite Brazil's mastery at almost every position—they still had someone named Ronaldo when its defenders weren't scoring "greatest goals ever"—I was convinced it would fall short, perhaps in the final. I thought that the team to beat them would be Italy. I was right four years ago and I would be right again. There was precedent (the 1986 and '90 finals had the same teams with different results).

Probably best then that I didn't make predictions. But it was fun to dip into soccer as a writer again. I had wanted to do more, but opportunities were still limited. In the back of my daily planner I would list my ideas for articles I wanted to write, whether about film, artists, architects, a world-renowned gastroenterologist, or soccer. From the year before, the list read: writer-director Peter Bogdanovich; Irwin Young, the godfather of many a New York independent film; boxing night at Jack Newfield's; artist Alexis Rockman; Joe McGinniss; the Old Firm derby, Glasgow's sectarian soccer rivalry; Lebbeus Woods, the experimental architect; and Len Ragozin and Len Friedman, the Marx and Lenin of horse betting.

Some sold, others—like the soccer ideas—didn't, but it was enough to get me on a two-week vacation. I returned to Italy.

I had always wanted to zigzag down the peninsula from north to south, veering from the Mediterranean coast to the Adriatic. The itinerary was such that I would land in Milan and return from Rome, but in between I'd improvise. I'd be there for two weekends, but only one, just two days after I arrived, would have a full Serie A schedule. The following weekend, the national team played a Euro 2000 qualifier but all the way in Udine, tucked inconveniently, for my journey at least, in the northeast corner. I landed in Milan on a Friday, and passed on San Siro, moving south to Genoa, where I would see Roma, my team, on the road this time, against Sampdoria.

I looked forward to seeing the stadium, Luigi Ferraris, since it was one of the few on the peninsula that resembled an English ground, a rectangle with no running track. It was easily identifiable on TV because of its burnt-orange pillars in each corner of the stadium. First, though, like that visit to Olimpico, there was the journey to the ground. It was a Sunday night game, so I spent the afternoon just wandering around the twisted alleys of the *centro storico*, the historic center. This being a Sunday in Italy, nothing was open. I made my way to the stadium early and double-checked with a police officer to make sure I was headed in the right direction. *Si*, he said. And then I asked something like, "Lo stadio, e pericoloso?"—Is it dangerous? No, no, he said. *Molto tranquillo*, he said, as if surprised and maybe even insulted. Then he looked at me, realizing I didn't speak his dialect—and Genovese was quite distinctive—and said, "Are you from Roma?" No, I said, I'm from America. "Oh, then you'll have no problem," he basically said. I think.

What I didn't say was that I was a *Romanista*. My guess was that I should keep that to myself. I leisurely ventured up to the stadium, had a sandwich somewhere, and entered a scruffy bar to have a beer and kill some time. As this was near the stadium, also known as the Marassi, it was bound to be filled with Samp *tifosi*. It wasn't as crowded as you'd imagine, and it wasn't filled with mere *tifosi*—fans—but *ultras*, the hardest core, sometimes violent fans. Just my luck.

When you do things alone in Italy, you stand out, and when you're in a smallish city, as Genoa is, despite its seafaring history, you're quickly recognized as a foreigner, not that there were many here. My ample nose could only camouflage me so long. I was given suspicious looks by this group of six of seven, women mixed with men, heavily pierced and tattooed. Somehow a conversation was struck. They emphasized that they were from an extreme fan group that sat behind the goal and they often clashed with opposing groups of fans. It turns out, they thought I was from Rome. No, no, I said in my limited Italian, I'm from New York, with southern Italian roots. They still seemed suspicious of me—why would an American go see Samp?—and they spoke no English and my Italian was as it always was: limited. What I did have was knowledge of Samp.

If I ever flirted with supporting another team besides Roma, it wasn't Milan, although I did admire its cool efficiency of the Sacchi years—not Juve, and not Inter, but Sampdoria. They had the coolest shirt in Italy, for one, and the team of the late '80s and early '90s—with Gianluca Vialli, Roberto Mancini, Attilio Lombardo, Toninho Cerezo, Srecko Katanec—was one of the best I'd seen. Those names, luckily, came to me quickly, as I started naming them one after the other, from Pagliuca in goal, through the defense, midfield, and ending with the great strike force of Mancini and Vialli. E Signor Boscov, I said. They were in shock. If there was any threat of menace, and it was hard to tell if there ever truly was—maybe it had been my imagination—it was now gone. I'd like to say they bought me a beer, but I don't think they did. I still wanted to get out of there, as I'd run out of Sampdoria factoids. Finally they left, still well before kickoff, to light their colored fireworks and wave their massive flags, and perhaps even get into it with visiting Roma *tifosi*. I was glad I was sitting in the *tribuna*, at about the midfield stripe. The stadium, as nice as it appeared on TV, was disappointing on the inside, like Olimpico. No amenities, nothing. The passageways were dark and uninviting. Whatever was sold—scarves, panini, beer—seemed to have been sold outside the stadium, where I'd met the *ultras*.

When I got to my seat, I wasn't going to do anything stupid, like cheer on the Giallorossi. If others did, and it was met with tolerance, perhaps I would do the same, but besides the away section, sequestered from the rest of the crowd via cage, more or less, no one was. Everyone, it went without saying, was for Samp. So I just sat quietly and tried to enjoy the match. But I didn't, couldn't. I was in the closet. And Roma lost, 2–1.

October 17, 1998
Asphalt Green
York Avenue
New York, New York

The Saturday after I returned, I was still on Italian time, wishing I was still there, wondering what to do with my life. It was an afternoon, and I was strolling aimlessly in my neighborhood, when I saw a guy, my age more or less, in an Italy jersey, shorts, Adidas Sambas, with soccer ball under arm, walking briskly. I followed him. I thought he might be walking to the Doss Soccer Supply to buy gear, but he cut over to York Avenue and made his way to the Asphalt Green, beside the FDR Drive, where NYU used to play.

For some reason it never occurred to me that there might be pickup games there, but sure enough. I watched from a safe distance near the fence. The guy I followed appeared to have a British accent, despite the Azzurri jersey. Some wore team colors, others didn't. Some knew one another, others didn't. Most seemed to be foreign and were good, but I thought I might be able to compete. I was in decent shape and had speed, which I would be able to use on the artificial turf. So I came back the next day, in gear this time.

The same guy was there, not in an Italy jersey this time, and he was welcoming and delightful. He was born and raised in London of Italian parents from Puglia, I believe. His name was Enzo, and he was a Chelsea man through and through. He kicked in a circle with some other guys: a Greek-Cypriot, who was the very unofficial organizer; a delicate Nigerian from the Ibo tribe, who had exquisite skills; a Tunisian and a Maltese, both of whom seemed as if they might have played professionally (U-21?) somewhere at some point; an older U-50 Brazilian who played as a classic winger, extending our already conceptual touchline even further, well into softball territory; and a couple of very good Americans. We played from football sideline to football sideline, starting at about six a side, crumpled T-shirts as goals, about three feet apart, no goalkeepers, and, well, since everyone was welcome, by late in the afternoon it verged on the preposterous, thirteen on thirteen or fourteen versus fifteen. At that point, we'd chat with each other more than play.

That first or second afternoon, as I sat back in a kind of sweeper position, another player stood beside me with his arms folded and watched the action at the other end of the field, by now a disorganized shambles. He watched the Maltese dribble through about seven defenders only to be stripped and said, "He'd be great if he played better." The first thing that struck me was that this stranger had just come up with a Yogi Berra-ism. The second was that he had an Italian accent. I asked him where he was from and he said Padova. I told him I had just been in Italy, had missed Padova, but that I wanted to go to the Cappella degli Scrovegni. He said, You know the Cappella degli Scrovegni?

We gravitated to the benches to towel off and drink some water and the conversation turned soon from Giotto but not to *càlcio*. Carlo, that was his name, made it clear that he hated *càlcio*, and hated Italy, and only liked playing to stay in shape—not for his own benefit but to appeal to women.

He'd clearly had his share. He looked like a model from Etro ads, messy, dirty blond, perfectly disheveled facial hair, green eyes, sculpted physique—he loved American football and actually played in an organized league in Padova. He said, Don't get me started on

Italian women. They are such a pain in my ass. Avoid them, and if you don't believe me, ask Domenico.

I'm new here, I said. Who's Domenico?

That's Domenico, he said, there in the Fiorentina jersey.

He called him over.

Domenico, Carlo said, this guy just came back from Italy and now loves Italian women. Talk some sense into him.

Domencio laughed. He was shorter than Carlo, had lived in Florence for a few years, but his father was from Calabria, he explained, and his mother was from Bogota, Colombia.

Yes, Domenico said, they are nice, many are very beautiful, but they are, how do you say, possessive? And if you don't call them, they all say, Where are you? Why you don't call me? Who are you with? Like this, no?

They are impossible, Carlo said. I can only be with American women now.

Well no, not impossible, Domenico said, but let's say difficult?

We met every Saturday and Sunday that fall and into the following winter, bundled up. Carlo always brought an American football and as I was the only one there who knew the game, had to run pass patterns for him—outs, hooks, slants, posts—so he could exercise his throwing arm and emulate Doug Flutie, who he would announce was the most underrated quarterback in the NFL. No one cared. Nor did I.

I preferred hearing Domenico's story of watching Italy-Nigeria in the second round match during the 1994 World Cup. It went like this: He took the afternoon off and, since he worked downtown, went to the Sporting Club in TriBeCa to watch it live. Italy was down 0–1 late in the game and was down to ten men after Zola was red-carded (for nothing, remember). It looked bleak, until Baggio tied it late, in the eighty-eighth minute. The Sporting Club was empty and Domenico was standing at the bar, too nervous to sit. When Baggio slotted home that goal, Domenico went berserk and only calmed down when extra time began. The bartender then presented him with something. Is this yours? he asked. It was Domenico's marriage band; it had flown off his hand during the celebration. They laughed together and wondered aloud if that was some kind of bad omen. Italy won the game; his marriage ended soon after.

June 6, 1999
The Hampton Jitney
Amagansett, New York

I opened the *New York Post* on the subway and read this on Page Six:

> Everyone knows Manhattan's movers and shakers flock to the Hamptons in the summer. Now publisher Little, Brown has hit on a way to capitalize on it. The house has arranged to have bound galleys of Joe McGinnis' [sic] new book *The Miracle of Castel di Sangro*, which has nothing to do with the Hamptons, placed on Hampton Jitney seats. "The publisher asked us if we would distribute some complimentary copies," says Tom Neely, Jitney marketing director. "We thought it was something our riders could enjoy as a treat for taking the Jitney, and I guess it serves the purpose of promoting the book." Of course, the *real* Hamptons movers and shakers fly out on helicopters.

I always read the *Post* on the subway, back to front, so I was at the end of my ride—and in a frozen state, even if it was June. I wasn't shocked that the book was out—I'd known for a couple of years that it was in the works and even tried to write about it—but that it was in the *Post*, on Page Six, and more shockingly that free copies were being given out to Hamptons folk. Huh?! What?! Why?! This was a horrifying thought. I'd never been to the Hamptons or on the Jitney bus.

Not because it wasn't beautiful—I had no doubt that it was—but because of what it implied. The Hamptons equaled status, sometimes real, sometimes imagined. It meant connections or possible connections. It meant wealth. It was the meritocracy inverted. There were no shortcuts to the Hamptons (unless, as the *Post* wrote, you went by helicopter) but it could be a shortcut, for instance, up a magazine masthead.

And worse, it divided New York, my great egalitarian city, into winners and losers, those who went to the Hamptons on insufferable, teeming, stinking summer weekends, and those who didn't, couldn't. (Tom used to call the amorphous city aroma "the New York smell," made up of the following: "Toss," he'd say and pause for effect. "Piss," pause again. "Vomit." Pause. "Wank!" with a horrified tone followed by a much longer pause. "And *shite!*") The ones who went away were winners, or so they thought, or so they planned to be, whether they had winning qualities or not. Those who couldn't, were losers, even if no one, ever, would put it in those terms.

And now, someone—a publishing executive, a marketing genius, an ambitious intern, who knows—decided that soccer, this sport for so long ridiculed, belittled, ignored, could be sold, even if copies were being given away for free to an affluent clientele. These new readers, it was hoped, would tell their friends and carry it under their arms, bring it to the beach, to brunch, bring it up at dinner parties.

What, suddenly, was the appeal, I wanted to ask? Was it the soccer part of it? But Second Division soccer? Was it the Rocky story? (Or was it Bad News Bears?) Was it the movie potential? Was it the "selling" of McGinniss? Or was it Italy? Was this a way to capitalize on the *Under the Tuscan Sun* phenomenon, even if the book took place in the less fashionable Abruzzo?

This wasn't why I loved soccer. I loved soccer because of Enzo, whose wife threw him a thirtieth birthday party that same month. A friend of his, also a lifelong Chelsea man, flew in from London, and at the end of the night presented him with a Chelsea jersey, signed by every current player—he had connections within the club—and had it framed behind glass. Enzo, in front of about thirty guests, broke down in tears. That's why I loved soccer, not for whatever its appeal might be to Hamptons dwellers.

I held none of this against Joe McGinniss. Was I a little jealous? A little. I wasn't a starry-eyed intern anymore, fact-checking *Among the Thugs*. I was published in major publications, had over seven years of *Esquire* under my belt, and was over thirty now. Joe McGinniss was twenty-six when he made his name with *The Selling of the President*. Why *not* be bold and think about a book? *And write what you know*. But who knew writing a soccer book was even an option, that anyone wanted one?

McGinniss, to be fair, wrote a terrific book. He could've followed a sexy name like Roberto Baggio, the player who ignited his interest, which appeared genuine, in 1994. He could've followed AC Milan or indulged the Tuscan fantasy and found some angle on Fiorentina. Instead, he bunkered down in a small town in, at the time, an insular region off the usual tourist map.

The writing of Buford's book still wowed me, especially that magnificent, brutal set piece in Turin, but McGinniss's book had a lot going for it. For one, it had great narrative drive, great characters, and a very gray, and I thought, brave ending. I had been cynical. Even while reading it, I was waiting for that "gotcha" moment—sure that McGinniss was "out to get" the Italians. He was so sweet at the outset—a sweetness that bordered on sentimental, that for me felt like a setup. Instead, he was fair and kind throughout. And you could argue that he does "get" the Italians at the end. But he saw what he saw. He could've had his happy ending and left it at that, cashed the six-figure movie-option check then and there. He could've kept the friends he made and stayed hotel-free, rent-free in Italy for the rest of his life. He chose not to; he chose not a dark ending—not for me—but a very real one. Soccer, yet again I thought, mirrored society, for better and worse, which was why it wasn't always fun, why it usually wasn't fun. McGinniss got that part, that soccer could often reflect the mundane, but he also had either a newcomer's or American's—or maybe it was an *American newcomer's*—view of soccer, a naïve one similar to what I once had when I first got into it (the only difference being that I was fourteen).

His road trips are refreshingly counterintuitive and take him to modernist concrete bowls or fields with erector-set-like seating, on the periphery of Italian cities, some of grandiose reputation. His Venice, the *càlcio* Venice, is off-putting, one that confounds stereotypes: "It's a dreary stadium surrounded by oil tanks in which twelve thousand of the fifteen thousand empty seats remained unoccupied." Watching the game there—a tedious one—felt as if he had "just spent an afternoon in Perth Amboy."

That part he can handle, but can he handle the truth?

The players, not brain surgeons but some terribly wise, tried to explain to him that sometimes life is like this in Italy (and, if I were on the team bus, I would have added India, Brazil, China, South Korea, Turkey, Nigeria, and yes, even Germany, and the United States). My own alma mater, NYU, once a power in college basketball, was stained by a point-shaving scandal. And much closer to Italy and more recent was Olympique Marseille in France's top division.

I didn't like McGinniss's self-righteousness at the end, but I understood it. Buford was repelled but also attracted to the ugliness he saw; when he finally had seen enough, he was still understated in his distaste for the hooligans. He tried, perhaps too hard, not to be judgmental. McGinniss, on the other hand, didn't just wag a finger, he was apoplectic—at the players, whom he'd grown close to, and at what he saw as a complicit Italian society. This from someone who'd written a best-selling book on Richard Nixon. It's one thing to throw a Second Division soccer game, I wanted to tell him, but another to subvert the U.S. constitution.

McGinniss rages, and the Italians, as ever, collectively shrug—*boh,* as Domenico would say. The only difference now was that they were encouraged to read about it in Amagansett. But why?

May 20, 2000
Roma vs. Benfica
New York/New Jersey MetroStars vs. Tampa Bay Mutiny
Giants Stadium
East Rutherford, New Jersey

Throughout the second half of the 1990s, Major League Soccer was there. It wasn't thriving but it was there, more in the background than anything else. Without tradition, without rivalries, without continuity among the players and coaches, the league felt like a chore for many of us American soccer fans. Not all; some were gung ho, almost proselytizing.

The evangelicals aside, most of us were glad a league was there, and we felt obliged to try to support it. I went to games, from the MetroStars' opener to a few games per season, but it always felt more like homework than anything else.

Giants Stadium was still a nuisance to get to; I never did warm to the place. Shea Stadium, the modernist behemoth that it was, could be four-fifths empty and it still had more character than the Meadowlands did. It had the Miracle of '69, the Beatles, the Say Hey Kid, the Pope, Joe Willie, and Bill Buckner on its timeline. And it was just off the number seven train.

But a new spring was here—a new year, a new decade, a new century, maybe a new day for soccer, whatever that might be—and Roma was heading to town, to play Benfica, who had many a Portuguese follower in Newark's Ironbound district. I had my nice memories of Benfica in 1988 and with my team coming in, it was a must see. I rounded up Domenico, George, and the two Sicilian brothers and we bought tickets.

If many of us still had a hard time taking MLS seriously, the league had its own inferiority complex. How else do you explain Roma-Benfica as the second game, the main event? Friendlies, and especially friendlies *after* the season, are mere walk-throughs, paychecks for clubs to tease their ethnic diasporas. We all knew it; it was an unspoken bargain. Otherwise, the league would risk the embarrassment that most fans—and there were almost thirty thousand this night—would leave if the international friendly went on first.

Both clubs arrived in a kind of emasculated state. The previous weekend, Lazio, Roma's despised city rival, won Serie A for the first time since 1974 and for only the second time ever, same as Roma. Sporting Lisbon, Benfica's own despised city rival, won the Portuguese league for the first time in eighteen years. This was the Cup of the Disgraced. And we were right, we cynical fans. The teams did saunter through the ninety minutes. It was completely forgettable. About all I could say is that I could check off another all-time great I'd seen in person: Aldair's fellow Brazilian with the perennial smile, Cafu, but even he wasn't his effervescent self. Why they even played, six days after the season ended, I don't know. It ended, I think, 1–1.

The opener was the better game. It went to extra time, 3–2 for the Metros. The reason to come early wasn't for any of the MetroStars; we could see them any time. They had Tab Ramos, a local who was still very good; the exciting young American striker Clint Mathis, who'd just joined the team; and now even Lothar Matthäus, whom I'd seen play in that World Cup quarterfinal loss to Bulgaria in this same stadium. Matthäus had been the first glamour signing for the New York/New Jersey franchise since Roberto Donadoni, though he already seemed, unlike the Italian, too cool for MLS. I remembered watching Donadoni in pregame warm-ups in that first season. I was sitting close to the field, second or third row, and could see in his face how deadly serious he took his job, his new team, this new league, even if there weren't many people there (which is why I was in the second or third row.)

Ramos was kind enough to relinquish his number 10 jersey for the German; he shouldn't have. He was a great American international and a legend in the tri-state area. Matthäus, efficient as he was, wore the number 10, but wasn't a number 10, with all that it symbolized. He was the dullest great player I can ever remember, without a soupçon of flair.

So Tabaré and, we would hope, Clint Mathis we could see anytime. Carlos Valderrama, now with Tampa and pushing forty, we could not. Crazy as it was, living far away from any kind of soccer epicenter, I'd seen Beckenbaur, Neeskens, Zico, Sócrates, Falcão, Rossi, Platini, Antognoni, N'Kono, Zoff, Maradona, Batistuta, Baggio, Higuita, Jorge Campos, Stoichkov, Totti, Klinsmann, and Andreas Brehme. If there was an international soccer Hall of Fame—and it was hard to believe there wasn't—they would all be in it. And near the top of that list, was Valderrama, one of my favorites. He played like no one else; maybe Platini and Zico were closest.

"El Pibe" was in his second tour with Tampa—he did a season with the Miami Fusion—but for whatever reason, I'd never seen him live. My viewings of Valderrama usually coincided with his appearances not for club but for country, for World Cup, qualifiers, and Copa América. It was always in that yellow shirt, with yellow Afro, that I'd see him dazzle in the midst of chaos. He seemed to have little interest in the field's wider corridors, content instead to ply his craft through crowded passages. This was the most difficult path, congested, and with the least amount of time to ponder. This is where he thrived and earned his living. The perfect term I could think of was an oxymoronic one, borrowed from the jazz musician Butch Morris, who called his method of conducting and improvisation "conduction."

Valderrama was the opposite of a traditional British player, who played it to the wings, crossed the ball, and was effective in the air. Valderrama used his head—all players must on occasion—but only if there was no alternative.

On this night, a champion playing on the undercard, a rock star as a warm-up act, he did what he did best, what he had done hundreds of times before: he created a goal. This time, not with a centimeter-perfect pass, or a dazzling dribbling solo to create opportunity, but with a chipped pass off a free kick.

It was like seeing Ali in the late 1970s against Earnie Shavers or Jimmy Young. Or Miles Davis in the mideighties. Not *the* Ali, not *the* Miles, but you couldn't turn away.

This was a number 10.

May 1, 2001
Sonny Mehta's apartment
Interview with Ryszard Kapuscinski
Park Avenue
New York, New York

In October of 2000, just before the disputed presidential election, I started a new job for a magazine we'll call *Week News*. I had a fancy title and worked on the website, when the web was still ahead of its time and not part of our every waking moment. One nice part of my job was that on my free time, which wasn't much, there was opportunity to write and publish. Not only for the website, but also for our international additions. There was an open-minded editor (not as common as you might imagine) who seemed to like the ideas I offered up. So I got to do one-page articles on figures such as the Dardenne Brothers, the Belgian filmmaking team; Raoul Peck, the Haitian director; Nanni Moretti, the film essayist; and the Canadian documentarian Damian Pettigrew.

All were labors of love. And then there was Ryszard Kapuscinski, who inspired admiration, but also fear. I loved his books, loved his insights, his writing, the life he lived. It was one I dreamed of as a young teenager reading the *New York Times* international section, with datelines from far-off places that even if in tumult still had great soccer traditions I could delve into in my spare time. The titles of his books seemed timeless and iconic: *The Shah of Shahs, The Emperor, Another Day of Life* (my personal favorite), and, of course, *The Soccer War*, a book that pulled me in immediately, even if it had little to do with soccer itself, or even the soccer war between El Salvador and Honduras after a World Cup qualifying match. I'd had my own fixation with Central America since Alexis Arguello, my favorite boxer, retired to join the anti-Sandinista Contras in his home country of Nicaragua (not, I would learn, a soccer country but a baseball one). From Nicaragua my interest spread throughout my teens to the entire region and by freshman year at NYU I was enrolled in a Latin American history course.

I knew nothing of the man except that he was Polish and had a severe gaze in his author photo, which was the same one in each of his books. So I was nervous to meet him, especially when the publicist said I should go to such and such an address on Park Avenue to the apartment of Sonny Mehta, the editor and publisher of Knopf, who had published his latest book *The Shadow of the Sun*, a beautiful compendium of short, poetic dispatches from his travels in Africa.

Turned out, Sonny wasn't home; no one was, except a housekeeper, and Ryszard. It was immediately clear that Kapuscinski was a complete gentleman. There was no ice to break, but I asked if he liked soccer anyway. Why, of course, he said. In a nervous fit I started rattling off names: Lato, Deyna, Gadocha, Boniek.

The look on his face was one of astonishment and delight. *Yes! Yes! But how do you know?* Now I was ready to turn on the tape recorder and interview him. I dated the microcassettes (5/1/01) and would keep them forever. It went on the website first, and a few weeks later, the international edition of the magazine ran a shorter, page-long version.

Soon after, I received a piece of mail with a handwritten envelope and lot of stamps. It was from Europe, Poland. *Poland? I don't know anyone from Poland.* Ah, it was from Kapuscinski. It read: "Dear Michael, It was so nice to meet you in New York and to have a lovely conversation. I am writing now to express my warm gratitude for the story which was written by you. . . . I am afraid I don't deserve so many compliments—nevertheless I am grateful for your generosity! I hope we will be in touch in the future. With kindest regards . . ."

September 10, 2001
Together
Lincoln Plaza Cinemas
New York, New York

It so happened that Monday was our slowest day of the week at my new job, and I could leave at a sociable time, maybe around six. On this night, while it was still light out, I ventured up to Lincoln Plaza Cinema, across Lincoln Center on Broadway, and bought a ticket to a Swedish movie called *Together*. It opened in August, but I had been on vacation and this was my first real chance to see it. I still followed film assiduously—in fact, I spent a few days of my vacation with my new Swiss girlfriend, Andrea, at the Locarno Film Festival—and kept track of every new movie that opened, great or small or foreign.

I didn't know much of what was in this movie except that it was Swedish and took place in the 1970s. I didn't know much about Swedish film outside of Bergmann—Lars von Trier, a new obsession, was a Dane—so this sounded like an opportunity to learn more.

It opens in November of 1975, when the news arrives that Generalísimo Francisco Franco has died. While there is no mention of the generalissimo's favorite soccer team, the post-hippie housemates celebrate wildly, even the two children, Tet and Moon. In this house, there are no Christmas presents, no meat, and no TV but lots of hair, on heads, face, underarms, and, thanks to a full-frontal scene, genitalia, male and female. There are also posters of Che, Mao, and the Tommie Smith–John Carlos black power salute.

Trouble, or deliverance, arrives when the working-class sister of one of the hirsute Maoists arrives at the house with her two children. She's been beaten by her husband—a plumber who wears a 1974 World Cup T-shirt with that great WM logo—and needs a place to stay. She's accepted—though her young son Stefan is called a fascist by little Tet—and immediately hit on by Tet's mom, who's recently become a lesbian and has fungal infection, her rationale for the full-frontal.

It's a hilarious, tender look of '60s and '70s ideology in its final days. From the kids playing a game of "Let's torture Pinochet," they soon transition to playing with toy soldiers, watching *Baretta* on TV, and chanting "We want meat!" with homemade placards.

Early in the movie, Stefan, who's devastated by his parents' separation, is mocked by local mean boys playing street hockey and is relegated to the chain-link fence, not allowed to play. I thought to myself: kids playing soccer would never do that; it's not in us. It's what I always liked about soccer; it was for everyone. I wasn't as good as the Brazilians, Nigerians, Italians, Maltese, and Tunisians I played with on Saturday, but I played, we played, even those not as good as me, even if it became twelve on twelve, or fourteen on fifteen.

Midway through the movie, when the most radical, joyless couple moves out of the house, someone says, out of nowhere, "Let's play football!" Stefan says he can't, that he's not good. His uncle implores him to join. And Stefan does. Finally he smiles.

And that, again, was that. Until the finale. The abusive husband/father returns, contrite it appears, with the help of a lonely, genteel old neighbor. There's yelling, there are doubts, there's still pain, and it's cold and there's snow in the front yard, but there's light and now warmth. And out comes the soccer ball. It starts with a one on one, with makeshift goals, then two on two, three on three, and it grows. There's joy and laughter, and plenty of goals by the way. Tet's mother, clothed this time, is in the kitchen consoling a repressed neighbor, when she says "Shall we join in?" "No," says the melancholy neighbor, "I can't play football." "Yes," says the radical, "everyone can play." ABBA's "SOS" begins to blare and the end credits roll.

Soccer, as I always maintained, could bring people, as in the title of the movie, together. I never left a theater happier. I couldn't wait to tell people the next day that they had to see this movie. I had ABBA's "SOS" in my head as I fell asleep. And I couldn't wait to see soccer again. Tomorrow there would be the first day of the new Champions League season.

August 6, 2002
Roma–Real Madrid Press Conference
Hilton Hotel
New York, New York

On September 11, soccer was actually played. And not by innocent little kids in some far corner of the globe who may not have known any better, but on its highest, most visible stage: the Champions League. After Heysel, nothing that happened in soccer shocked me anymore. Why or how anyone would even want to watch or play in a game on that day or the days that followed is hard for me to fathom. I was working virtually all day for about two consecutive weeks, editing stories from our reporters at Ground Zero and getting them up on the website as soon as possible. I didn't even have a chance to mourn. On the day of the eleventh, I didn't, couldn't, put any food into my system until late into the night at the office cafeteria, and did so just to get the energy to continue working. I think if I had eaten any earlier, I would have thrown up.

The next day, games were cancelled, but it would still be hard for me to put any kind of faith in soccer again, that it would bring out the best in people, even if I thought that the night before, whistling ABBA's "SOS" after the movie.

September 11 happened to be the first day of the Champions League group stage and Roma hosted Real Madrid. People, over sixty thousand, for some reason, turned up. Real won that game, I'd find out, and went on to win the trophy in May.

Three months later, the two teams that kicked off the tournament on that day, would play a preseason friendly at Giants Stadium. It was for charity, to benefit the global fight against HIV/AIDS and the day before the players were invited to the United Nations to meet Secretary-General Kofi Annan. A worthy cause, but being that they had played each other on 9/11, and were now in the metropolitan area, wouldn't a 9/11 charity have been more appropriate? Soccer was always big in northern New Jersey; they couldn't have the now parentless kids meet Zidane and Totti, run around with them on the field? Was that too much to ask?

All that aside, this game bothered me. As much as I wanted to see top-class soccer live, I wasn't the biggest fan of the big European powers coming across to play in preseason exhibitions. It seemed to me that with the expansion of the Champions League, top players were playing too many games already. To drag them across six (or more) time zones to the United States in the month of August and have them play in ninety-degree heat and humidity, seemed almost cruel and unusual. Sure these elite clubs could play some of their reserves, but ticket prices were steep and American enthusiasts surely didn't want to pay top dollar to watch only kids from the u-19 squad. I thought these clubs, if anything, should extend their off-seasons and have their players recharge their bodies and minds. I'd rather they be on a beach in Seychelles than in a blistering New York or Washington summer. Yes, I'd craved these games in summers past and put down my money to see them; people like me created the demand. But I was ambivalent about these preseason extravaganzas, as I was, more and more, about soccer in general.

What I thought didn't matter. There was money to be made. And Roma was coming to town, for the second time in three years. After Lazio won only its second title in 2000, Roma, to prove that they weren't in competition with the rest of Serie A but merely trying to save face against its city rival, won the very next season. It was a great team. Totti was coming off a fine performance for Italy in Euro 2000 when he outplayed Zidane in the final, despite the tragic loss, and led a team with players like Cafu, Gabriel Batistuta, and Vincenzo Montella. They were so good, the Japanese great Hidetoshi Nakata, one of my favorites, came off the bench. Roma had usually played attractive soccer and often had dynamic coaches: Nils Liedholm, Sven-Göran Eriksson, Zdeněk Zeman, and Ottavio Bianchi, who won with Napoli. Now it had the more pragmatic Fabio Capello, and despite all the talent, it was he who had assembled it and deserved much if not all of the credit. In the season that just ended, he had Roma in second, just a single point behind Juventus.

Real Madrid was Real Madrid, as grand a club as could be found in the history of the game. Capello had coached them for one season, 1996/97, and won the Primera Liga. Roma was lucky to have him.

I made sure to get a press pass for the game and was granted one. In fact, for my job, I wrote a large World Cup preview back in May and got other staff members to contribute opinions and analysis in nearly real time during the tournament. I even appeared as an expert on CNN International before the tournament began. Too bad no one saw it; or maybe it was for the best, as I predicted that Cameroon would be the first African nation to make the semifinals. But the job, ever since September 11, had become more and more demanding, requiring ten-hour days, at least. The night before the game there was a press conference and luckily it was nearby, at the Hilton Hotel on Sixth Avenue, a short walk away.

There was, on Roma's side of the dais, Capello, Christian Panucci, and Damiano Tommasi; and for Real, Coach Vicente del Bosque, Luís Figo, and Fernando Hierro. Capello and Hierro, and then Panucci and Hierro, gave one another hugs so genuine and heartfelt, it was moving to watch. They hadn't been through war together—you had to be careful how you used such metaphors these days, and rightly so—but they'd been though Classicos.

As great as these figures were, I was most interested in Tommasi, and not because it was the name of a character in *L.A. Confidential*. No, Tommasi represented a certain kind of player I liked. Dependable, ego-free, without drama or histrionics, and intelligent. He was, in other words, the anti-Totti. Not that I didn't love Totti, but he was a diva and all that came with that. In fact, I was so impressed with Tommasi's mien, I bought two Roma jerseys, the Kappa design, with his name and number, which, defiantly, was number 17, the equivalent in Italy, as Domenico informed me, of our 13.

So when the press conference was opened up to questions, I had two ready for Tommasi. The World Cup in Japan and South

Korea was a good one, with great moments, and the most beautiful for me was Senegal's counterattack goal against Denmark that went the virtual length of the field in about fourteen seconds. (If Denmark provided so many memorable moments for me—in 1984, '86, '92, and '98—this one happened to be at their expense.) It was wonderful to see the tournament in Asia for the first time, it was the World Cup after all, but start times on the East Coast—usually in the wee-est of hours—made it difficult to watch as many games as I normally would have. Work, and making a good impression at work, mattered more this year. One game I did watch live was South Korea–Italy, in the second round. It was exhausting, which had nothing to do with the early kickoff time. So much happened, good and bad and off-the-wall, I'd never felt so enervated after a match, even when I played.

Tommasi was involved in a pivotal play. A few minutes after Totti received a second yellow for what Ecuadoran referee Byron Moreno considered a dive, Tommasi scored a goal, a "golden goal" that would've ended the game, but was whistled for offside. It was Italy's fifth disallowed goal in three games. So at the press conference my hand went up, and I asked Tommasi what he thought of the call against him. It was two months in the past—for some ancient history, for others still too recent to contemplate—but Tommasi gave the response I had hoped he would. He said, through a translator, something to the effect that these things happen, people make mistakes, life goes on. He didn't talk about being robbed or conspiracies, though I wondered what Hierro, sitting across the dais, would have answered to a question about South Korea's win over Spain in the match that followed. But Tommasi was a prince and wouldn't lower himself to such talk. I liked him more now.

I didn't get to ask my other question: Why did you guys play on September 11? Tommasi didn't dress for that game, why I don't know. Maybe because he believed in doing the right thing—something I had hoped—or maybe he was just injured. When the press conference was over, Tommasi quietly and quickly left the room. I followed him. I wanted to hear more. I wanted to tell him, not as a fan so much, but as an admirer, that I appreciated the way he carried himself for Roma and for Italy. But he was quick, darting down one corridor, then another, then one more, until there was a fork in the hallway. I lost him, but maybe it was for the best.

The next night was the game. I didn't go. I felt that work came first and there was always a story coming in that needed to be edited and posted on the website, even if it was primarily a weekly magazine. The web was becoming more and more relevant. When I first started this job, writing for the web was perceived as second class, though no one would say it. But almost overnight, especially since 9/11, it became as important. I couldn't risk dropping the ball, being out to lunch (even literally, as I almost always ate at my desk), or being out at a soccer game, even if it was an 8:00 p.m. start.

It was too bad I'd miss seeing my own team, and too bad I'd miss Real with Roberto Carlos, Zidane, Raúl, Steve McManaman, Fernando Morientes, Figo, Guti, and Claude Makélélé. But it was also a shame they had played on the darkest day of our lifetimes.

November 9, 2003
Parma vs. AC Milan
Stadio Ennio Tardini
Parma, Italy

In October, I left my thankless job. No matter how many good things I wrote, no matter how prepared and present I was, never out to lunch or even at soccer games at 8:00 p.m., I wasn't someone the elite top editors wanted to see succeed. What I wasn't good at was dividing and conquering and forming alliances with people at the top. Others were.

When, on the eve of the Iraq invasion in March, I wrote a cri de coeur saying what a mistake this would be, what long-term fallout this would have, that Iraq had nothing to do with 9/11, that Congress and Big Media (and by extension, us at *Week News*, though I didn't say it) hadn't done our job. I ended it by writing, We should be ashamed of ourselves.

I wanted to publish it on the site, but was nervous about it, too. I knew I'd get hate mail and who knew what else. America and most at-large news organizations were on board, as were most of their intellectual heavy hitters. One of our star political commentators who was known for being gutsy, outspoken, and very liberal said to me over the phone that she wished she had the guts to write what I wrote. I knew then I'd made a mistake.

Seven months later, I rolled up my *Bonnie & Clyde* poster with Warren Beatty and Faye Dunaway and left the building, never to return to that sunless, joyless block on Fifty-Seventh and Broadway ever again. If, for whatever reason, I needed to walk by it, I'd cross the street.

Besides, I'd been seeing Andrea and she was spending more and more time in her native Switzerland. I decided to go see her for a month or so, decide my next move, and while there, visit Domenico in Italy. When I'd met him in October of 1998 he was working for an Italian company in White Plains. It paid well and he lived in a nice spacious studio apartment on Fifty-Third Street just off First Avenue. By 2001, things at the company began to sour, to the point where he would tell me that he was burning files on behalf of his boss. Domenico loved the U.S.—he went to the University of Texas at Austin, a proud Longhorn—and loved New York, but decided it was time to go back to Italy. His late father was originally from Calabria in the deep south, but his mother, originally from Bogotá, and sisters remained in Florence where his father had opened a men's clothing store.

He ended up being a close friend, and New York was odd without him. I stopped playing soccer at the Asphalt Green and didn't watch as many games in bars and restaurants. We remained in touch and decided to meet somewhere in Italy for a Serie A game.

We did. With Milan being somewhat in the middle between Zurich and Florence, San Siro was an obvious meeting point, but for whatever scheduling reason, that couldn't happen. Maybe I didn't want to see Inter; for me, Milan was always the more dynamic team, no matter what star players the Nerazzurri bought. On the one weekend we could both make it, Parma looked liked the best bet, and it was Milan that were the visitors. It might not be the same as seeing them in Stadio Giuseppe Meazza, but I was happy to see them in my first Serie A match in five years.

Domenico took the train north, just about an hour and a half. My journey was longer, about six hours, but it was a beautiful ride, first through the Gotthard Tunnel and then magically on the other side of the Alps to Ticino, the Italian-speaking canton of Switzerland. From Lugano, Milan was just thirty minutes away and there you get to change trains at Milano Centrale, one of the most glamorous stations in Europe.

Parma was a new city for me. I'd been to Emilia-Romagna in 1998, to Bologna, maybe my favorite city in the country, where, I was told, basketball is more popular than *càlcio*, and to Ferrara, for a pilgrimage to Antonioni's hometown.

The game was Sunday, and we met on a Saturday afternoon. It rained all day and all night. We had no choice but to stop into cafés for a lot of food and drink. Not that this was a bad thing; Emilia-Romagna, for many travelers and critics, has *the* best food in the country, and it gave us a chance to catch up.

The next day, the sun didn't exactly come out, but it stopped raining more or less. We walked from the city center, where we had shared a room in a small, tidy pensione, and walked to the stadium. First there was the matter of food (again) and it appeared that everyone was eating food outside of the stadium, from trucks. We did the same. (When in Parma . . .) Emilia-Romagna, and specifically Parma, is famous for, among other delicacies, cheese and cured meats (Parmigiano-Reggiano; prosciutto di Parma). The sandwiches were far better than any you'd get at a "gourmet" shop in New York or even Zurich, a city that knew good food. I had a sausage and pepper sandwich—but more elegant than the

Mulberry Street variety—and Domenico had mortadella. There was still cold Peroni left so we shared an airily light piadina of bresaola and rucola. Maybe these rinky-dink Italian stadiums didn't have food courts inside because they didn't need them. Maybe the food trucks had such fresh, high-quality ingredients that fast food from concession stands just didn't make sense. Maybe going to a game, meant watching, concentrating, on the game, the tactics, not strolling the corridors on a cheese fries quest.

As we stood and ate, the Milan team bus went by and entered the stadium, only about fifty or sixty minutes before kickoff. When we went in, it was clear that seating had been added in certain areas, probably as Parma became one of the success stories of the 1990s. Just a few years earlier, with Gianluigi Buffon, Fabio Cannavaro, and Lilian Thuram, the club was a legitimate title contender, along with the Milan and Roma clubs, Juve, and Fiorentina. The Seven Sisters they were called.

We invested in the best seats in the house—midfield and high up in the steep *tribuna*—since this was my first time seeing Andrea Pirlo in person, and I was determined to watch him as *regista* (literally, director), the deep-lying playmaker role. Besides his skills, his vision, his ability to anticipate patterns before they materialized, I admired his demeanor; the man never, ever, smiled. Did he love his work? I don't know. Did he find joy in it? No idea. But he was serious about what he did and did it at a very high level. I appreciated that. You'd often hear commentators in the U.S. say that athletes were supposed to "go out there and have fun." I had nothing against athletes who actually had fun. Cafu would play all ninety minutes, running up and down the right flank, with a smile on his face. But soccer was serious. Not serious business—although it was becoming more and more of a business each year, each decade, and probably always was—but just *serious*. Soccer was fun some of the time, joyous, too, but it was serious, and Pirlo was deadly serious.

When we got to our seats, they were occupied. Like my trips to Olimpico in 1995 and the Marassi (aka Stadio Luigi Ferraris) in 1998—there were no stewards or officials to help you find your seats or to assist in any way. We took two free seats near our own and if someone asked us to move, we would have to do the same. It didn't happen. We were left alone. Maybe everyone was in the wrong seats.

The stadium may have been ramshackle but there was no tension in the crowd. There were Japanese tourists in our section (perhaps to see the splendid, effortless Hidetoshi Nakata) and even fans with Milan scarves. In Genoa, I didn't wear Roma colors, and I was glad I didn't. This was civilized, but it was almost soporific. The sandwiches, I had to admit, were the highlight of the afternoon. It ended 0–0; not that this was necessarily a bad sign, not at all, but Pirlo had an indifferent afternoon, and the more I watched soccer, the more I realized that great players often did. If you were lucky, there'd be a moment or two. Pirlo, I could see, gave up the ball more than you might expect. He'd produce an errant pass once or twice a game, it seemed, sometimes in his own half. Often a teammate, Gennaro Gattuso usually, and a supreme defensive line was there to provide cover. This didn't make him any less great, but it was more evidence that statistics would never work in soccer. If you measured his "pass percentage," heaven forbid, it might not be as high as you'd expect, but when he made the perfect pass it created opportunity. Today, he didn't.

November 23, 2003
FC Zurich vs. FC Aarau
Stadion Letzigrund
Zurich, Switzerland

It was nice to be out of New York for more than a week or two and I looked forward to settling into and learning more about Zurich, the city of exiles, of James Joyce, Lenin, Trotsky, Wagner, Ignazio Silone. But first, it was time to see soccer. As a close reader of *World Soccer* in the 1980s, I recognized Grasshoppers as the

Yankees of Switzerland. They'd even show up in the European Cup and hold their own against Europe's elite. I also knew of Young Boys Bern, Servette, Basel, Xamax, and Sion. But when my girlfriend told me that FC Zurich was playing at home this particular weekend, I had to admit that I didn't know there was an FC Zurich. I knew that FIFA was here, just as I knew that UEFA was in Nyon, across the country in the French-speaking western part of the country.

Yes, she said, they weren't as good as Grasshoppers but they had a long history and played in a different stadium, which was even closer to where she lived. She wouldn't go—she hated soccer—but she gave me exact instructions: Take the 33 bus to Albisriederplatz and transfer to the No. 2 tram just one stop. The stadium was right there. I tried to convince her again to come with me, but, although she grew up playing tennis and skiing and going to the occasional Grasshoppers match with her father, she didn't have time for sports. Art, and especially photography, was her focus.

So I went, with the awful feeling that I could get lost at any and every turn in this new city. On the way there, one of the bus stops was named Zwinglihaus, for the Swiss reformer Ulrich Zwingli, who still defined this city in ways beyond the naming of churches or landmarks, even if he'd died in the sixteenth century.

Albisriederplatz was a circular space well off the city center—the *Altstadt*, where Zwingli railed against the papists at Grossmünster—but it looked very European to me upon first glance. There was a *Bäckerei*, a *Konditorei*, *Metzgerei*, and *Apotheke*. Just what you'd imagine. I wasn't sure where I should wait for the tram so I just stood near two guys with soccer scarves, which are unmistakable whether you know a team's colors or not.

I walked up and bought a ticket. This wasn't difficult as the game was against Aarau, another team I'd never heard of, and not well-attended. That and the fact that the stadium was the most downtrodden I'd ever seen. For one, there was, for soccer fans, the dreaded running track that kept us far from the action. There was a good excuse at least: Zurich still hosted a world-class track meet once a year in August. And besides the track, the stadium wasn't even in an oval. In the area behind the goal, where the track curves, the stands didn't curve with it, but instead made a point. This made the stadium into an odd oblong hexagon, if there is such a thing.

Then behind the goals there were terraces, with no seating and only the concrete steps and uneven placement of stanchions, just like the old English grounds, where this was now abolished. In fact it reminded me of a smaller version of the photos I'd seen of Heysel Stadium in Brussels. It looked like the equivalent of steerage. The whole atmosphere felt bleak and unwelcoming. It was so quiet that the two Armenians I'd been talking to the whole game actually waved to one of the players, Arthur Petrosyan, an Armenian international, and he easily spotted them in the crowd and waved back. After the game he talked to them from the field with them standing at their seats. Maybe it wasn't so unwelcoming after all. Was I judging a book by its cover? Was this stadium, so full of the kind of quirks that Americans had lovingly tried to re-create in baseball the last ten years, a treasure or a dump? I wasn't sure. And I wasn't sure I'd be back.

November 30, 2003
Grasshoppers CZ vs. Young Boys Bern
Hardturm Stadion
Zurich, Switzerland

The FCZ match was, like many games, forgettable; the stadium was *not* forgettable. It was disappointing but not something I'd easily forget. I was glad I went. The following week, Grasshoppers Club Zurich, GCZ, were home. This time, I didn't ask my girlfriend to come with me; I begged. I wanted to go with someone. She gave in. It must have been true love.

She'd been here, years before, with her father. He was a GCZ fan and brought his daughters to Hardturm every so often. I'd met him just recently, but he only spoke German and Swiss-German; I spoke neither, though I tried. I muttered, "Ich gehe Letzigrund für FCZ und ist sehr gut" (I go Letzigrund for FCZ and it is very good). He was unimpressed, both with my German and that I'd actually go to an FCZ match. "FC Zuri ist scheisse," he said simply (FC Zurich is shit.)

I could've let the conversation—if you could call it that—end there, but I kept on. I didn't know much about Swiss soccer—they hadn't been in a major tournament recently—but I did remember the 1994 team. They were grouped with the U.S. and played each other in the first World Cup match under a roof, the 1–1 draw (and gorgeous free kick from Eric Wynalda) in the Pontiac Silverdome.

I rattled off names—Stéphane Chapuisat, Alan Sutter, Ciriaco Sforza—but still he seemed unimpressed. He likes *fussball*, and he still likes GZ, my girlfriend said, but he prefers skiing and does part-time work for the Swiss National Ski Team. Ah, I said, then you must remember Pirmin Zurbriggen and Michela Figini. Only then did I get a smile out of him.

So I wouldn't have a ready-made soccer buddy in Zurich, but today I had company. We took the bus, the same No. 33, but to the other side of the railway tracks, to Escher-Wyss-Platz, the heart of the industrial quarter that was beginning to be transformed into Zuri West, a gentrified zone of all-night raves, bars, and restaurants. Hardturm was beyond Escher-Wyss, about four tram stops or a pleasant twenty-minute walk beside the tram tracks. Even better, and special to Zurich, was that, on the other side of houses and warehouses, was the Limmat River, with a walking and cycling path that made you feel miles away from the city. An industrial landscape on one road, nature along the other.

We walked along the tracks, and tucked into an obtuse angle, barely noticeable, was the stadium. One thing it had going for it was that without a running track, the seats were right on the field. It wasn't as dilapidated as Letzigrund—each section of the stadium looked like it was added in a different decade—but wasn't what you'd expect from an affluent city like Zurich.

If everything in this city was expensive at least there wasn't price gouging at the concession stands. If a *stange*—a draft beer in Swiss-German—cost five francs at a bar, it was the same at the stadium. (A *stange* was the only reasonably priced item in all of Zurich.) And it was better than Bud Light. And there were hamburgers here, a tough find in Zurich. More people, singing, away supporters, a good view of the game, better food, and companionship made for a better experience. It wasn't Bernabéu—though I'd never been to Bernabéu—but this felt the way European soccer should. At last!

Part 3

THE ENLIGHTENMENT, 2004–2012

Football is the last sacred
ritual of our time.

PIER PAOLO PASOLINI

A team is above all an idea.

CÉSAR LUIS MENOTTI

Stadion Hardturm Zürich
UEFA Champions League, 2. Qualifikationsrunde
FC ZÜRICH - RED BULL SALZBURG

Tribüne Nord EG 1+4   Reihe   Platz
Sektor C Presse   14   22

Ticket berechtigt zum einmaligen Ein
VERBOTEN: Büchsen, Flaschen,
Feuerwerk, Fahnenstangen, Laserpoi

Media   Veranstalter:
                        Betriebsgesellschaft FC Zürich AG

Mittwoch 26. Juli 06. 20:15 Uhr

TICKET   TICKET   TICKET   TIC

CLASH OF THE TITANS
MetLife STADIUM
MEDIA

CBF   VS   AFA

BRASIL

JUNE 9, 2012
EAST RUTHERFORD, NJ

No Field Access   No Locker Access

2012 · MEDIA · 2012

CHAMPIONS LEAGUE

MIXED ZONE
FC BASEL 1893 – AS Roma
28. September 2010
PRINT

EVENT CODE	SECTION	ROW	SEAT		EV
MS0803	130	6	1	N-CW	EMS
$ 85.00	LOWER TIER		85.00		CN
All Taxes incl. if Applicable		ADM 3	SUBJECT TO REVERSE SIDE		

CHAMPIONSWORLD & NJSEA

130			
SECTION			13
AC 11%	AS ROMA		AC5
6	VS		
ROW SEAT	LIVERPOOL		N
MED512H	GIANTS STADIUM		
1JUN04	TUE AUG 3, 2004 7:45PM		

UEFA.com   UEFA-

Stadion Letzigrund Zürich
UEFA Champions League 2009/10 - Group Stage

Dienstag
8. Dez. 09
20:45 Uhr

FC ZÜRICH - AC MILAN

Normalpreis

Zugang B16	Block 16	Reihe 5	Platz 14	Package-Ticket

Dienstag
8. Dez. C
20:45 Uh

Stadion
UEFA Champ
FC ZÜRICH

Türöffnung: 120 Minuten vor Spielbeginn
Wir empfehlen die öffentlichen Verkehrsmittel zu benutzen.

Veranstalter: 3. Vertragspartnerin des Kunden: Betriebsgesellschaft FC Zürich, Zürich

Auftragsnummer 500-5041-21974-0-1-6   ibn

May 1, 2004
Curva Nord
357 East Eighty-Sixth Street
New York, New York

May Day has never created the havoc and protest in the United States that it has in Europe. You'd hardly know it was a holiday celebrated around the world. Today had added significance, too. Ten new nations—eight from the former USSR—were admitted into the European Union. The EU now had a population of 450 million, which the media said over and over made it the world's largest trading bloc.

In New York, it was just a Saturday, a nice spring Saturday—nice enough to wear a soccer jersey, my 1998 Roma version. I was strolling around my neighborhood, when I saw, on the southeast corner of Eighty-Sixth Street and Second Avenue, a few steps from the last vestiges of the old Yorkville Germantown—Schaller & Weber butchers and the Heidelberg Restaurant—a teenager handing out leaflets. This wasn't unusual; restaurants and small businesses did this all the time.

But the young man, after eyeing me up while still crossing the street, appeared intent to give me one of these flyers. He went a few steps out of his normal orbit and handed me one, without saying anything. I took it, as I always did—I never liked making people who did jobs like this feel invisible—but when I looked down at it, I couldn't believe what I was seeing. It read something like "Grand Opening of the Curva Nord, for soccer jerseys and accessories, 357 East 86th Street, just off First Avenue."

Curva Nord was the famous—and for some, like me, infamous—area behind the goal at Roma's Stadio Olimpico that was reserved for the most rabid of Lazio fans. Roma's hardest-core sat, or rather, stood, in the Curva Sud in the stadium they shared.

Being that I was in a Roma jersey, I was stunned and thought that someone was playing a kind of practical joke on me. But I was on a lazy stroll; who knew I was going to cross toward the southeast corner of Eighty-Sixth and Second? I easily could have crossed to the west side of the block. I continued to stare blankly at him for a moment—did I know this kid? Had I played soccer with him at the Asphalt Green?—and he at me, also unsmilingly. I slowly kept walking south toward Eighty-Fifth Street, trying to figure out what just happened. What of this Grand Opening? There was already the Doss Soccer Sport Supply store on Ninetieth and First. But if it was called Curva Nord, it must be someone from Italy who had opened this store. Who else would give it such an insider name? A name many soccer fans wouldn't even get? It would be like naming a store the Kop. Some people would get it, more than Curva Nord, but some wouldn't. Some would be confused. A big sign saying Soccer World or the Soccer Shop or some such would be so much easier and maybe even better for business.

There was such a shop, besides Doss, in downtown Manhattan. It was called the Onion Bag and was in the East Village off of Third Avenue, an advantageous location considering it was just a short block away from the premier soccer bar in all of New York, Nevada Smiths, with the friendliest Irish bartender in the city—which is saying a lot—named, appropriately, Happy Jack Kean.

This shop was owned by a Brit. It was a small, well-kept place with a lot of team jerseys, books, and VHS tapes and DVDs. So naming a soccer shop Curva Nord, whether I liked Lazio or not, was brave, I had to admit. I'd have to go in and meet the owner of this place, who must for sure be a crazy Italian. I wouldn't visit today, not with my Roma shirt, in case he really was insane.

When I did go in, I discovered a small place with, like the Onion Bag, jerseys, shorts, and DVDs, but also scarves, key chains, a few team balls, lapel pins, novelty T-shirts, and retro team warm-up jackets. There was also a TV that played Greatest Goal DVDs in a loop, and on the walls were 1974 team photos of Brazil and West Germany. It was, in a word, a dream hangout.

When I walked in, warily, there were no customers, just a big Asian guy behind the counter. I said something like, Nice store. The initial dialog was cautious. We were like two fighters in the first round. The owner is a Lazio fan? I asked. Well, I am the owner, and yes, I'm a *Laziali.*

I was stunned. I was certain only Italians, from Rome and the region of Lazio, supported the club, a club famously hostile to foreigners. We talked and talked. It turned out that his name was Brian, and he was from Seoul, South Korea, but his parents were in the diplomatic corps and he had spent many of his formative years in West Germany. There he became a fan of the West German and Italian national teams and of the club teams Lazio and Schalke 04. He pronounced the city of Gelsenkirchen with a proper German inflection. He seemed to have endless knowledge of the 1974 World Cup, his first. He would, he said, bring in some of his own VHS tapes and DVDs of that tournament and, better still, he had games from the 1972 and 1976 European Championships.

He told me that he had been running a stationery store in this space and one day, just to cheer himself up, put up a Lazio jersey in the window. This store hadn't registered with me; it was in my neighborhood but slightly off my path. People would come in and ask him if he sold soccer shirts; he said no. But they kept coming in, asking. He did informal market research and still answered no, but if he did have some, would they buy them? Everyone said yes.

Brian lived in New Jersey and knew well the soccer store in Bergen County run by former beloved Cosmos players Hubert Birkenmeier and Andranik Eskandarian. He knew them just from going in there a lot and talking soccer, and he bought a bunch of jerseys just to see if he could sell them. Brazil, England, Man United, Real Madrid. Eskie gave him a discount. They all sold and now he was going to give the soccer thing a full-time go.

The fact that I was a *Romanista* didn't matter to him. In fact, he was impressed I had come to the team because of Bruno Conti, whom he admired. Brian's knowledge of the sport was deep. Passion is an overused word, but he was that, too. More than that, he was a soccer thinker. I hadn't met anyone like Brian in a long time, maybe ever. He was the reason I loved soccer. Yes, this was the dream hang out.

June 13, 2004
European Championships
West Eighty-Third Street
New York, New York

After several years of not hearing from David, my former colleague and keeper of the soccer flame in this city, I'd been back in touch with him. Another big tournament was upon us, and he suggested we watch some of the European Championships together. We wasted no time and watched England-France on the second day of the tournament, but not at any old bar. David, as he had told me, was old friends with Paul Gardner, the soccer writer. It was Gardner, the writer and editor of that game program for the FIFA-UNICEF World All-Star Game in 1982, who did so much to ignite my interest in this game. He could be crotchety, David warned, but ultimately was generous and kind.

He said there would be other "soccer weenies" there, too. *Sorry, a soccer what?* He had used the term "Euro-snob" in the '90s, post-MLS launch. I didn't like that term and didn't consider myself one, but I understood what he meant. But "soccer weenie"? It was a term I'd never heard before and didn't like now that I had. When we journeyed to Giants Stadium or played pickup games or I screened my VHS tapes, I didn't consider us "weenies" or "nerds." We were more than "fans"—soccer had been so difficult to find for so long that it had an underground feel to it. You had to be dogged in pursuit of it. And we were. Maybe "obsessives" would be how I would describe us. But there was nothing "weenie" about us. I hadn't seen David these past years, so maybe he'd been under new influences. It was a term that didn't sound like his.

These "weenies" were Steve, whom I already knew from Argentina-Nigeria in 1994, U.S.-Mexico in 1997, and my VHS nights; and another writer, also named David, an American who loved West Ham. And there was nothing "weenie" about West Ham.

Paul was wonderful, and yes, crotchety—he was on deadline for *Soccer America*, it should be said—but welcomed any and all. David wasn't good with introductions, but the other David appeared quick and easy with strangers and we had an immediate rapport. Before the match began, David began handing out a new book to all of us, one that his company published, though he'd had, he said, nothing to do with it. The book was called *How Soccer Explains the World* by Franklin Foer.

Our collective reaction was, Huh? What? We were writers, too; at least Paul, the other David, and I were (as was Steve back in the NASL days). How did *Foer* get to write a book on soccer? Who was this guy? As the Gershwins wrote, nice work if you can get it.

David said he wrote for *Slate* and the *New Republic* and was the brother of the wunderkind novelist Jonathan Safran Foer, and son of the famous antitrust lawyer in Washington. He assured us that he had nothing to do with commissioning the book and went out of his way to tell us, as if to soften the news, that Foer had never played the game, something I wouldn't have held against any writer. Or was he implying that Foer was . . . a weenie?

Foer's book was similar in its approach to Simon Kuper's *Football Against the Enemy*, a classic in the soccer cannon. Each chapter was a reported piece—each a substantial magazine article, essentially—that told an interesting story, most of which (not all, but most) would be familiar to a soccer enthusiast.

The book was good; I inhaled it in two sittings the following couple of nights. But most of the stories were basic knowledge—Soccer 101, you could say—backed up by travel, interviews, observations, and good writing. All things I was skilled at, though I'd like to think that I'd refrain from lines about how Italian men "smear on substantial quantities of hair care products."

So how did Foer, a relative newcomer to soccer, according to David, get the book deal, and not, for instance, me (or the other David or Gardner)? Well, he pitched it. It was that simple. I was napping; he was proactive. I suppose his (and his agent's and his publisher's) lack of deep knowledge of soccer and its back story, its subtexts, its mysteries, worked in his favor. In their collective assessment of the reading public, they imagined it would sell, and with some marketing oomph and a review in the *New York Times*, it did. The title was off slightly—we all thought, that day in Paul Gardner's apartment, it should have read *How Soccer* Reflects *the World*—but it was catchy and you could already imagine editors for smart magazines using it in pun headlines.

Maybe this was good in a way. Maybe, if I discovered a new foreign passion—cricket, say, or capoeira—I could turn it into a book deal.

I wouldn't have thought to pitch a book that included a chapter on the Old Firm derby, since I'd already read about it so often. I'd imagine my friends or an editor saying, "Tell me something we don't already know."

That's why I loved soccer—there was always something I didn't know. So when Croatia came strolling out for one of the matches I was watching with the same group at Gardner's apartment—we watched a bunch of games there during the tournament—one of us, I forget who, said something to the effect of "I hate that jersey of theirs," referring to the unusual red-and-white checkered design. When I asked why, it was explained to me that the checkered pattern was taken from a coat of arms within the Croatian flag (that much I knew), but it harkened back to the fascist regime that was aligned with the Nazis. Every time I saw the Croatia jersey after that, I couldn't help but remember that afternoon, us around Paul Gardner's TV.

August 2, 2004
Guggenheim Museum
1071 Fifth Avenue
New York, New York

August 4, 2004
Roma vs. Liverpool
Giants Stadium
East Rutherford, New Jersey

If there was one sight I never thought I'd see, it would have been AS Roma captain and legend Francesco Totti in a museum, any museum, but especially one in New York. This is not to typecast athletes or entertainers. I once saw New York Knicks great Bernard King at the ACA Gallery on Fifty-Seventh Street in the midnineties for an exhibit of Romare Bearden's work. When I was at the Vatican Museums in Rome, I saw R&B singer and producer Babyface (whom I realized, as I looked at him, would be known in Italian, if I'm not mistaken, as Faccia di Bambino).

But Totti? The previous year, a book of jokes about Totti, edited by Totti himself, was published with profits going to charity. The book was a bestseller. Among the jokes were these:

When someone said to him "Carpe Diem," Totti replied, "I'm sorry, I don't speak English."

The three hardest years for Totti: first grade.

Totti tries to finish a jigsaw puzzle. It takes him almost four months. Then he turns the box over and reads: "From 2 to 3 years." He says, "Ah, so now I'm a genius!"

On the field, though, there wasn't a player with a higher aptitude. He could anticipate situations before they happened; had the unteachable quality of vision; and, like a Michael Jordan, was wily in how he psychologically worked referees. This all took smarts and shrewdness. But when he wasn't playing, he spoke in a thick Roman dialect, more of a leap from textbook Italian than you'd imagine, and was known to speak not in clichés, like so many athletes did, but as a child might. Thus the joke book, with proceeds going to the elderly of Rome and the homeless children of Congo.

Yet there he was in the Guggenheim, twisting his neck this way and that to take in Frank Lloyd Wright's spiral. Not that he was there for the exhibit—Mondrian to Ryman: The Abstract Impulse was showing—but for a reception, two days ahead of Roma's friendly against Liverpool, hosted by Diadora, the maker of his club's kit. The company unveiled the *giallorossi* special Champions League jersey, which was neither *giallo* or *rossi*, yellow or red, but green, an army fatigue-colored green, that borrowed from one of the three clubs AS Roma was formed out of in 1927. I got my hands on an invite and took the twenty-five-minute walk from my apartment.

At some point, I was within arm's reach of the man himself, Totti, who was crunching on celery sticks. What should I say? That I was a big fan? That I admired his skills? Did he really dive in the 2002 match against South Korea? What did he think of the Guggenheim? Of New York? He seemed entirely approachable, comfortable with who he was, mullet and all. There would be the language barrier, so was it really worth it? He didn't speak English—that was for sure. I thought of what Nick Hornby wrote in *Fever Pitch*: "They're the players and I'm the fan, and I don't want to blur the boundaries. . . . Professional footballers are as beautiful and unattainable as models, and I don't want to be a middle-aged bottom-pincher." So I said nothing.

The game was two nights later. David, as he was wont to do, got a bunch of tickets. It was the twentieth anniversary of the infamous Roma-Liverpool European Cup final that Roma lost at Olimpico on penalties, though this seemed a coincidence. It appeared that no one cared about the sport's past, which surprised me since so many new fans seemed highly educated and you'd think would appreciate context. But to them it was all about the now. What happened to "What's past is prologue" or "The past is never dead. It's not even past"?

Joining us, David told me, would be Mike, our former colleague from *Esquire* who we went with to the Bulgaria-Germany quarterfinal in 1994, and who in the years I'd lost touch with him, became quite the serious fan; Mark, a legendary magazine editor; an English friend of David's who was an accomplished women's player and coach; and Franklin Foer, who would meet us at the stadium. I hoped I'd get the chance to talk to him firsthand about his book.

Since I couldn't wear team colors at the Guggenheim event, I was determined to wear them for the game. We wouldn't be in the press box but in the stands. David as usual scored good seats, about sixth or seventh row near midfield—so I'd be free to cheer for my team.

I had this new army-green jersey that Diadora gave out, but it was so awful I chose the traditional-colored jersey. I had so many that for one of them I had the name F. Fellini, as in the director, printed on the back. He was from Rimini, on the Adriatic coast, made famous in *Amarcord*, but he immortalized his adopted city in 1972 with the very strange essayistic film *Fellini Roma*. When you have twelve jerseys you can goof around with at least one.

Mark, the editor, was a delightful gentleman. He didn't have to be; so many New York editors were the opposite unless you were somebody worth knowing. He even said something like, Hey, cool jersey. Are you a Roma fan? I said yes, have been for quite a while now, and he seemed interested. Like all good editors and writers, he was curious and didn't pretend to know it all.

When we got to the stadium, we kicked around in the parking lot and then met Franklin and Mike, who was now a TV executive. I exchanged pleasantries with Mike—I always liked him even if we were never close—and I think he too complimented the jersey, but as David was always bad at introductions, he didn't introduce me to Franklin—or Franklin to me.

When we went to our seats, it happened that I was sitting at one end with Mark, and Franklin was at the other end focused, it seemed, only on Mike. David and his British friend were in the middle.

At half time we all may have mingled, I forget, but even if we did, he and I didn't cross paths or exchange glances. A few strangers in the stadium said to me, Cool jersey. Foer didn't seem to notice. At the end of the game, he went his way, Mike his own, and the four of us went back to Manhattan together. We had plenty to talk about and ended up having beers on Eighty-Third and Third, near my apartment.

The pub had several different identities since I'd been in the neighborhood, but it was always a bar, with glass doors that opened onto the sidewalk. On warm nights like tonight, the doors were always open. As we drank away and talked about soccer and the magazine world—I'll never forget this—a rat, a sizeable one, ran in and scurried around the bar. Besides me and Mark, no one appeared to notice.

August 18, 2004
Switzerland vs. Northern Ireland
International Friendly
Stadion Hardturm
Zurich, Switzerland

Euro 2004 was over. It was oddly bookended by two games between Portugal, the host, and Greece, which was only in its third major tournament and, until the opener, had been winless in these tournaments. When the final arrived, it seemed certain that Portugal, which still had members of its Golden Generation, would avenge that aberration in the first game. Instead, the Greeks won their third straight knockout match by 1–0. Otto Rehhagel, a German, had perfected an Italian system that even Italians didn't trust anymore after getting burned again and again, defending a one-goal lead.

There were beautiful new stadiums that appealed more to architecture critics than fans, there were great goals (Ibrahimovic's deft flick against Italy comes to mind), and even a good conspiracy: the

Denmark-Sweden 2–2 draw, at least in the eyes of Italy. England had Gazza in tears in 1990; Italy now had a bawling Cassano.

Fans were shocked, some even outraged, that Greece won. But why, I wondered? The object of the game is simple: to score more goals than the other team, and that's what they did, without once having to go to penalty kicks. Rehhagel had a plan and his team executed it to perfection. How could you not admire that?

With Greece winning, I thought of Gus Constantine, the NYU coach. He wasn't a flag-waving Greek, not publicly anyway, but he loved soccer and was a proud Greek American, and though I had lost touch with him, I knew he was happy. I was happy that he was happy, wherever he was.

There was also good company to watch games with. Domenico moved back to Italy, but David and I made several trips back to Paul Gardner's place with Steve and David, the author. Paul's apartment was filled with books, great books in world literature. He was a wine drinker, and spoke both Spanish and Italian. A cultivated guy, and the sort you wanted to be around. I wondered why he only wrote for *Soccer America*—no knock—and why only about soccer. He seemed capable of so much more. If he had a doctrine—and he could be doctrinaire, more so in person than in print—it was all about attacking soccer and scoring goals. Hard to argue with that. You could bring up defending or goalkeeping but at your own risk. He might go into a diatribe. And he favored (I don't think that's the wrong word) Latin players, especially the South Americans, over all others. It was nice to get to know him.

Brian at the Curva Nord shop became a fast friend during the tournament—his store was a daily hangout for dozens of aficionados—and we watched a bunch of games together, one being England-Switzerland. We watched it across the street on First Avenue at Fiona's.

Switzerland was in its first major tournament since 1994. Now that I was familiar with some of its players and more of its soccer culture, I was glad it was back on the international scene, despite getting only a draw in its three games. A month after the Euro, I was back in Zurich. I found some freelance editing work to take with me and would do a long stay there while working on a book proposal. Summers in Zurich can be quite wonderful; the winters not so much. December through February are so cold and dank, the soccer season takes a two-month break. The bonus is that the season starts in July, when it's perfect to sit outdoors, sip a cold Feldschlösschen, enjoy a *Wurst mit Senf*, and watch a game. It made me want to teach the Swiss Ernie Banks's famous catchphrase: "Let's play two!"

This August, there was an added treat: an international friendly—usually played in Bern or Basel—was coming to town, Switzerland versus Northern Ireland. Maybe it's because I came to soccer during the 1982 World Cup, but internationals were special to me. And also because of '82, how could I not fondly remember Northern Ireland, the seventeen-year-old Norman Whiteside and Martin O'Neill?

My girlfriend was excited for me but she wouldn't be going; that much was clear. It was one thing to go back to see the team her father supported when she was a child, but it was another thing, and an awful one at that, to cheer on the Swiss national team. For her, this was too embarrassing. I got my ticket a few days early; I couldn't miss this. The Euro may have just ended, but qualifying for the 2006 World Cup would start in a few weeks.

The weather was, as I had hoped, perfect. I stopped for an espresso at Spheres, a glass-and-steel bar and bookstore in Zuri West, my favorite spot in the city, and walked along the Limmat at a leisurely pace before I turned in at Hardturm. I bought my ice-cold *stange*, my wurst, and stared at the still sun-splashed field. All good, except that with maybe four thousand attendees, the crowd was small.

How could this be? How could the entire city *not* be into this game? Andrea had said that Zurichers were the least nationalistic in the country. It was the city not only of Zwingli, but also of the Dada movement, the student riots of the early eighties, one of the great heroin markets in the nineties, and today it was famous for its thriving and mostly legal red-light district. I was learning more about this new country all the time, and hearing more and more that to other Swiss Zurich was a cesspool. (Damn nice cesspool, I thought.) The feeling was mutual. You rarely saw the famous red flag with white cross in the city, even on August 1, their version of the Fourth of July. If you wanted to be part of the festivities—which marked the founding of the Confoederatio Helvetica of 1291—it was best to go to the central cantons. And these celebrations were increasingly becoming theater pieces for the Swiss People's Party (SVP), a growing right-wing movement led by the charismatic Christoph Blocher.

Even the fans at this game didn't look like city folk, but more from the provinces. They chanted "Hopp Schwiiz!" (Go Switzerland!), but you could barely hear them. The match ended 0–0. Was I demented, I wondered to myself, not only coming to see this game, but looking forward to it the way I did? Well, no. I just loved soccer.

June 18, 2005
MetroStars vs. Columbus Crew
Giants Stadium
East Rutherford, New Jersey

Brian and I had talked about going to a match since we first met at his store the previous year. Finally, we choose a MetroStars game. It was a beautiful night for a game but not many fans showed up. It's one thing to watch a game with four thousand at Hardturm or Letzigrund with their modest capacities, but Giants Stadium held over seventy-six thousand. On this night it had sixty-eight thousand *empty* seats, and it was a reminder again that MLS, besides sounding like a disease—ALS, MDS, MS—sometimes had the feeling of spinach (though I actually liked spinach, sautéed in garlic and olive oil with a squeeze of lemon).

I went to a few games per season—sometimes more—though the journey to the Meadowlands never made it especially appealing. If only the Metros could play at Shea or Yankee, despite the crooked dimensions, or even Randall's Island, where the Cosmos originally debuted.

One thing I liked about going to MetroStars games was that it was a parade of international jerseys, all except the red-and-black verticals of New York/New Jersey. It was the red and black of Milan, the black and blue of Inter, the red and white of Arsenal, of Liverpool, of Man U, of Bayern. The blue of Chelsea, Cruziero, France, Italy, Japan, U.S. away. The white of Real, Santos, Fulham, England, Germany. The green of Ireland and the green-and-white hoops of Celtic and Sporting (a real fan could spot the difference immediately). The white and black of Juve and Newcastle (and a fan knew the relationship).

The year before, I wrote an article for the *New York Times* Style section on two new retro Holland jackets, one by Puma, the other by Adidas. I explained how Johan Cruyff, who had a deal with Puma, ripped out one of the famous Adidas three stripes, something the new Puma jacket slyly alluded to.

For this game Brian wore the *celeste* of Lazio and I wore my *giallorossi*. We thought it would be funny. The previous year, a Roma-Lazio derby was suspended in the second half under the murkiest of circumstances. "Only in America"? This was a case of "Only in Italy." It started when Roma *ultras*, an emissary group of three, somehow not only got onto the field but approached team captain Francesco Totti and told him a young Roma fan had been run over by a police car outside the stadium and that his bereaved mother insisted the match be stopped. And it was. Only the story wasn't true. It was a ruse to stop the game, apparently to show the federation how powerful the *ultra* groups could be.

It sounded like a one-act farce by Dario Fo: *The Accidental (But Fake) Death of an Ultra*. I was watching live at Nevada Smiths, not knowing what the hell was going on. Brian, whom I didn't know at the time, was at the match, in the Curva Nord, with his Lazio friends. He clashed with police afterward amid tear gas, and it wasn't the first time. He told me it was nothing compared to the student riots in Seoul, to which he'd returned, in the 1980s. He showed me video that he took from the Olimpico on his cell phone. I didn't know much about the Seoul student riots, but this looked intense. By chance, David was also at the game in Rome. Nothing like this happened in Cosmos Country, or even Highbury, for that matter, not anymore.

So when Brian and I went to the MetroStars, we thought we'd get a rise out of some of the sharper-eyed fans, a big Korean in a Lazio shirt, a skinny guy in Roma colors. No one got it. There were knowledgeable MetroStars crowds; this wasn't one of them. For whatever reason—I think there was a promotional day, maybe something having to do with school kids—there were more parents at this game than I had ever remembered. For the entire first half, little kids ran up and down the aisles, through the rows, in the concourses. Their mothers yelled at them. Brian turned to me at one point and said, No one's watching the game.

For the second half, we changed seats. We had not only an entire row of our own but an entire vast section of red seats. Toward the end of the game, we saw Alexi Lalas, now the MetroStars general manager, walking through the stadium in a suit, dejected. We felt bad for him. He may not have been Franz Beckenbauer but he'd had a distinguished career, played in two World Cups, had nearly one hundred caps for his country, was the first American to play in Serie A—Serie A at a high point—scored a goal at San Siro, and was one of the big names to help get MLS off the ground in those early years. Lalas had a lot to be proud of. A move to coaching or the front office seemed like a logical next step for him; he always seemed bright and articulate. And now he was overseeing this: the eyesore of sixty-eight thousand empty red seats and hyperactive kids using the aisles for food fights. Lalas, we agreed, deserved better.

May 1, 2005
Palermo vs. Chievo Verona
Stadio Renzo Barbera
Palermo, Sicily

Andrea and I had talked about going to Sicily for a while, and we knew the best time to go was in April and May. We got a cheap flight from Zurich to Palermo, rented a car, and spent two weeks making it up as we went along.

I warned her in advance a couple of days after we arrived that there was a game, and I was going to see it, whether she wanted to or not. This time, she was up for it since it was Italy; it had to be better than Zurich, no?

The only hotel we booked was in Palermo, the Hotel Posta, one block removed from the fascist-era post office, almost comical looking amid the city's dilapidated grandeur.

From the beginning, the small hotel staff seemed friendly. After we checked in, I asked, in my limited Italian, if it would be difficult to get tickets to Sunday's game. Yes, it would—*molto dificile*, the man behind the desk told me. This made sense. Attendance in Italy had been down for years, but this was Palermo's first season back in Serie A since 1973, and the club was playing well. My disappointment clearly showed, and I suppose the man, my age more or less—Nicola was his name—who turned out to be the owner, wondered why. So he asked. And I told him. What should have been a sentence or two turned into a long, emotional conversation. He himself did part-time work as a sports photographer and would be just off the touchline for a local paper. We left it that I'd try my luck at the stadium and maybe buy from a scalper—though I couldn't express this concept in Italian without it coming out all wrong. He implied it would be a long shot, but he'd give us a ride to the stadium. He still seemed in shock that an American, of all people, would be familiar with Luca Toni, Fabio Grosso, Andrea Barzagli, and Christian Zaccardo.

That was on a Friday. I called the stadium box office the next day, and still nothing, sold out. By Sunday morning, I'd given up. I even wondered if it was worth heading all the way to the ground with the hope of finding two tickets—and two tickets together.

My girlfriend was okay with it either way, as we were already having a great time. The day before, we saw Palermo's outdoor markets in their full glory, fresh fish, vegetables, fruits, meats, nuts. We saw the eclectic Duomo and the catacombs. And at night we found out at the last minute that there was a Ravel and Satie concert at Teatro Massimo. Andrea recognized it as the theater in the final scene in *Godfather III*, which I hadn't seen. We walked up, bought amazing seats for just fourteen euros and heard great music. So to this point, Palermo had already been a delight. We left the hotel that morning with no destination in mind except to wander and get lost.

About ten or fifteen minutes from our hotel, we stopped for an al fresco cappuccino—it was still morning, and one rule I did abide by was the Italian one that cappuccino should only be served until noon—and admired a baroque church. Baroque was everywhere on the island and we were looking forward to the southeast, especially Noto, for more of this.

Suddenly, a car sped up to the café and screeched on its breaks. It was Nicola. He jumped out of his car, beaming. In Italian, he went on and on, so fast we didn't know what he was saying, until he took out two tickets. Long story, he seemed to imply, but he landed these and there would be no markup, only face value. It seemed too good to be true, but we forked over the cash—not that much, about forty euros each, for upper deck, midfield—thanked him again and again, shook hands, and offered him cappuccino. He had to go, but said he'd pick us up at the hotel an hour and a half before the game.

Incredible, Andrea said. My own American mass-media conditioning about Southern Italians kicked in, and I wondered aloud if the tickets were real. With all the play about the Mafia back home, you start believing the deplorable stereotypes, even the ones about your own people. Andrea said, Stop it, he's the owner of the hotel, he's going to pick us up and probably drive us back, we'll see him tomorrow morning. He knows what real tickets are, they are real, shut up. She was right. I felt awful.

He turned out to be a wonderful representative of his city. He drove us to the stadium, along with his wife and another friend, who couldn't have been kinder. He told us where to enter the stadium, and said he'd meet us here after the game to drive us back.

When we got to our section of the stadium, there were men, mostly men, sitting on the stairs smoking cigarettes. When we got close to our seats, I could see that they were already occupied. We sat in two empty seats nearby, just as Domenico and I had done in Parma. No one bothered us. Maybe assigned seats in Italian stadiums were merely suggestions, like the old joke about red lights.

Andrea may not have liked soccer, but she appreciated the unvarnished, noncommercial, almost rule-less quality of the whole experience. There weren't even a lot of souvenirs in pink and black—the club's colors, and how appropriate—being hawked. It was the opposite of Zurich or even a sporting event in New York. Where so much of tourism these days felt packaged and commodified, this felt like a real experience. There were, it was safe to assume, no other Americans or Swiss among us, not even many Chievo fans from Verona.

After the game, Nicola met us where he said he would and with his friends gave us a late-night driving tour through Palermo and the local mountain, Monte Gallo, above. Then we drove back into the city and headed to one of the few late-night spots still open, an old *focacceria*, where the grilled intestine sandwich was the specialty. I passed—innards aren't my thing—but drank a cold beer. When we got back to the room, we said something like, Wow, what a night. It's a good thing we ran into Nicola yesterday; what if we hadn't been there?

My girlfriend paused. Then she said this: But wait, how did he know where to even find us yesterday? We could've been anywhere. Right?

June 11, 2005
Italy vs. Ecuador
Giants Stadium
East Rutherford, New Jersey

It seemed as if soccer was getting more popular by the month. Still, it was a surprise when I got an e-mail one day from an enthusiastic young guy named Ben saying that he was the managing editor of a new American soccer magazine and asked if I'd like to contribute. He and the editor, a colleague of his at *Slam* magazine, the hip-hop influenced basketball monthly, had been given the green light to do something similar for soccer.

My answer was obvious and immediate: Yes, I'd love to contribute. There were a few assignments available, one on Alessandro Del Piero, one on Kaka, and another on Luca Toni, who'd just finished the season with Palermo with twenty goals—one that I saw live—and helped them to a sixth-place finish and qualification for the UEFA Cup. The talk was that he could be Italy's star forward in next year's World Cup. For the profile on Toni, which I accepted, I went to the Meadowlands to see a friendly between Italy and Ecuador. I would have gone anyway, but I needed to get a quote from either Toni himself or the coach, Marcello Lippi.

I didn't like sitting in the press box, but if I had to, I had to. One thing was clear: there was no rooting. It made it less fun, but I respected the rules: no cheering, no chauvinism, and no team colors. I went in navy slacks and a burgundy polo shirt. Italy looked awful frankly, as they often do in these situations. Ecuador wasn't much better. Luckily for me and my story, Luca Toni scored on a header. I wondered if Nicola was watching back in Palermo. I doubted he was, knowing the Italian apathy toward friendlies, especially during the summer.

Truth was I didn't much care for Luca Toni as a player. Italy often likes the big-small striker partnership. I preferred small ball, in every sport. The small player seemed to be able to do more that turned out to be memorable, whether it was Zico, Maradona, Platini, Baggio, or Valderrama. There were exceptions. I liked tall and graceful, like Jan Ceulemans, Michel, and old videos of Cryuff and Beckenbauer. And who could forget Saeed al-Owairan from 1994? About the only big, powerful striker I grew to like was Eduardo "El Tanque" Hurtado, an Ecuadoran who played for the MetroStars for a couple of years in the nineties. (That was another problem with the New York/New Jersey franchise; no one seemed to stay on for much longer than a year or two.) What I liked was that there was no obfuscation about his game; he was just as his nickname explained, the tank.

With Luca Toni, who did that silly thing with his hand to his ear after he scored, I'd have to think hard to come up with something new to write, and at least his headed goal today would give the article currency.

Throughout the match, I simply took notes. It was hard to get excited about it anyway: It was a friendly a year before the World Cup. The few Italian journalists there were hardly noticeable. Not the Ecuadoran press; they whooped and hollered and cheered their team as if they were sitting behind the goal. Unprofessional? Either nobody told them or they didn't care or that wasn't the unwritten rule in their country. Maybe their honesty should be viewed as refreshing. Certainly, of the American journalists there, many would have loved to see Italy lose but would never come out and admit it. No one lost; it was a dull 1–1 draw.

Under the stadium, I went to a small room, where Lippi held a press conference. I stuck my hand in the air with my tape recorder and asked whether today's goal solidified Toni's position as a starter on the national team for next year's World Cup.

An interpreter reiterated the question in Italian, and Lippi, looking at me, answered back in his native tongue. I was never keen on Lippi, but he was distinguished: from his name (think painter Filippo Lippi), to his white hair, to his spectacles. He could've passed for a doctor or museum curator. I couldn't completely follow what he was saying, but I nodded along as if I did, as if he was explaining something of great import. It turned out he wasn't, just one cliché after the next, which is why I didn't want to cover sports the way a beat writer would.

But I got what I needed. Now the part I always dreaded: the long trip back home, first to Port Authority. And, since I had to stay for the press conference, would I make the last bus? Or would my recurring nightmare of being stranded there come true this time?

I made it, on one of the very last buses back. It was almost full to capacity but there was a free aisle seat about three rows from the front. I always brought reading material for such occasions and pulled out the Saturday *New York Times*.

I was quietly reading when someone tapped me on the shoulder. I say tap, it was more of jab, one that I immediately recognized as adversarial.

I looked back and a young Latino man, younger than me—maybe Ecuadoran, maybe not—seated diagonally behind me, asked, Are you Jewish? Just like that. He didn't say it in a tone of, Excuse me, are you Jewish? Because we're South American Jews and you actually look like a friend of ours . . . No, that would have been friendly and perfectly fine. He didn't even say, Excuse me, but are you Jewish? Just in the most aggressive way, Are you Jewish?

Huh? I didn't understand? Was it my nose? What was he getting at?

I answered his question calmly and truthfully. I said, No, I'm not Jewish. His friend next to him at the window seat was leaning forward, glaring, and looked prepared to lunge at me. What the hell was this? And I turned back around. But then I thought I should have said, And what if I am? Is that a fuckin' problem? Why would you even ask that, dumb ass? The entire ride back I was thinking of what I could have said or should have said. Then I said to myself, No don't even engage them in intelligent debate. Why even risk escalation? What would you have done?

But what would they do when we got off the bus? Would they say something else? How ridiculous would this be to get into an altercation over—what exactly? I knew anti-Semitism still existed; I never imagined I'd be a victim of it.

To think that if I hadn't had to sit in the press box, I would've worn my 2002 Italy jersey, and would not have been mistaken for Jewish. Or maybe I would have? Or maybe they liked Italians less? When the bus stopped at the Port Authority—now so safe it was creepy and would have been ridiculously ironic if, after all these years, I got attacked there now—I didn't hurry out of my seat. I let them pass and got up right after them. When they got off the bus, they kept going. I was relieved.

If I'd said something else to them, and maybe I should have, it probably would've ended up in a confrontation. For what? Because they didn't like the way I looked? Or didn't like what they thought I looked like? This wasn't supposed to happen at a soccer game. Or maybe it could only happen at soccer, where, as I'd read over the years and seen, some thought it the perfect arena to let their inner bigot hang out. A shame, really, especially in the United States.

July 30, 2005
Stade de Suisse Wankdorf
Bern, Switzerland

I'd always been fascinated by stadiums, even ugly ones like Shea. On family vacations, I always gazed lovingly at Robert Moses's grandiose monstrosity beside the Grand Central Parkway on the way to LaGuardia or JFK. When we went to Montreal in 1980, I insisted we take a guided tour of Olympic Stadium. I did the same for the Superdome when we went to New Orleans. And there was the lucky coincidence that there was a soccer doubleheader at the newly opened BC Place Dome in Vancouver in 1983.

One of the first books I bought from Soccer Learning Systems all those years ago was *The Football Grounds of Europe*. I'd flip through it—each had a significant history, it seemed—not thinking I'd ever see many of them.

One stadium in the book that I almost had access to was the Wankdorf in Bern. As a student of the World Cup, I knew it was the site of the 1954 final between the storied Hungarians and underdog West Germans. Not only did the match make athletic shoemaker Adi Dassler in demand—his company, Adidas, gave the German team the option of changing into screw-on cleats at half time—but Germany, the West anyway, unofficially rejoined the world with its victory. It was a part of European history I thought could've been made in Hollywood; and in fact a movie *had* been made about it, though not in Hollywood, a few years before, called *Das Wunder von Bern* (The Miracle of Bern).

I'd seen Young Boys Bern play in Zurich a couple of times already, and I'd been to the capital, but Wankdorf was torn down in 2001, a couple of years before my regular visits. In midsummer of 2005, we went to visit Andrea's friend Maya in Bern, the main purpose being to see the new Paul Klee Museum designed by Renzo Piano, who also did the Beyeler Foundation in Basel.

Piano's new building was on the edge of the city, and its gentle, undulating roof suggested the rolling foothills of the surrounding landscape. For me, it looked like an aquatic center. The sports arena wasn't foreign to Piano. He may have achieved star architect status from the Pompidou Center in Paris, the Menil Collection in Houston, and Potsdamer Platz in Berlin, but he also did Bari's Stadio San Nicola for the 1990 World Cup. Who knows how much this commission was for—I'm sure he didn't starve—so it was disconcerting to learn from the genteel, mostly older staff members, that they weren't getting paid; they were only volunteers.

It so happened that this weekend was also the grand opening of the brand new Stade de Suisse, built on the Wankdorf site. Switzerland would be co-hosting the 2008 European Championships and the Wankdorf was over seventy-five years old.

There was no game this weekend, but there was a free open house, for any and all to come in and walk around, have a wurst or a beer, and see the new space. Andrea wasn't interested and, being it was a beautiful afternoon, preferred to go swimming in the Aare River. So Maya and I took a slow walk out to the stadium. She didn't like *fussball* either, but was a Bern native and was proud of the sleepy capital.

Stade de Suisse was a completely new stadium, nice, almost perfect. Roomy seats, wide corridors, modern bathrooms, great sightlines, you were right on the field. It was small—with a thirty-two thousand capacity—and I thought that it would be the perfect size for an MLS stadium, especially for the MetroStars. As much as I thought it would be great to see a game there, especially in Euro '08, I still wished I'd seen the old Wankdorf Stadium. On our way out, my friend told me that they kept the old clock, the old-fashioned Longines game clock that I had seen in black-and-white photos of the 1954 World Cup final, and might install it as a kind of museum piece outside the stadium. How appropriate would that be in the capital of Confoederatio Helvetica? Orson Welles said famously in *The Third Man*, "In Italy for thirty years under the Borgias they had warfare, terror, murder, and bloodshed but they produced Michelangelo, Leonardo da Vinci, and the Renaissance. In Switzerland, they had brotherly love; they had five hundred years of democracy and peace and what did that produce? The cuckoo clock." This wasn't a cuckoo clock, but what a clock it was. At least something was still sacred.

March 9, 2006
Olimpiastadion
Berlin, Germany

Of all the great capitals of Europe, the one where I felt most at home was Berlin. It wasn't a friendly place, but it wasn't unfriendly either. I liked Paris, especially the layout of it—in my mind, I called it "the city of cities"—but it could be stodgy and unwelcoming. Rome was both chaotic on the one hand and obsessed with rules—like where you could and couldn't sit while drinking coffee—on the other. Nor was it especially friendly. The last time I was in London, the friendliness often felt phony and it seemed as if it had sold its soul, like my hometown had. In fact, London felt a little too much like New York.

I still loved all of those cities, mind you, and only wished I could afford to get to them more often, but Berlin felt less judgmental and more open, not open for business in a Giuliani/Bloomberg post–9/11 kind of way, which was fair enough—*We're open for business! Spend money!*—but open to new thoughts and other possibilities.

I'd already been to Berlin previously, around this time of year in 2004. It was March, around my birthday, and windswept. I enjoyed the former East, endless and endlessly fascinating. Now, in 2006, my sister came in for a week, and I took the train up from Zurich to meet her for a few days. Like two years before, Hertha was on the road, but there were guided tours of the Olympic Stadium. Hertha played there, sure, but it was historic for other reasons, specifically the 1936 Olympiad and its dark undercurrents. On a brighter side, it would also host the World Cup final in just four months.

My sister's itinerary differed from mine but it dovetailed for the Neue Nationalgalerie—we both loved Mies—the Reichstag, the TV tower (the Fernsehturm), and, yes, she'd be up for the Olympic Stadium. It made sense that I would see my first German stadium with my sister; she was the first person I watched soccer with and that was *Soccer Made in Germany*. I never remembered Hertha in those years. It was always Bayern, Köln, Stuttgart with the Forster brothers (her favorites), and Borussia Mönchengladbach.

We took the subway out there and the depot reminded me of the Shea Stadium/U.S. Tennis Center stop on the No. 7 train. As we approached the stadium—God, it was freezing—I already became uncomfortable. Uncomfortable because I already felt attracted to it, even if I knew this to be the centerpiece of fascist architecture and, with the adjacent Maifeld, the rallying point of fascism itself. So was Tempelhof Airport, but that was also celebrated for the Berlin Airlift.

The stadium had balance and substance. No one was around—it was like being on the set of a science-fiction movie—and the closer I got to it, the more other worldly it seemed. We bought tickets and by now there were about six or seven other people in this vast open space. A few were Japanese. (I wonder what *they* felt.) There was no tour guide; they just opened the gates and let us wander. The inside was blighted by an awful royal-blue running track that covered over Jesse Owens's path from 1936.

To see the Olympic Bell Tower outside the stadium made me attracted once again—and repulsed once again. It was a sight, one you'd never forget, but less than seventy years ago, not very long in the scheme of history, it had been a place where the masses were worked into a frenzy.

Let's go, my sister said, this is getting to me.

March 22, 2006
Germany vs. United States
Westfalenstadion
Dortmund, Germany

A couple of weeks later, the U.S. team had a friendly against Germany. Both were bound for the World Cup and both had reasons to be optimistic. The U.S. was coming off its best finish in a World Cup since 1930, when it reached the quarterfinals and lost narrowly, 1–0, to Germany. It was a game the Americans could've and probably should've won. The U.S. team beat Portugal, tied South Korea, and beat Mexico, and was filled with young precocious talents that didn't appear at all intimidated by the occasion. On the eve of that 2002 tournament, an editor at GQ called me and asked who was going to be *the* American player of the tournament. I said there could be a few—Clint Mathis, DaMarcus Beasley, Brian McBride—but I'd put my money on twenty-year-old Landon Donovan. He said okay, call him and write three hundred words on him; we'll do a full page. I did, and it ran.

Here in '06, Donovan was back, as was Beasley, McBride, and Bruce Arena, the coach. Germany were the hosts and since the Miracle of Bern had won three World Cups, finished as runners-up four times, and in the top four another two more times, plus won the European Championships three times, and finished second in that tournament twice. Absolutely extraordinary. They were, in other words, almost guaranteed a spot in the semifinals, and if they got there and the bracket went according to plan, they would play at the famously intimidating Westfalenstadion in Dortmund, where the national team had never lost and had eleven wins and a draw.

I was in Zurich, and an editor at ESPN *Magazine* suggested I run up to see the game in case some kind of news broke: if Clint Mathis scored a hat trick, if the U.S. actually won, if a riot broke out.

None of those things happened: Mathis had been in good form, but had a quiet game; the U.S. lost badly, 4–0; and no riot broke out. On the contrary, the American fans who were there were model away supporters, politely drinking beer in a designated area in the city center.

Not that there was much else to do. Dortmund is a small city in the industrial western Ruhr area, a region packed with great soccer clubs. Borussia is everything. When I left my two-star hotel, I asked the husband and wife owners if they were going to watch the game. They said they only cared about Borussia. They were season-ticket holders and decorated the hotel's small lobby in team photos and pennants.

The stadium is Dortmund's main attraction, known as the opera house of German football for its steep and still all-standing terrace behind the south goal. That I didn't see. For internationals it's converted to an all-seater. Still, you could see why the national team was undefeated here. Full, or nearly full, as it was tonight, made for as imposing a setting as I could imagine in soccer. The U.S. was never going to win here.

I sat in the outdoor press area. At half time, I went inside to warm up and get a hot coffee or tea. There was a line of journalists, all

German as far as I could tell, and I couldn't quite believe my eyes: they were on line for beer. There was an older gentleman, manning a massive beer keg. He kept the valve open and moved one cup after the next in a seamless motion under the spout.

I didn't want beer that night; it was too cold, and I didn't want my judgment compromised in case Mathis did score an improbable second-half hat trick and I needed to run down and get a quote, but I was glad I was seeing this. It wasn't the American way to drink in the press box, but it was what the locals did apparently. They wouldn't sanitize for the sake of the visiting Americans. It was the triumph of the local over the global and as beautiful as anything on the field that night.

June 12, 2006
The Great Lawn
Central Park
New York, New York

Since I'd reconnected with David in 2004, we'd often meet on Central Park's Great Lawn for what the English would call a kickabout. I could see, as the years went by, that Americans were subservient to the English when it came to soccer, adapting the English vernacular and gestures regarding the game. I, for one, was not, adamantly so, but if ever there was a perfect word, it was "kickabout." Like playing "catch."

Not that I, or he, actually used the term, nor, thank goodness, said "footie." But it's what it was; we kicked it back and forth, to and fro, often practicing our juggling skills in between. We didn't have a choice; no soccer games were allowed on the Great Lawn since it had been refurbished, beautifully, I might add, in 1997. The Parks Department's argument, and it often ended up as an argument, was that cleated shoes would tear up the grass. Within five minutes of setting up a three on three, four on four, or the like, a park official would break up the game. I suppose I couldn't blame them. The grass was spectacular. Why they didn't restrict the wearing of cleats for softball players, especially outfielders, was another story.

Anyway, as the weather in the spring of 2006 warmed, as the World Cup approached—always my favorite time, even more than the tournament itself—David handed me a book as we met for one of our first kicks of the season. It was called *The Thinking Fan's Guide to the World Cup*, and was published by a division of his company. It was made up of thirty-two essays, one on each country in the upcoming tournament.

Wait a second, I'm a fan, I'm a thinker, I'm interested in all that surrounds the game, always have been, why wasn't I asked to contribute? David said he had nothing to do with it, but that the editors, Matt Weiland and Sean Wilsey, didn't listen to his recommendations and didn't include him, either. Or Paul Gardner. So I shouldn't be insulted. But why don't you try to review it? he said.

I'd have to read it first, and did, like Foer's book, in two sittings over a weekend. It's hard to pitch book reviews—they're usually assigned—but I pitched the *New York Observer*, a paper I hadn't written for since 1995, when I did a front-page, two-thousand-word profile of Albert Murray, the writer and intellectual. Right away, the book editor, one who was highly regarded, it should be said, gave me the green light and it ran on June 12.

I applauded the parts of the book that I found "surprising, informed, erudite, funny." As a whole, though, it didn't "feel like a sincere quest to share an appreciation of the game and all that surrounds it; it feels more like showing off to impress really smart friends. It feels clubby, not inclusive."

I thought it was an entirely fair review, as did the *Observer* editor, whose edits were minimal.

David soon informed me that Franklin Foer was editing a World Cup blog on the *New Republic's* website—by invitation only. It felt exclusive and cliquey, everything that soccer, to me, wasn't. I didn't own it—heck, I didn't own anything, a house, a car, a bike, and certainly not soccer—but the new "thinking fan," they didn't own it either.

It would have been nice to contribute, but the following week, the *Observer* ran a long feature that prominently featured Foer. The piece, written by Lizzie Ratner, the daughter of real estate mogul Bruce Ratner, was on "the soccer Jew."

"Laydees (and gents)," the piece read, "meet the Soccer Jew, that intellectual, kvetchy, *Granta*-reading guy who also happens to possess an encyclopedic knowledge of Ronaldinho's every kick. With one foot planted firmly in the nerd camp and at least a few toes dangling in the jock sphere, he is the strange, hybrid Creature of the Moment."

My friend David was at the center of the piece—or "the Grand Rebbe of the New York Soccer Jew movement"—and had a string of hilarious quotes. He had invited me to Playwright Tavern, where the scene of the piece was set during the U.S.-Czech World Cup match. I was asked for a quote, but it wasn't used. The piece went on:

> This kind of self-conscious chatter is common in this season of high-intensity soccer, particularly on the various invite-only World Cup blogs, like Mr. Foer's the Goal Post, which reads like Talmudic commentaries on every team, player, kick and tumble of the tournament. Call them virtual soccer yeshivas (they even don't let in girls!). On these blogs, soccer fiends can proffer their theories, indulge their brainy urges and yet still be guys, which is perhaps the ultimate sign of the Soccer Jew. They can be dorky and sporty all at once.

Where I fit into this, who knew. But if I wasn't quoted or handpicked or invited, I'd move on. I wouldn't let this stop me. I thought I'd be bold and pitch an editor at the *New York Times Week in Review* section a few World Cup ideas. She wasn't interested in them, but a few days later, she got in touch and said they were looking for a piece on how different nations dealt with defeat. Was I interested?

Of course. Being persistent and industrious paid off. I got to talk once again to Nick Hornby, whom I'd met in the midnineties, and got him to sign a bound galley of *Fever Pitch*. *For Michael, Even if you prefer càlcio.* And I got Eduardo Galeano, the Uruguayan author of *Soccer in Sun and Shadow*, to contribute, too. Authors of two of the best soccer books ever written. I was happy. The piece appeared with my byline on page 1 of the *Sunday Times Week in Review*. My voice had been heard. Now I could enjoy the World Cup, my favorite thing, ever, in life.

July 26, 2006
FC Zurich vs. Red Bull Salzburg
Hardturm Stadion
Zurich, Switzerland

The day after the World Cup ended, I was headed back to Zurich to see Andrea. Two weeks later, qualification for the Champions League was already underway. Since those first Swiss league games in 2003, I was a regular at both FCZ and Grasshoppers. I knew I had to choose—there was a whole, long story about my Mets and Yankees affiliations—but the fact was, I just loved going to games in Zurich, even in the odd little stadiums.

Better still was that FC Zurich not only had a terrific team but, with Letzigrund undergoing full renovations for the 2008 European Championships, the club was playing in Hardturm, which was better for soccer. FCZ had won the league just two months before on the final game of the season, away to Basel—in the ninety-third minute on a goal by Iulian Filipescu, a former Romanian international. There was a pitch invasion by raging Basel supporters who attacked the FCZ players. They'd never heard of Bobby Thomson in Zurich, but if they had, this was their Pafko-at-the-wall, the Giants-win-the-pennant moment.

FCZ had a great coach, Lucien Favre, who was a disciple of Arsène Wenger. Among his best players were the young trio of Gökhan

Inler, Blerim Dzemaili, and Xavier Margairaz. There was also an even younger Almen Abdi; veteran Hannu Tihinen, the captain of the Finnish national team; Alhassane Keita, a Guinean forward; Alexandre Alphonse, a goal-scoring Frenchman; and Rafael, a Brazilian. My personal favorite was César, just César, another Brazilian, who was kind of the midfield schemer. I would go to games and just focus on César. If I'd ever made it as a player, I would have wanted to play like him. He never got near the Brazilian national team to my knowledge, but he was so nonchalant and graceful. He didn't have good speed; instead he'd lope, keep control the extra half note, head up, and make the pass that needed to be made. It's the way I dreamed I could play.

Red Bull Salzburg was in town for the second qualifying round of the Champions League. The visitors had their own assets, if not in bold face. The first pretty-good get by the Austria beverage company was to acquire coach Giovanni Trapattoni, who brought his old Inter player with him as an assistant coach, Lothar Matthäus, whose cup of coffee with the New York/New Jersey MetroStars was more like a single shot of espresso, standing up at the bar. Then they acquired Niko Kovac, born in West Berlin and captain of Croatia's national team. There were flashier Croatian players of that era—Robert Prosinecki, Zvonimir Boban, and Alen Boksic, all at the top of any list of great players of the era—but none was smarter than Niko Kovac. He and his brother Robert played throughout the Bundesliga and were imbued with not one but two great soccer cultures: the efficiency and pragmatism of Europe's highest-achieving country, and the guile and dash of the south Balkans—Yugoslavia wasn't known at one time as "the Brazilians of Europe" for nothing.

These three men alone had deeper reserves of knowledge than many entire teams. No matter how youthful and precocious FCZ were, beating this club, even new and rebranded as it was, would be difficult. They had their own bright young talent, and a Swiss. Johan Vonlanthen was a twenty-year-old who had burst onto the scene in Euro '04 with a goal against France that made him the youngest player ever to score in the European Championships. He was of Colombian descent and looked as if he could be the future of the Swiss national team, along with the three young FCZ players.

Zurich came out like the home team, aiming not only to win the game but to end the two-legged matchup before half time. And they went up 2–0 by the twentieth minute, through Keita and César. But it also felt naïve. They missed chances but kept pouring forth. By the thirty-second minute, Vonlanthen scored. Zurich attacked, it created, its effort was commendable, but despite it ending 2–1, the feeling in the stadium was that it was a missed opportunity.

The Austrians—not that there were many in the squad—got their precious away goal and appeared happy with the result. So did their traveling supporters. But here's the thing: they waved their huge flags and wore their jerseys not in the new Red Bulls colors, but in the violet and white of what they once were, and had been for over seventy years, SV Austria Salzburg.

You didn't have to be a Trotskyite to feel for them. Their team was gutted, even the colors and the team name. It was one thing to do that to the MetroStars, founded in 1996, but to do that to a club founded in 1933, which had won the title and the cup several times and made the final of the 1994 UEFA Cup? How do you just spit that out? At least the Dodgers remained the Dodgers and remained blue. I was surprised any fans even made the long trip to Zurich. Would you, if your team, its tradition with it, were obliterated? It was easy in one sense to criticize the rebranded Champions League; then again, this was the best live game I'd ever seen. And it wasn't technically the Champions League. Maybe it only got better from here.

August 18, 2007
New York Red Bulls vs. LA Galaxy
Giants Stadium
East Rutherford, New Jersey

If there was an annus mirabilis in my soccer life, it was the unlikely year of 2007—post–World Cup, pre-Euro—and condensed into the last five months. There were my first games in the Bundesliga and Premier League, a U.S. international abroad, a brand new Letzigrund, a UEFA Cup, and a derby.

It started fantastically with MLS, and, there was no other way to put this, the "David Beckham Game." It ended up being—cue to the titanic voice of NFL Films' John Facenda—*The Greatest Game Ever Played.* At least in MLS.

David, who else, got tickets, a bunch, in the front row of the mezzanine. I was never a fan of Beckham's. He was good, very good, but not great in my opinion. He was good looking, great looking, but so were a lot of players. He could "bend it," but so could a lot of players. Pirlo scored twice from free kicks in a World Cup qualifier against Scotland and he didn't erupt into an international sensation.

It didn't matter what I thought; Beckham was a phenomenon, and maybe MLS officials were right and he would be good for the league. Already MLS was slowly getting more of an international flair. Little things, like ads in front of jerseys, made it more like our favorite teams from abroad. (And what's more American than splashing around corporate logos?) New MLS stadiums were being built, smaller, more intimate, with fans virtually right on the field. The term, a new one as far as I remember, was "soccer-specific stadium." Now there was Beckham's influence. Welcome to MLS 2.0.

The parking lot prematch may have been the cusp of a new day, but it felt like old times. Four on fours, five on fives everywhere, juggling, trickery, meat on the grill. And there were a lot of us, sixty-six thousand. Pirlo, as great as he was, couldn't bring in that many by himself. It was the difference between Aphex Twin and U2.

It's hard to explain what happened next. It was more like a basketball game. It went something like this: Juan Pablo Angel scored in the fourth minute; LA tied it two minutes later, with Beckham assisting from a corner (he shushed the crowd, many of whom had been booing him); two minutes after that, LA's Carlos Pavón scored from a Beckham free kick; Clint Mathis tied it just before the half.

Jozy Altidore made it 3–2 New York; "LA amazing chance missed!" I scribbled in my pad. Altidore scored again in the seventieth minute; a minute later, Landon Donovan closed it to 4–3; in the eighty-second minute Edson Buddle put in a rebound after Beckham's corner was headed off the crossbar; 4–4 now at that point—"Tom Arnold is at the game," I wrote. Next, Mathis fired a great shot, and Angel put in the rebound, 5–4, which is finally how it ended.

Really, could you have scripted it better? In fact, that's what it felt like, a script, a Disney script. It was so crazy and "exciting" it felt fixed. Beckham's first game for New York? You can't be serious, as a former soccer player turned tennis star once said. But let's say it wasn't fixed. What it was, was sloppy. This wasn't soccer I wanted to see. It may have been exciting for nonsoccer fans, for the moms and dads, but for knowledgeable fans, and there were a lot of us, we didn't need such superficiality. It felt like a Hollywood blockbuster, an entertainment, with predictable plot, explosions, and a built-in sequel.

September 22, 2007
Fulham vs. Manchester City
Craven Cottage
London, England

A few days later, I was off to London. My girlfriend had an artists' residency there, and I would spend the last two weeks with her in the East End before we'd travel back to Zurich together.

Tom had settled back in London for good and I alerted him that I was coming. He was married now, with a couple of kids, and was a lawyer for a very big corporation. I last saw him in 2003 when he had spent a few months in Washington DC working for the American branch of a London firm. He had come up to New York for a weekend and we watched a Fulham match at Nevada Smiths. He had told me about the first seasons in the Premier League—yeah, it was great and all but something was missing. Those rides with the lads to Burnley or Swansea, rain pissing down, singing for Don MacKay's black-and-white army, nothing could beat that, even the top flight. But on that morning in the nearly empty bar, he let out the loudest YEAH! I'd ever heard when Fulham scored. Before I left, he had me sign a petition to save the Cottage. It wasn't the first one. He'd mailed one to me years ago, in 1996, just after I got back to New York after my visit. It came in an envelope marked—and this was better than *World Soccer* arriving all those years before via Royal Mail—"On Her Majesty's Service Department of the Environment." It was dated August 15, 1996. "Dear Mr. M Agovino . . ." The rest was sixteen pages in legalese—British legalese—without Tom's wit or any reference to Don MacKay or the black-and-white army or any jokes at the expense of the Welsh. But I kept it as a remembrance. How could you not, with an envelope that read "On Her Majesty's Service"?

Tom thought that if the supporters' club had representatives in the United States, especially New York, that this would somehow be a sign of strength. And maybe it helped in some small way, as Fulham remained in its cozy home ground. I couldn't wait to see the inside for the first time.

He was a season-ticket holder with his boyhood friend Dave, whom I'd last seen in 1996, at Aldershot-Fulham. Tom and I hadn't been in touch much since that day in 2003 when we'd said goodbye at Penn Station. He assured me that he'd have a ticket for me for the upcoming game against Man City.

In the meantime, there were other games; this was London, the greatest city for soccer in all the world, it had to be said and accentuated. I might not have been enraptured by the English league as so many Americans were (especially lately), but London—with its concentration of clubs, over a dozen within the city limits, many of those in the top two divisions, all with long and distinctive histories, very loyal supporters (something else I had to admit), and its wonderful grounds, like five or six Fenways in one city—was the first wonder of the soccer world. In the 1980s when I used to fall asleep late at night with *World Soccer* over my chest, hoping I'd dream of soccer, I conceived of London as the first-ever city to host a World Cup. If the Olympics could do it, why not soccer?

Back then it was a silly dream. But now, with all-seater stadiums, Sir Norman Foster's refurbished Wembley, and the brand new Emirates, this was actually conceivable. The Cottage, the Den, the Valley, Loftus Road, they could all host early-round matches, plus there was Stanford Bridge, White Hart Lane, and Upton Park.

So there were plenty of games in town during my two weeks. The problem was money. Living the freelance life could be nice—I got a taste of living day-to-day in Europe—but it was stressful too. *Where's my next pay check going to come from?* I was, as ever, on a shoestring budget.

The stadium I had most wanted to see was gone: Highbury, which was all but dismantled. Arsenal was playing a Champions League match midweek against Sevilla so I thought I might go. As I had in the past, I sometimes wrote to the press office requesting a credential. I sent links to my soccer work, and always did have in mind to do a story on soccer tourism, especially Americans going to Europe to see live matches, which I'd been hearing more about. That former colleague, Mike, David had told me, had jetted to London in the past few years to see games. I didn't hear back until the morning of the match. This was the response:

Hi Michael,

Can we please have confirmation that the piece you write on Arsenal will not be detrimental to the Club in any way.

Also, as it is a travel piece you are intending to write, could we provide you with some information on our Stadium tours?

If this is all ok with you, and we can see the print [sic] before it goes to print, your pass is fine for this evenings [sic] game.

Please let me know asap.

Kind Regards,
Communications Department
Arsenal Football Club

I wrote back "asap" and said thanks but no thanks. I would never present something I wrote for vetting other than to an editor and certainly not the subject. Nor was I ever asked as much by the U.S. Soccer Federation, the two Zurich clubs, or anyone else. I was kind of shocked and disappointed. I really wanted to go to the game and, yes, write about it somewhere, sometime. So I took the tube up anyway and thought I might find a stray ticket at the box office or find someone selling a single ticket at face value. If not, there were scalpers—*touts* in this part of the world.

I got to the Arsenal stop early. The game was sold out and no one appeared to be selling. There was still time, so I asked for directions to Highbury and was pointed the short distance. Just about all of it had been taken down, but a portion of the Art Deco main façade was still up. At least I saw that. I walked back to the Emirates and found a few touts, older men, which surprised me, with real London charm. I got into a long conversation with them—they were incredibly friendly—told them I was from New York, loved soccer, loved London, named virtually the entire Arsenal team from 1989. They were impressed, though didn't seem attached to Arsenal. Why should they be? They were businessmen. I got them down from something like 125 pounds to 80 or 90 pounds. It was still a lot of money for me. I told them I'd think about it and come back. I didn't. I knew I'd regret it, but I was financially guilty just being here. I walked away, a little sad, as, by now, fans paced toward the stadium with excitement in their step. But there was still the promise of the Cottage.

Tom delivered. He didn't take a cent, and the ground was as elysian as he had assured me all these years. It was a little box astride the Thames. "And there," he said, "is the Cottage itself. You helped save it, Mikey."

When I asked who Fulham's new coach was, Tom told me it was the oddly named Northern Irishman Lawrie Sanchez. "The same Lawrie Sanchez that coached Northern Ireland the last few years?" "There's only one," he said. "I saw his team play Switzerland in a friendly." "You actually went to a Swiss–Northern Ireland friendly?" "Yeah." "You've gone mad, Michael."

The Fulham game turned out to be thrilling, everything you'd expect from a Premier League match: 3–3. Tom's season-card seats were behind the goal. Peter Schmeichel's son was City's keeper, Martin Petrov was a constant menace and scored twice, Micah Richards looked a star in the making, and Danny Murphy tied it. We cheered for Clint Dempsey; that day I was from Nacogdoches. We hugged strangers.

There were six goals, but it didn't feel cheap, like the 5–4 MLS game. It felt earned, well-played, atmosphere off the scale; even the hugging of strangers felt organic. I had resisted the Premier League, or rather the Americans who paid attention only to the English game, but the appeal, up close, was clear to see. All evidence of hooliganism appeared to have been expunged, even though Tom told a story of being caught in a riot a few years earlier when he and his father had to leap behind someone's garden shrubs to hide from a charging mob.

After the match we went to a gastropub with an Italianate menu. I wanted a local lager, but they didn't have any.

October 17, 2007
Switzerland vs. United States
St. Jakob Park
Basel, Switzerland

The United States had become, without any big announcement, a lock for each World Cup. There might have been the difficult away game in Tegucigalpa or Kingston, and always in the Azteca, but Mexico and the United States were as automatic as Germany and Brazil in their respective regions. Advancing deep into the tournament was the problem. The CONCACAF Gold Cup was more of the same competition. Wins in the World Cup, and in Europe, were the most elusive.

So booking a friendly against Switzerland, at Basel's St. Jakob Park, its biggest stadium, was a good test. The Swiss would be co-hosting the Euro the following year and didn't have to go through the difficult qualification process, meaning it would take a friendly like this seriously. Fortunately I was there and made the acquaintance of a smart young blogger named Adam Spangler who ran a website called ThisIsAmericanSoccer.com. I told him I was in Zurich and he suggested I go to Basel and write about the game.

A few days before, Switzerland hosted Austria, the other co-host for Euro 2008, in one of the first games at the newly refurbished Letzigrund. I went; how could I not? It was a completely new stadium and the difference was astonishing. I remembered that first visit in 2003 and how shocked I was at the configuration and condition of the ground. Now it appeared sparkling and light as air. The strobe lights, once in four Brutalist clusters, were now evenly spaced wisps, and this without any star architects involved, as Zurich was one of the world's few moneyed cities at the time that didn't feel the need to be validated by a Gehry or Piano. The stadium still had the running track—the opening event at the new stadium was the annual Weltklasse—but for the Euro, temporary seats would be built on top of it. For Swiss Super League games and international friendlies like this, the track would remain.

Maybe it was the unusually charged-up Zurich crowd—many probably there for the stadium—maybe it was the underwhelming neighbor to the west, but the Swiss looked as good as I'd ever seen them. The final was 3–1. Tranquillo Barnetta, a left-sided midfielder for Bayer Leverkusen in the Bundesliga, assisted on all three goals. He was known by what the Swiss referred to as a *secondo*, meaning a second-generation immigrant. If it sounded like a pejorative, it wasn't. The first wave of immigration was from Italy (even if Italian is one of the four official Swiss languages) and later Spain and Portugal, men who usually went into construction and contracting. They assimilated easily, worked hard, and their children spoke perfect Swiss-German.

Barnetta was a nice boy, the kind of athlete you wouldn't mind your sister dating. He and other *secondos* appeared to be the future of the Swiss national team. More and more were from Africa, Turkey, and especially from the former Yugoslavia, who arrived as asylum seekers by the early 1990s and were not as docile as the immigrants from western Europe. There were so many young people of Balkan descent that it was even having an impact on the Swiss-German language—itself a mostly unwritten dialect—as South Slavic slang, cadences, and rhythms were considered cool and became part of many young people's vernacular, not unlike hip-hop speak to young Americans. The far-right party of Christoph Blocher had, if not gained in popularity, stayed in the headlines of the freebie tabloids that were ubiquitous on the trams.

Switzerland's future pointed toward diversity, and, you'd imagine, a wider pool of soccer talent with improved results that could go with that. A miniversion of the French national team perhaps. Or perhaps not. At least not when the Americans came to town. As good as the Swiss looked against Austria was as bad as they looked against the U.S. Only 16,500 showed up in the Herzog & de Meuron–designed St. Jakob's Park—all the starchitecture was in Basel—and they booed their team off at half time and full time. Michael Bradley scored the only goal in the eighty-sixth minute in an ugly game but a brave performance for the U.S. team. Winning ugly was something it needed to learn how to do—the hell with winning over new fans.

A few hundred Americans went crazy in the upper deck. It seemed now that wherever the U.S. Men's National Team played—known as the USMNT, an acronym I don't remember in the 1980s or '90s—there were American fans. When it could barely get fans at its home games, it now had traveling supporters, and loud ones. The year before I'd written a history of the national team's uniform—an identity crisis, I called it—for Slate.com and it got the most response of anything I'd ever published. In Basel, the Americans chanted "Fred-y, Fred-y" when Adu came on late and, for some reason, "We will, we will, rock you!"—something else I'd never heard at U.S. soccer, but somehow worked better than "USA! USA!"

November 24, 2007
Bayern Munich vs. Wolfsburg
Allianz Arena
Munich, Germany

If there was another old arena I was desperate to see, it was Munich's Olympic Stadium. The 1972 Olympics had its own dark history with the murder of the Israeli athletes. Looking back at it, like Heysel, you wonder how the hell the games were allowed to continue.

But the stadium itself looked beautiful, set into the ground, not towering forebodingly above it, and enveloped in a beguiling mock netting. I don't know, maybe because it was lovingly shot in *Heading for Glory*, "a mosquito net where soon the gnats of fate will sting." Or from the *Soccer Made in Germany* telecasts. Or from Euro '88. Why the running track didn't bother me while watching a game on TV from this stadium was hard to say.

I also wanted to see the city of Munich, had for a long time. Our friend Maya in Bern had met a guy from Munich and they went up for occasional weekends, one of which they invited us.

By now, the Olympic Stadium was no longer in use—Bayern and Munich 1860 moved into the brand new Allianz Arena, built for the 2006 World Cup—but it was still standing as was the Olympic park.

If there's a drawback to seeing a city with a native, it's that you experience the city as they've experienced it—a good thing, sure—but there's little time for improvisation, unexpected discovery, or even your own itinerary. We went all over the city but somehow the old stadium eluded us. There was wurst and beer and German meatballs, which looked like they could've been the precursor to the hamburger, and more beer and *Weisswurst* and pretzels and still more beer on Sunday morning—the morning—that my Mediterranean stomach couldn't possibly fathom.

And there would be soccer, Bundesliga *fussball*. I wrote ahead to the Bayern press office, as I had with Arsenal, with links to my soccer stories and requested a media credential. They got back to me immediately and granted me one, no questions asked, no demand to not publish something unflattering about the club or to vet anything I might write before it went to press.

A couple of weeks ago, when Andrea and I channel-surfed in Zurich, we came across a sports report on one of the German networks. Even on her most basic of cable packages, she got channels from every direction: Austria, France, Italy, and Germany. For each one, when she came upon sports, with the exception of Roger Federer, she tried to speed past them before I noticed. Not this time. We watched as Uli Hoeness, former Bayern great and part of West Germany's 1974 World Cup winning team, and now a club executive, held a press conference and started raging. Andrea interpreted and said he was angry at the fans, angry that they were angry, about what they perceived as a sterile atmosphere in the new stadium.

He was as animated as I'd ever seen a German, flailing his arms around almost like a Neapolitan. There was a saying, recycled, that

Munich was the northernmost Italian city, likely because of its strong Catholic traditions—they greeted one another not with *Guten Tag*, as in the rest of Germany, but *Grüss Gott*, God greet (you), which was popularized by the Catholic Church. Maybe because I had seen the northernmost Italian cities, going to and fro from Switzerland, but this was just tourism speak that gets repeated by others who think it's original. There's nothing Italian about Munich, even the Catholicism, especially the Catholicism.

But I did appreciate Hoeness's emotion. His father was a sausage maker in Bavaria, and he knew where he was from. He told them, more or less, to shut up, that the club had worked hard to give them a beautiful new stadium.

I also appreciated that the supporters raised their collective voice and had a venue in which to vent. What Americans often forgot was that the *c* in FC stood for "club," and these weren't just teams, but clubs you could join. In baseball, the phrase "ball club," especially from my father's generation, was thrown around as if it were a synonym for "team." It was quaint, "ball club," but these were teams, franchises. The fans had no voice. In Europe they did. They would protest at training sessions, sometimes violently; at the stadium; and sometimes in official gatherings with the club officials.

Fans in the U.S. could complain on sports-talk radio twenty-four hours a day, but they didn't have organized political power. This was refreshing. Now I wanted to see the new stadium.

I was all for tradition and preservation, and I did miss seeing the Olympic Stadium on TV, but when I saw Allianz Arena, frankly, I didn't know what the fans were so upset about. It was a beautiful stadium, another job well done by the Basel team of Herzog & de Meuron, whose National Stadium in Beijing for next year's Olympics looked like something new altogether. (St. Jakob's Park, in their hometown, was more low key, though perfect for soccer.) It was a little far from the city center for my taste—it had that hovering-in-the-middle-of-nowhere quality (or maybe nonquality)—but there was a subway stop close enough. The façade was lit red for

Bayern games and blue for 1860, so the shared utilitarianism was creatively sidestepped.

Inside, it was the perfect configuration for soccer, like the Basel stadium. It was packed, loud, and vibrant. There were food and souvenir stands but not every thirty feet as in so many new American stadiums. It didn't hurt that the press box, or press area (like Dortmund, it was outside), was the best seat in the house. It was cold, but the vantage point was perfect.

I was an outsider but, if nothing else, the back and forth between Hoeness and the supporters seemed healthy. And the team was as stylish, efficient, and substantial as anything produced by Bayerische Motoren Werke, the other illustrious institution in Munich. (Funny then that Audi was one of the club's sponsors.) Khan, Ribery, Altintop, Toni, Roberto, Van Bommel, Klose, and Lahm beat their former manager Felix Magath, now at Wolfsburg.

When I did my research on Wolfsburg, I noticed it had an American on the roster named Kamani Hill, a Californian who starred in two seasons at UCLA. I looked forward to seeing him play against Europe's elite. Maybe because Magath's father was a U.S. serviceman from Puerto Rico, the coach might be a valuable mentor for a young American. But he didn't play that day, nor was he on the subs bench. He hadn't played much that season and although it was brave and, to me, proactive to abandon a U.S. university for, in my opinion, the best league in the world, I had to wonder if it was better to play regularly, anywhere—college, MLS, the Swiss league—than to watch. He'd learn a little by osmosis—from just being there and training with elite players and a great coach, who had a European Cup Final–winning goal on his CV—but players need to play, and in big games, not just training games or B-team games. From afar, I wished Kamani Hill only the best. At least he hadn't taken the easy way out.

November 29, 2007
FC Zurich vs. Toulouse
Stadion Letzigrund
Zurich, Switzerland

The day after the Bayern match, we were back in Zurich. As much as I liked Munich, it was good to be home—as Zurich, or Zuri, as the locals called it, felt like my second home by now. It was known as "a little big city," though some locals found the smallness a curse. For me it was a blessing. When I'd lived in the Bronx, I had to give myself an hour and fifteen minutes to get anywhere in Manhattan. When I moved to Manhattan, I still had to give myself at least a half hour, and if I was headed Downtown or to the West Side (or both, like my beloved Film Forum) I had to allow forty-five or fifty minutes.

Both stadiums in Zurich were close, Letzigrund even closer than Hardturm. Because there was a midweek game, I was on my way back. It would be freezing, just like it was in Munich, but I'd have company this time. A Swiss acquaintance who lived in New York was visiting his parents and he was an FCZ supporter. We agreed to go together. So few of Andrea's friends liked *fussball*. Her father did, but in the time I knew him he'd told me he was for Grasshoppers, then Basel, and now he was for Barcelona. At least he was consistent in his loathing for FCZ. (What I slowly realized, as the years went by, was that he loved skiing most of all. He was a part-time coach and administrator of the Swiss National Ski Team and would accompany the cross-country squad to tournaments every weekend in wintertime. He even had an official team van, with the huge Swiss Ski logo on the outside. He had another car, but took the team van everywhere, even to pick us up at the small train station in his town outside Zurich. People stared at us—at red lights, in traffic, on the highway—as if we were rock stars. If they'd only known that, no, Didier Cuche was not in the van, that it was only me, and that I had never been on skis in my life, nor was I about to learn on a freelancer's budget and no health insurance.)

This night would be a UEFA Cup match, against Toulouse. It wasn't my first. In September 2005, on a beautiful fall day, I'd gone to Hardturm to watch Grasshoppers play a team called MyPa. Since my *World Soccer* obsession in the 1980s, I was pretty good at identifying clubs, at the very least what country they came from, if not city and color. But I'd have to confess I'd never heard of MyPa. It turned out that MyPa was from Finland, about eighty miles north of Helsinki. Like the friendly versus Northern Ireland, hardly anyone was there. I sat near the touchline and could hear the players call out instructions to one another. All I remember about MyPa was that they had a Brazilian and his name was Ronaldo. Maybe this said everything you needed to know about soccer in the twenty-first century.

I was ambivalent about the UEFA Cup. It seemed as if the trophy that the great Maradona lifted in 1989 had become superfluous. The relaunch of the Champions League had eventually expanded, more like a business than a sporting competition intended for the best of the best, to include second-, third-, and fourth-place teams, depending on the country, teams that would have competed in the UEFA Cup in Maradona's day. The Cup Winners' Cup had been discontinued as a stand-alone tournament, so maybe it was time to end the UEFA Cup.

On the other hand, the clubs that excelled in the Champions League were not necessarily the pedigreed or the most innovative or had the best youth systems—Ajax and Benfica had once been elite but no longer had a real chance of winning it anymore. The winning teams now were the ones that spent the most, the Super Clubs. The novelty of the new Champions League, born in 1992, felt at times as if it was wearing off.

Maybe the UEFA, with smaller clubs and their realistic budgets, was where the stars of tomorrow would be on display and perhaps where more tactical chances would be taken. To appreciate it, you might have to dig a little deeper, get beyond the artifice, ask more questions, watch a bit more carefully—it wasn't all going to be as obvious as watching the *galácticos*, whether they be from Madrid, Milan, or Manchester. It's nice to look at super models but there are women whose beauty is more subtle and reveals itself slowly and in different ways.

So many American fans, when it came to the international game, were frankly star fuckers. They knew, more or less, only the top four teams in England (Man U, Chelsea, Arsenal, Liverpool); the top three in Italy (Milan, Inter, and Juve, barely); the top two in Spain (Barça and Real); and the top one in Germany (Bayern). Call it the Big Ten. There was nothing more unoriginal than to see another Chelsea jersey on a Manhattan Saturday afternoon.

Watching the more modest clubs you'd have to do a little more homework, maybe think like a scout. Or just forget all that and sit back and enjoy the game. There were actually good games, and quality soccer, that didn't involve Zlatan Ibrahimović.

This game wasn't a forgotten gem of the ages. The Südkurve was bursting and impressive; the game less so. I remember it being merely okay, and so cold—even with two pairs of socks, long underwear, woolen hat, and layer upon layer—it was hard to concentrate on the match.

What I considered FCZ's dream team had been broken up, the best players sold for good money. Inler had gone to Udinese in Serie A, Dzemaili to Bolton Wanderers in the Premier League, Margairaz to Osasuna in La Liga, and Coach Lucien Favre went to Hertha Berlin in the Bundesliga. My favorite, César, went to Al Ahli in Dubai. He was already twenty-eight and this was likely his last chance at a substantial paycheck. I couldn't blame him.

Zurich still had the Finn, Hannu Tihinen, and Raffael—who both scored in the 2–0 win—though the rumor was that Favre was going to bring the Brazilian with him to Hertha during the transfer window. Almen Abdi was the new midfielder who would get plucked, then Eric Hassli, a burly but skillful French striker, or as they called it in German—and I loved this—a *Stürmer*, one in the midst of a storm.

Toulouse had a rising star named André-Pierre Gignac, a Cameroonian international named Achille Emana, and Swedish striker Johan Elmander. Like I said, it was okay. Not as great as the Champions League elimination match between FCZ and Red Bull Salzburg. I left the stadium desperate for anything hot or of high proof—it ended up being schnapps at Albisriederplatz—and still not sure what to make of the UEFA Cup. I only knew from the program that in three weeks, FCZ would host Bayer Leverkusen in the last game of the first round, and I was already kicking myself that I'd be back in New York.

December 9, 2007
Grasshoppers vs. FC Zurich
Stadion Letzigrund
Zurich, Switzerland

The art crowd in Zurich that Andrea was so much a part of could have a too-cool-for-school air. The feeling was that sports and football was beneath them. One friend of hers said it outright—*All this fussball, it's horrible. Horrible, I tell you*—and planned to leave town during next year's European Championships and sublet her apartment. So it was refreshing to meet an artist—and a substantial one—who was actually a fan.

Andrea met him during her London residency over the summer. Uwe was his name and he was represented by galleries in Zurich—one of the best—London, and New York. His reputation was growing, it seemed, by the month. Before I met him, I'd asked Andrea over the phone what team he supported. She had no idea, she didn't ask, nor did she care, but she said when he talked of soccer, it would nearly bring tears to his eyes.

When I met him he couldn't have been nicer. Turned out he was in the right city. He was a Chelsea fan and, as if he sensed my next question, said he had been since the '70s. He was also, and this surprised me, a fervent Grasshoppers supporter.

If creative types did favor one of the city's teams, they appeared to lean toward FCZ, long associated with the working class, while Grasshoppers was known as the club of the moneyed elite.

One reason my girlfriend was happy for his midcareer success—and the success was both critical and financial—was because he came from very humble roots within Zurich's working class, a working class that was once abundant but was now fading. She told me that early in his career he had been shunned by city and canton foundations that awarded artists' grants.

He *should've* been for FCZ but he wasn't. I liked people who surprised me, who didn't spout conventional wisdom and conventional choices. He said the class aspect of the two clubs was overstated, that the overwhelming advantage in support that FCZ had enjoyed in recent years was only because they were more successful and had become trendy, that so many in town declaring allegiance to FCZ were newcomers. He detested this.

I didn't get to see a game in London with him—I don't think Tom would have permitted me to go into Stamford Bridge—but we promised to keep in touch back in Zurich. A few days before I was set to return to New York, he called us and said he had two tickets for the GCZ-FCZ derby.

We wouldn't be sitting with him, which I regretted since I would love to have experienced the game through his eyes—it was a home game for GC—not so as to have a good laugh while watching someone squirm, gesticulate, and froth, but because I'd never met a Grasshoppers fan who cared this much. I was glad there were some still around. I still, to be honest, hadn't chosen a side. I leaned toward FCZ, but I had no ill will toward GC. I couldn't, after all, forget the inviting, intimate atmosphere of their stadium, or former stadium, Hardturm, now closed for redevelopment. (In a bit of role reversal, it shared FCZ's stadium, Letzigrund.) I believed what Uwe said was true, about a lot of bandwagoners aboard the FCZ tram. Zurich was the better club, but I didn't want to go with the winner—that was never in my nature.

Either way, I wanted GC to thrive so that on derby days like this one, the stadium would be throbbing and soccer in the city would matter. Some days it didn't appear as if it did.

As for the class division, I always veered between classes. My family wasn't working class but we were around the working class. We weren't upper class, but occasionally had a moment in its sphere. We were middle class, sometimes in upper-middle-class circles, but we lived in a place that became lower middle class, which I suppose put me in the middle-middle class, and thus I was still figuring out, after four years, which Zurich club to align with.

My baseball allegiances between the Yankees, from my hometown borough, and the Mets, my first true childhood team, were equally as tangled. But that's for another day.

What bothered me about this derby was not what I sometimes saw as indifference. It was something as simple and immediate as the team colors: both clubs wore blue (in nearly the same shade) and white. FCZ was all white with blue trim; GC's shirt was half white, half blue, taken from a Blackburn Rovers supporter who founded Grasshoppers in 1886. If there were two teams in the same city with more or less the same color scheme I didn't know them.

Couldn't one be red or green or orange or even violet, like Toulouse and the former Salzburg? Or even pink, like Palermo?

June 9, 2008
Romania vs. France
European Championships
Stadion Letzigrund
Zurich, Switzerland

I had seen a World Cup match in my home city; now there was the Euro in my second city. Because this was Switzerland, the ticketing process was as perfectly organized as the SBB, the national Swiss rail line. Combined with the lack of a thriving scalping culture and the small stadiums—Vienna's Ernst Happel Stadion would be the biggest at fifty-one thousand—I knew it would be next to impossible to get tickets. I didn't get any assignments to write about it—soccer writers were, if you'll pardon the pun, coming out of the woodwork, it seemed—and the Swiss people I did know weren't selling tickets. This was, for them, their own once in a lifetime, like World Cup '94 was for me. I couldn't blame them. But dammit, I was going to get into at least one game. I'd find a way.

For them, and even for me to an extent—as the Swiss became my second team in the tournament—the European Championships had an ominous start. Just before half time of the opening match, their captain, best player, and greatest goal-scoring threat, Alex Frei, went down injured. As soon as he pounded the turf with his hand, I knew it was serious and that he'd be out for the tournament. It reminded me of Vinny Testaverde going down in the opening game of the 1999 season for the Jets. He, too, pounded the turf, and he was out for the season.

I was at a party, a nice party, thrown by a Swiss guy I'd met a couple of years earlier. I had been on the Great Lawn in Central Park with David when we came across a juggler par excellence. David spotted him first and did a speed walk straight toward him. He was bald and wore white Nike Brazil shorts. While he juggled, effortlessly and exquisitely as if the ball was a reverse yo-yo on his foot, David began questioning him: "Hey, Brazil, Brazil, are you from Brazil?"

Without looking up, still juggling, he said, "No, I'm from Switzerland." David said something like, Talk with this guy, he knows Switzerland, and he walked away. I remained, and though I was a pretty good juggler, this guy, René was his name, was better. It turned out he played on the youth teams of FC Luzern, close to where he was from. I knew the area a little and we juggled and talked for hours, and remained in contact, in New York, where he worked for an international consulting firm, and back in Zurich, when he returned.

His friends at the party were a refreshing change from the usual art crowd I was surrounded by. Here there was no affectation, just good food, cold drinks, and love of soccer. After Frei went down you knew what was coming. And it came in the seventy-first minute, the Czech goal. I felt their pain. The Czechs had bushwhacked the U.S. in the opening game in the 2006 World Cup—and in 1990 as Czechoslovakia. On the field, they were ruthless. Everyone went home depressed.

Two days later, Zurich hosted its first game, Romania versus France, and I was off to Letzigrund to look for a ticket. I went early—it was a beautiful day—and checked the box office, walked up and down Badenerstrasse, the main avenue where the tram line ran. Nothing, until about twenty minutes before kickoff. I heard a British accent speaking on a cell phone and talking about an extra ticket. I interrupted him, and said, just like this, "Yo man, you got an extra ticket?" Yes, he said, he might. He got off his call and made another call to see if his friend was coming. The friend wasn't, and the ticket was mine—bless him—at face value, 120 Swiss francs, almost the same in dollars. I hadn't spent this much on a ticket since the 1994 World Cup semifinal at Giants Stadium, but it could've been worse.

The seat was in a Romanian section in the fifth row. To add more seats to Letzigrund, organizers had built a platform over part of the running track and added several rows. This is where I was, and the view was awful. I suppose it was good that this was the dullest match maybe ever. In recent memory, Switzerland versus Ukraine in the second round of the last World Cup was bad, but being it was an elimination match that went to penalties, at least it had drama. This was the opening game for both teams, and literally nothing happened. Nada. The Romanians were out for a 0–0 draw and the French, despite an all-star lineup, couldn't be bothered.

Not that it mattered for me. I was there. I got in. That was the point. I wanted to see a game, especially in Zurich, and here I was. I knew, as soon as I left the stadium, that I wouldn't remember much. What I do remember is this: at the beginning of the match, during national anthems, as we all stood, there was a folded twenty-Swiss-franc-bill with the image of composer Arthur Honegger at the feet of the woman in front of me, and maybe even more tucked within it. I had a running joke with Andrea: No matter how often I found money in New York (and to her astonishment, I did so quite often) I never once found money in Zurich, in all the time I'd been coming there. It was an affluent city, but a frugal one, where money was never talked about, never seen, but mattered. *Fucking Zwingli,* I'd say, and she'd laugh and laugh. *Can't even find a five-franc piece in this town of UBS and Credit Suisse. Bastards.* She'd laugh again. *Your mother from the farm country, that's what made your country great.* We're both laughing now—*not these Zwingli fuckers. Ha!*

So here these Romanians come to town from one of the poorest countries in Europe and a woman, maybe here on a wing and a prayer, has dropped at least twenty francs, possibly several twenty-franc bills. So during "La Marseillaise" I tapped her on the shoulder and, in English, said, "Excuse me, miss, you dropped some money." She thanked me, in German.

October 25, 2008
Zidane: A Twenty-First Century Portrait
Brooklyn Academy of Music
Brooklyn, New York

When I opened the *New York Times* on Friday I wasn't surprised to see that the Zidane documentary had opened. It had been released in 2006; in fact, it showed at the Cannes Film Festival and Art Basel, the renowned fair, where it was screened at St. Jakob Park. I hadn't seen it there—wish I had—but while book-and-magazine browsing later that year I saw Zidane, of all places, on the cover of *Artforum* magazine. I once reviewed a Jay McInerney novel for *Bookforum,* a spin-off of the brainy *Artforum,* and always enjoyed my subscription, but I wasn't a regular reader, or even an occasional one, of *Artforum.* I'd heard it said, from artists, mind you, that you needed advanced degrees to make sense of the writing. Still I picked this one up immediately. Zidane wasn't a favorite of mine, but it was soccer on the cover—a beautiful cover—of an eminent publication. It was not a desire but a necessity, even for the steep ten-dollar newsstand price, for my expanding soccer shelf.

The cover work was from the artists Douglas Gordon, a Scot, and the Algerian-born Philippe Parreno, who set seventeen cameras on Zidane during a Real-Villarreal match in April 2005. Manohla Dargis's review in the *Times* was well-written and well thought out, like all of her reviews. She didn't appear to have any knowledge of soccer but, in this case, that didn't matter; as any good critic, she was open-minded and judged it as a piece of art, which is what it was. She wrote,

> The movie's close-ups demonstrate that Zidane's body is more spectacular than most, though, notably, he spends much of his time waiting and walking. The game unfolds in fits and starts, with none of mainstream narrative's orchestrated rhythms. For soccer fans, the game is probably inherently suspenseful; for the rest of us, suspense arises from our hope (expectation, anticipation) that this body will cease waiting (like us) and starting moving (like a star).

I went the next day. I reread the *Artforum* cover story by Michael Fried, with a weighty sidebar by Tim Griffin. Fried writes,

> In short I see *Zidane* as belonging to the absorptive current or tradition that I have elsewhere tried to show has played a central role in the evolution of modern art. *But:* Zidane's participation in the match is not depicted as involving a total unawareness of everything other than the focus of his absorption—in particular, an unawareness of being beheld that has been the hallmark of absorptive depiction from Chardin and Greuze in the eighteenth century to André Kertész's pictures of people reading and Walker Evans's subway photos in the twentieth.

Griffin wrote,

Whereas Barthes in the '50s called wrestlers epic players in a realm characterized by "the drenching and vertical quality of the flood of light," a football player such as Zidane now operates in the densest microcosm of contemporary post-Fordist society—a spectacularized workplace designed almost exclusively for sight; a landscape premised on immanent reproducibility, the likes of which entices, say, a communications giant like Rupert Murdoch to purchase Manchester United.

(Okay. I guess this wasn't the venue to mention that Villareal's unspectacular but brilliant holding midfielder Marcos Senna shared so many frames with Zidane, either just in the foreground or background with the protagonist, especially in the first half.)

I admired Zidane, but I preferred flair players of smaller stature. France, on that 1984 European Championship team that made such an impression on me, had three in the midfield: Platini, Tigana, and Giresse. I always felt I should've liked Zidane more, or maybe because I always felt pressured to like him more. When I would bring out his red-card stomping of a Saudi player in the 1998 World Cup, no one seemed to remember. It's normal for a player to lose his cool or even commit an egregious foul on rare occasion. It's something else to step on someone. It was a statement. When I brought up Zidane's transgression to some fans, it's almost as if they simply didn't want to remember, despite it being in the World Cup. (Perhaps they didn't waste time watching Saudi Arabia; after the al-Owairan goal in 1994, I would never miss them.) This bothered me about some soccer fans, especially newer ones; there seemed to a rancid mix of selective amnesia and a lack of historical context.

I'd admit that Zidane was the best player—I always avoided using the nebulous, hackneyed "of his or her generation" in any field—from 1996 to 2006. And, all credit to him, he did it in the biggest of games—the Champions League final, the World Cup final, and the 2006 World Cup quarterfinal versus Brazil—about as high a compliment that comes to mind.

At the same time, more than most in soccer's Cooperstown, wherever that may be, Zidane seemed to disappear for long spells in matches.

It may not have been their intention—it is, as Dargis wrote, a "formalist exercise"—but this is shown by the filmmakers. He is, in their lens, or seventeen lenses, a paradox: engaged but indifferent; present but someplace else; his gaze intense but faraway; focused but preoccupied; at work but at rest; placid but volcanic; graceful but violent. How ironic, then, what the film foreshadowed.

I wondered if a camera—or seventeen of them—were set on a Xavi or Pirlo or Messi if they would be so often at rest. They might not be sprinting up-and-down forty-yard patches for very long—soccer players rarely need to, nor would it make much sense—but they would be calling for the ball, if not verbally then by gesture, with more regularity. Or the ball would find them. Of course, in the Villareal game, when Zizou needed to produce the moment of invention, he did. Invention and madness.

December 8, 2009
FC Zurich versus AC Milan
Champions League
Stadion Letzigrund
Zurich, Switzerland

Besides FCZ versus Red Bull Salzburg, technically only a qualification match, I'd never been to the Champions League. FC Zurich had to qualify again this year, but this time it did. I don't know who came up with the phrase "Be careful what you wish for," and I don't know if they were familiar with the concept of the group of death—which I'd heard for the first time in 1986 for the World Cup, group E—but I wouldn't be surprised if they were a soccer fan, or Swiss. FCZ wound up with Real, Milan, and Marseille. The first game was on live in the U.S., and I watched it in my New York apartment. It was weird. All those trips to Letzigrund and now I was seeing it on my TV on a weekday afternoon. They lost to Real, 2–5, but played well in spots. (It was 2–3, until the eighty-ninth minute.) Then they went to San Siro and shocked Milan, 0–1. Wow. When it lost twice to Marseille, and 1–0 in the return with Real, FC Zurich was eliminated.

I was in Zurich in November and the first half of December and the only Champions League game FCZ hosted in that time was the last one, against Milan. The game meant nothing for FCZ; it would finish last in the group regardless. Milan needed a win to guarantee themselves a spot in the knockout phase. I didn't have a ticket but would do what I had done at the European Championships: go to Letzigrund and wink at the soccer gods.

Even if the result mattered little to the locals—and that it was freezing—fans weren't giving up their tickets. Teams like Milan and its rock stars—on this day Ronaldinho, Pato, Pirlo—didn't come every year. But I got one ticket, again for face value, one hundred francs, again a horrible seat, second row behind the corner flag, with all of that running-track real estate between me and the field. As I texted nonsensically to a friend back home, he should look for me on TV "in the corner of the oval," as this, too, was on live in the States, still a kind of a shock to me at a macrolevel. (More of a microshock was Milan's performance on this day. Pirlo looked listless, his team enervated. The match ended 1–1. Milan couldn't get the three points it needed and only advanced after Real beat Marseille.)

There had been virtually nothing in the eighties and now FC Zurich was on live twice within a few months. Today there was almost too much soccer. My friend George would send me an e-mail every Friday with the soccer listings, just for the weekend. This was a recent one:

October 30, 2009

FRIDAY

U-17 World Cup, Mexico-Japan, 2:00 p.m., ET Galavision

SATURDAY

England, Arsenal-Spurs, 8:30 a.m., ESPN2

Germany, Stuttgart–Bayern Munich, 10:30 a.m., GolTV

England, Bolton-Chelsea, 11:00 a.m., FSC

Spain, Getafe–Real Madrid, 12:55 p.m., ESPN Deportes

England, Manchester United–Blackburn, 1:30 p.m., FSC

Spain, Sevilla-Xerez, 2:55 p.m., ESPN Deportes

Spain, Osasuna-Barcelona, 3:00 p.m., GolTV

Italy, AC Milan-Parma, 3:30 p.m., FSC

Spain, Athletic Bilbao–Atlético Madrid, 5:00 p.m., GolTV

Netherlands, Vitesse-Eindhoven, 5:00 p.m., ESPN Deportes

Italy, Juventus-Napoli, 6:00 p.m., FSC

Mexico, San Luis–Monterrey, 7:00 p.m., Telefutura

Colombia, Huila-Junior, 7:15 p.m., GolTV

England, Sunderland–West Ham, 8:00 p.m., FSC

Mexico, Indios-Puebla, 8:55 p.m., ESPN Deportes

Mexico, Tigres-Estudiantes, 9:00 p.m., Telemundo

Mexico, Atlas-Pachuca, 11:00 p.m., Telemundo

SUNDAY

Australia, Sydney-Wellington, 2:00 a.m., FSC

Netherlands, Feyenoord-Ajax, 6:30 a.m., ESPN Deportes

Italy, Livorno–Inter Milan, 9:00 a.m., FSC

U-17 World Cup, USA-UAE, 10:00 a.m., ESPNU, Galavision

Spain, Almeria-Zaragoza, 10:55 a.m., ESPN Deportes

England, Birmingham–Manchester City, 11:00 a.m., FSC

Brazil, Palmeiras-Corinthians, 1:00 p.m., GolTV

Mexico, Toluca-Queretaro, 1:00 p.m., Telemundo

MLS playoffs, New England–Chicago, 2:00 p.m., FSC

Spain, Coruna-Gijon, 3:00 p.m., GolTV

Argentina, River Plate–Lanus, 4:00 p.m., Fox Sports Español
MLS playoffs, Chivas USA–Los Angeles, 5:00 p.m., ESPN2
NCAA women, Santa Clara–Portland, 5:00 p.m., FSC
Mexico, América-Chiapas, 6:00 p.m., Univision
Italy, Palermo-Genoa, 7:00 p.m., FSC
Mexico, Santos-Pumas, 9:00 p.m., Telefutura

A few weeks before that e-mail, I couldn't help but jot this down, on October 14, from an ESPN SportsCenter broadcast: "Ecuador needed a win to qualify, but you don't just go into Santiago and beat up on Chile." I never, ever, thought I'd hear glib references to South American World Cup qualification on American TV. What used to be something you had to search for in foreign languages, on video-cassette, in hard-to-find European magazines, through penpals, and on channels so coarse-grained they recalled David Hemming's stills in *Blow-Up*, was now something everyone of a certain educational level was expected to be at least conversant in. What used to be something subversive, a secret international brotherhood, a band of outsiders, who for the occasional ninety-minute spell, were insiders, was now mainstream and trendy and ubiquitous, 24/7.

The international brotherhood part—that seemed gone. In its place was unleashed vitriol, conveniently behind made-up online-screen names. A couple of weeks before, on November 16, two days after the first Ireland-France World Cup playoff qualifier, this was posted on ESPN Soccernet's comments section, a reference to the 2006 World Cup final: "Zidane butt the guy because he was saying racist comments, everyone knows Italians are racist. They joined up with the Nazi's in ww2, come on."

To some, only certain groups cheated (and they were usually from southern Europe and South America), forgetting when an Englishman or a Frenchman did something untoward, as Thierry Henry would a mere two days later in the "Hand of Gaul" incident.

And then there was the sheer quantity of soccer—granted combined with quality, but still. It was as if there were four or five basketball leagues roughly equivalent in quality and atmosphere to the NBA and you had access to all of them, in addition to leagues not quite in that class but still pretty good. Plus, there were international competitions, both club and country. No matter how much you loved basketball, it would be a challenge, especially if you had other interests—if you liked movies, say, and read books, enjoyed art or music, cooked a meal now and again, watched the news, or actually played sports. How much was enough? American neophytes turned, automatically, to England, believing the oft-spouted claim that the Premier League was "the best in the world." The writing of the overeducated literati and nerds felt smarter than thou, precious, show-offy, free for anyone to read, but really just between themselves.

There were clear good guys and bad guys in both camps, the newcomers and the soccer nerds/weenies. It was the Bush Doctrine as applied to international soccer—you were either with them or against them—and it lacked maturity and nuance, something that would never be tolerated in baseball or basketball or even tennis coverage. As much as I saw the English league as overhyped, the best writers and commentators were writing out of England.

The Internet—which should have enabled worthy curatorial efforts on soccer, and did here and there—ended up being the curb outside a bar at closing time, a place for vomit, and when there's nothing to throw up, up comes bile.

Was it better now? It should've been—everyone was insisting that it was; how could you *not* be with the program?—but I wasn't sure.

June 3, 2010
Kinsale Tavern
1672 Third Avenue
New York, New York

June 8, 2010
Goal!
BAM Rose Cinemas
Brooklyn, New York

Whatever soccer had come to represent, and however ambivalent I had become about it, didn't matter every fourth year at World Cup time. It's what had made me a fan—a believer, you could say—all those years ago. No one, not the media, which I was still on the periphery of, not corporations or sponsors, not Russian oligarchs, not Gulf gazillionaires, was going to take away the joy. "The joy": that's how I described it in an essay I wrote earlier in the year for *Tin House*, the literary quarterly. It was the longest piece I'd ever written on soccer. The longest piece I'd written on anything—over five thousand words—and I ended it with just that, the word "joy."

And the months, weeks, and days before the World Cup was my own Garden of Eden, a quadrennial spring training, full of energy and hope and new narratives. This, too, I wrote about, for a blog I would be doing for the *Atlantic Monthly*'s website, set to launch the following week. I used the *Tin House* piece plus a bunch of preview material I wrote for ESPN *Magazine* (much of which I did at my father's bedside at Carolinas Medical Center) and pitched myself as a World Cup blogger. It wouldn't pay much, but I'd have a voice, and for now that was the most important thing. My father was better, for the time being, and I could enjoy the World Cup.

A week and a half before the opening match, there was a party for a new World Cup book. David cowrote a history of the tournament with a Brit named Roger Bennett, whom David had introduced me to at the 2007 TriBeCa Film Festival. Roger, cowriter of another book called *Bar Mitzvah Disco*, was a charming Liverpudlian—and, I was happy to discover, an Everton fan—who produced a soccer documentary, *Sons of Sakhnin United*, that was screened at the relatively new but already prestigious film festival. It was directed by two Americans—Christopher and Alex Browne—and it was a fine piece of work. Nothing was whitewashed. I knew a little about Israeli soccer—Asher, in the NYU days, talked about it some, but he was more obsessed with the Belgian league and Mechelen. In an ESPN *Magazine* piece I did in 2000, I looked into it some more and proclaimed it would be a major player on the world stage—but I didn't know *that* much. I suppose my assumption was that it would be free of the bigotry of Europe. Turns out, I was wrong. Supporters of the club Beitar Jerusalem spewed chants as vile as any as I'd heard, maybe worse since some were aimed at the Prophet Muhammad. There was no attempt by the filmmakers to bowdlerize, and that was admirable.

Like so much quality work being done on soccer—and there was more and more, despite the pseudo-intellectual dreck—*Sons of Sakhnin United* deserved a wider audience in the United States. So did Simon Kuper's latest book, *Soccernomics*, which just had its American release and party at Kinsale Tavern. I couldn't make that, but for the next night's celebration at the same bar, David asked if I could comb through my VHS collection—Kinsale still had a VCR—and bring a few videos so they could be played in the background on the big screens. I think I brought *The Boys from Brazil*, *Ten Faces of Platini*, the 1982 Italy-Brazil game, and *All the Goals from World Cup 1994*, which was the only one that ended up being played—in a loop. You could do worse than watch Hagi and Dumitrescu have the gumption to take it to Batistuta, Ortega, Simeone, and the stately Redondo—over and over and over.

I still wanted to write my own book on soccer, but I was beaten to it again. I did some behind-the-scenes work on it for David, and the party had a good energy. David was a regular at Kinsale, and I thought it was a nice touch that he'd celebrate his book, and the upcoming tournament, at a real soccer-centric spot—as opposed to, say, SoHo House.

Paul Gardner was there; so was David, the writer; and Steve, whom I hadn't seen since the five of us watched all of those Euro 2004 matches together. Steve invited anyone and everyone to come with him to see *Goal!*, the 1966 World Cup film, which was playing at the Brooklyn Academy of Music's cinema house—and he was treating for Junior's cheesecake afterward. I'm there, I told Steve, and for Junior's, too.

I'd never seen it in its entirety and being that it was really a film, not a FIFA-endorsed corporate product that the World Cup documentaries have sadly become, I was eager to see it on a big screen. We went on a weekday afternoon—my favorite time to see movies and one of the very few delights left of the freelance life—and it was a pleasure. It was beautifully shot. It was big, everything about it, and glamorous, and one of those films I wanted to walk into. The tracking shot of Argentina's Antonio Rattin walking around the field after he was shown a second yellow was worthy of Altman or Welles.

It was part of a minisoccer film festival, occasioned by the tournament, and there was a British reporter outside the theater asking people questions. She was from the *Independent* and asked Steve and me, basically, why we were there. "Beautiful game hits fever pitch in the USA," read the headline the next day. Steve was not only quoted, he became the lead! And Junior's was Junior's; the cheesecake, the cheesecake.

August 10, 2010
United States vs. Brazil
New Meadowlands Stadium
East Rutherford, New Jersey

When Shea Stadium closed, I cried. No, sorry, I bawled. I was alone in my apartment and had just watched the Mets season come to a tragic end. This was followed by former Mets greats walking out onto the field and waving to the fans. And it was raining. I'd fallen out of love with the Mets ages ago—in their greatest year ever, 1986—a relationship that had turned to hate, but that was amicable again.

It was still my first childhood team, pre-Vikings and Knicks and Rangers. And well before the Cosmos and AS Roma. Shea was the first place I'd attended any sporting event, and I had happy, happy memories of the place with friends and family, no matter how imperfect, how windy, how ugly a structure it was. That was September 2008. The following year, Giants Stadium held its last game, replaced, like Shea, with a new stadium that would go up in its parking lot.

When Giants Stadium closed, I didn't watch. I didn't cry, that's for sure. I might not even have known it was the last day/game of its existence. In the end, with all the MetroStars–Red Bulls games, plus the Cosmos and international friendlies, combined with my divorce of the Mets, I may have attended more games at Giants Stadium. No matter how many there were, whether there were more games than at Shea or not, I never warmed to it. Shea may have been out of the way compared to Yankee Stadium or Madison Square Garden, but at least it was on a subway line. With Giants Stadium there was always the angst, not so much of getting there—the Port Authority terminal was always reliable for that, and it had evolved into a gleaming shopping mall—but the recurring nightmare of possibly being stranded in the flat nothingness of the Meadowlands, with only highways skewering the marsh. There were memories, sure: that first game, always the first game, on that August night in 1982, to see the world's best; going with my parents and sister in 1983 to see São Paulo and Fiorentina; a year later in the deluge for U.S.-Italy; the World Cup in '94, a quarterfinal and semifinal, at that; "the Beckham game," with David and friends. But, well, I couldn't explain it. It was in the middle of a parking lot, but so too, was Shea, more or less. It was a sterile building, but Shea was a Robert Moses, modernist monstrosity, the anti–Ebbets Field. Yet Shea made me weep; Giants Stadium didn't.

So when I went to the new stadium, still unnamed and known as the New Meadowlands Stadium, I went without nostalgia. When I got there, I couldn't even place where the old stadium was. More to the point, the traffic was suffocating—making it by kickoff was now iffy—so there was no time to reminisce, only to notice that the new building looked like a massive vertical parking lot; a parking lot within a parking lot. Herzog & de Meuron got it right in Munich; this, I didn't know what this was or what it aspired to be. Not that this was the moment for architectural criticism; Brazil was in town to play the U.S.—hence the traffic—and it was the Seleção's first game under new coach Mano Menezes after a disappointing World Cup. At the same time, many thought, it could also be the final game for U.S. coach Bob Bradley, after a semisuccessful, semidisappointing tournament.

It was a disappointing World Cup in many ways. There were few matches of great drama, but there was senseless debate about vuvuzelas; a cynical final; and only 2.27 goals per game, the lowest since the infamous 2.21 of 1990. Then there was the commentary. The broadcasts on ESPN were just fine and the mainstream media's coverage improved greatly. What was most infuriating were the highbrow blogs, mainly from the websites of otherwise smart magazines (stealing the idea of Franklin Foer and the *New Republic*). It was achingly hip, privileged publishing geeks trying to outdo other publishing geeks, and it defined pretension.

My blog/column at TheAtlantic.com—which began with a piece in May on the twenty-fifth anniversary of Heysel—was short-lived. I knew something was wrong when I wrote about Chile's eccentric coach, Marcelo Bielsa, otherwise known as "El Loco." (If I ever did start a blog on soccer, I told myself, I'd call it El Loco, in honor of maverick figures like René "El Loco" Higuita and now Bielsa, who played a frenzied high-press, attack-minded 3-3-1-3 formation.) I thought my take was a smart one, and it was linked to a blog written by my Chilean novelist friend Alberto Fuguet. But the next day, another piece on Bielsa ran on another soccer blog on the Atlantic site, one mimicking the *New Republic*'s, with in-crowd writers. It was as if I wasn't even there.

I was glad when the whole tournament ended. I watched the final with Brian and some of his friends in a third-floor Korea Town bar he was now running after he had to close the soccer store on Eighty-Sixth Street. It was nice to spend the final with him rather than bandwagon Spain fans, but the World Cup and the neo-fans and commentators, the know-nothings, who began to appear lately, left a bad taste in my mouth, one I wasn't sure would ever leave.

That's why it was so nice to see Brazil's sunny shirts come to the City. It may have been August, but it was spring, a time for rebirth and to fall for soccer again. On the bus from the Port Authority, I ran into George, a young Mexican American fan who was working his way through college at a place that served grilled chicken in my neighborhood. He was a shy young guy—reminded me of myself at his age—and seemed to be a fan for all the good reasons, not for networking opportunities, not to make a buck off it, not to dazzle the chattering classes. Brazil was in town (!!!) and what more could a fan want?

For others, the U.S. team was the marquee name, and that was fine, too—and in the long run even better. I arrived the previous night after visiting my parents and took the M60 bus from LaGuardia Airport to 125th Street. It was the cheapest way to get into Manhattan, a mere swipe of the MetroCard, and there were (hand on my heart) three Sam's Army guys who had probably just arrived at LaGuardia for the game, talking about the latest Bob Bradley gossip—would he stay or go? *Possibly to Aston Villa.* I was going to pipe up and say that if he does, the USSF should hire Martin O'Neill, a serious, but likable man who did a great job with Villa, who was fluent in English, won a European Cup with Nottingham Forest, and played in a World Cup for Northern Ireland. (*O'Neill is in the net, and the ball is offside!*, in those once-famous words of Toby Charles.)

But even if this was Queens, the most international section of any city in the world, there didn't appear to be many soccer fans on the crowded bus. Not that I wanted to make assumptions, but I saw faces that were tired, overworked, underpaid, and didn't appreciate having to stand and be nudged by tourists' luggage. So it didn't feel right to chime in and give my opinion on the USMNT coach to complete strangers a few rows away. It would've felt as if I was talking past people, or over them, literally and metaphorically. It would've felt like the opposite of Ugly Americanism: an imperious ugly internationalism.

The New Meadowlands Stadium—its interim name while a corporate sponsor was found—was filled to as close to capacity as possible, and (though, again, I don't like assumptions) I was certain—and delighted—that this had nothing to do with the novelty of the stadium, but for the soccer. What stood out about the stadium was four massive screens that showed the ESPN telecast, along with the commercials, for McDonald's, Castrol, Dick's Sporting Goods, the next Red Bulls game (tomorrow versus Toronto; I'd be going to the one after that).

What stood out about the match was the American naïveté. After the United States' second-round World Cup loss to Ghana just six weeks earlier, Landon Donovan said right after the game that his team was naïve. He was right; Americans were still sanctimonious when it came to soccer. This notion of "diving"—falling to the turf, sometimes feigning injury, to get a foul called in their favor—was abhorrent to Americans. They saw it in black and white, like the English did, as cheating, not about being savvy and wily. Why would Americans, in their national pastime, applaud a shortstop who is a foot off second base while turning a 4–6–3 double play? Or ditto for the first baseman who drags his foot off the bag? Or a catcher who slyly brings his glove six inches closer to home plate after he catches it out of the strike zone? Or an outfielder who knowingly traps the ball but tries to sell it to the umpire? Or the charge/block flopping in the NBA? And the home calls? And the make-up calls? Or in football, our real national pastime: Didn't Lester Hayes, make Stickum famous? And the rest of the Oakland

Raiders didn't look to flout every rule and yet won thousands of fans across the country? Forget about college sports, which earned millions of dollars thanks to free labor—the most anticapitalist, anti-American concept imaginable. Why Americans suddenly became self-righteous when it came to soccer, I still couldn't figure out. So in just the third minute, when Landon Donovan was nudged from the side in the penalty area, he should've gone down. The referee was at least thirty yards behind the play and in truth, Landon was thrown off balance, but he stayed on his feet—noble, sure—but he could've gotten the call. What was even more naïve was that after Brazil cleared, Landon—I was a huge fan of his since writing about him for GQ in 2002—threw his arms up in protest, the international penalty appeal. But it was too little, too late. As delightful as Brazilian players are, they would've gone down and put the onus on the referee. And if Landon did get the call? Well, Brazil probably still would have won; they were that good.

All 77,223 of us could tell the grandkids that we saw the young Neymar and Pato—both nearly legendary already—score goals, the second a thing of sparkling improvisatory invention conceived by a quartet. We'll tell them that it could've been more than 0–2 if not for the woodwork and Brad Guzan.

After the game, the press rushed in to hear Bob Bradley: Was it too much too soon after the World Cup? What were your impressions of Neymar? On Brazil? And your future? When does it need to be decided?

Do I need to reference my shorthand and reiterate his answers? As always with Bradley, it seemed like a funeral, which didn't make him a bad coach. He was a good coach, but there was nothing quotable. There was no news about his future, he said; there would be more discussions, he'd be here till the end of the year, looking forward to the next game.

Okay.

Then he left the press room—on field level in the new stadium with only glass separating it from obsessive fans—and most of the

American media troupe left with him. I stayed. How could you not? Mano Menezes, in his first match for the most celebrated national team in the world, was due next. The questions, and his answers, were just as predictable as Bradley's. That is until a question came in English, not so much a question but a pronouncement, or an order; and it came from—who else?—Paul Gardner, one of the only English speakers who remained. I was in Barcelona in June of 1982, he began, on that fateful day when Brazil lost to Italy, the beginning of the end of *joga bonito*. Will you, Mano Menezes—and this is me paraphrasing—return to the Brazil the world wants, or will you continue the dreary, and now failed, philosophies of Dunga?

I scribbled down this: "These moments are reference points. The idea is to be in the spotlight and that's how we plan this project." And then I wrote, to myself, "another bad answer or bad translation." And bad longhand on my part. At least Gardner tried to elevate the press conference to a discussion of ideas.

All I knew was that I'd never want to have Mano Menezes's job, no matter how well the team played in his debut. He had one job and one job only: to redeem Brazil's reputation but also to win the World Cup, at home, in 2014. Anything less and the poor man would be excoriated for life. I'd already made up my mind and decided Brazil would never win the World Cup in 2014, especially not in 2014—precisely because it was at home and the pressure would be unrelenting. No matter how Neymar and Pato developed and no matter how good Menezes might be as a coach, someone would feel the pressure at some point in the tournament and make a game-changing mistake. And since I loved historical precedent, I told anyone who would listen, that it would happen in the final, at the same Maracanã as it had in 1950.

August 14, 2010
New York Red Bulls vs. LA Galaxy
Red Bull Arena
Harrison, New Jersey

Four days, two new stadiums. It took a while for MLS to transition from outsized NFL behemoths to stadiums of more appropriate dimensions—appropriate for now. (There'd come a time, I was certain, in ten, twenty years, that MLS would outgrow these little gems and move back to the NFL coliseums.) We'd heard about a soccer-specific stadium for MLS's New York/New Jersey franchise for years. It took what seemed like forever, those last years at Giants Stadium painful, but it arrived in March of 2010.

I'd missed the opening matches in early spring and was then immersed in the World Cup. It so happened that my first game at the new stadium was against the LA Galaxy, which was also the team's first official sellout of an MLS game at the arena. A sellout, with plenty of empty seats in the corners and at the very top of the second deck.

It wasn't the 5–4 spectacle of 2007 but it had a lot of worthy elements. The stadium was as close to perfect as I'd seen. It wasn't as easy to get to as I'd heard—you had to take the PATH train from Herald Square or points south and then change at Journal Square—but then I live on the East Side of Manhattan and any journey west of Central Park ended up being time consuming. And the stadium was a bit of a walk from the closest train station, with nothing around it. But inside, they got it all right. Even the press box—which at Giants Stadium and the New Meadowlands Stadium was insulated behind soundproof glass so you hardly knew you were at a sporting event—was, like at Allianz and St. Jakob Park, Hardturm and Letzigrund, in a designated area within the stands. You were able to feel the energy, anger, joy, and frustrations of the crowd. And it was situated about seven rows up, around midfield, with a good view of the field—maybe ten or twenty rows higher would've been ideal but I wasn't about to complain.

It so happened that my press seat was behind the LA bench. David Beckham was still with the Galaxy (hence the sellout), but was injured and wouldn't be playing (hence, perhaps, the no-shows). He was in team sweats, and a fan a few seats over from me, just outside the press area, was heckling him—nothing clever as some fans could be, especially at baseball games, where you sometimes had to laugh even if it was bordering on crude. I figured Beckham would just ignore it, but he gave the half turn (at first) and then, when it continued, the full turn, almost standing, with his finger to his ear and a furrowed brow, looking at the guy and mouthing "Huh?" The guy shut up.

Before the game, there was a sign of the maturation of MLS and of American soccer culture: the farewell to Clint Mathis, who had recently retired. God, that was fast, I thought; it seemed like just the other day that he came out with the mohawk in the 2002 World Cup. He was only thirty-three, but had knee trouble. He bounced around a lot, with two tours each in LA, Real Salt Lake, and New York/New Jersey, plus stops in Colorado, Germany, and Greece. He was hardly a Red Bull (or MetroStar) but had several good years here, including a famous sixty- or seventy-yard slalom-run goal. He said to the crowd over the loudspeaker: "Thank you so, so much. The name has changed, the organization has changed, but the fans have always been the same." There were a few banners in tribute to the Georgia boy, including "We (heart) Clint." He took a photo with Tab Ramos and expressed his gratitude to the fans behind the goal.

There had always been a small hardcore group behind the goal at Giants Stadium, but here in the new stadium they were more substantial and empowered. When LA's keeper Donovan Ricketts lined up to take a goal kick, they made a kind of collective hum—like a college place-kicker charging up for the kickoff—and upon contact, the hum reached a crescendo and in unison they chanted "You suck asshole!" I remembered hearing that college football-like pre-kickoff hum on TV, but couldn't make out what they were saying. Now, in this stadium, it being intimate, it having a roof over the stands, and me being there, the chant felt well-articulated and loud. Everything felt loud here, whether it was the cheers for Clint Mathis, the player introductions, or the protests to a fifty-ninth-minute yellow card for Juan Pablo Ángel.

I imagined the chant would make club and league officials uneasy. I'm sure they wanted "atmosphere" but still maintain the clean-cut "soccer mom" demographic. "Atmosphere," as we know in Europe and South America, can go over the line and involve banana peels, racist chants or banners, bigoted gestures, and crude humor. Can you control what people say or sing or chant? Or what tattoos they wear? Or what they think? Did Duke University officials ban the student body from chanting, when the Blue Devils were losing a game, "It's alright, it's okay, you will work for us someday"?

On the one hand, I thought the "asshole" chant could be the start of something gloriously hateful. On the other, I thought it showed no creativity. The Duke chant was classist but it required thought; this wasn't and didn't. I thought of a few precursors, besides the kickoff in college football: "Yank-ees suck!" from Red Sox fans; the occasionally heard "ass-hole, ass-hole" moan/chant in the NBA sung the way Red Sox fans belted out "Dar-ryl, Dar-ryl" in the 1986 World Series; and when I was young, Jet fans at Shea Stadium chanted "Ho-ward sucks" during Monday Night Football. But somehow those worked; combining suck *and* asshole didn't.

Maybe this was the start of something good and boisterous, maybe the start of something messy. We wanted "atmosphere," we got it. In a small stadium, things are more intimate, which is good (at one point, fans were pointing up toward one of the boxes, the rumor being that Tony Parker was at the game), and bad (Beckham heard those insults—so unoriginal I didn't even jot them down—and in the eighty-ninth minute, three young guys made their way onto the field and ran eighty yards.) Careful what you wish for?

In the tunnel and locker-room area after the game—and no, I don't remember who won the game, nor did I jot it down in my notebook, nor have I looked it up online since—I saw two other American soccer legends: LA coach Bruce Arena, who was much bigger in person than I imagined, and one of his assistant coaches, Cobi Jones, the ex-U.S. international, who along with Holland's Marc Overmars was the fastest player I'd ever seen. It surprised me, then, how much weight he had gained. And I didn't say or think this to make fun of him in any way—I always liked Cobi Jones—but it was just another reminder of how fast time went by. There, too, was David Beckham, posing for photos with the staff, and kids of the staff maybe. He may have been injured, but he was in impeccable condition. What struck me were, of all things for a soccer player, his shoulders. They were broad and square and statuesque like a baseball player's, but in much better shape, maybe out of vanity, maybe out of potential endorsements—both probably—but more than anything because he was a great professional. Not a great player, not anymore at age thirty-five, but one who cared about what he did and came prepared. Arena had said at one point that Beckham trained hard every day. He had never been a favorite of mine—I thought he was another good-looking, overrated British brat—but the older he got, the more he earned my respect.

As I left the stadium and walked toward the PATH train—no longer did I have to worry about being stranded in the middle-of-nowhere New Jersey—there were still plenty of people milling about the stadium. It was a stunning day, and it occurred to me that while in the past at Giants Stadium you'd see a plethora of jerseys from different international clubs, now I saw mostly Red Bulls jerseys. Or Galaxy, No. 23.

October 25 and 26, 2010
The Future of Football
Dolder Grand Hotel
Zurich, Switzerland

By the end of September, I was back in Zurich. It was ironic. With Andrea's having the most basic TV package, which only showed Bundesliga 2 (played at a very high level *and* in nearly full stadiums, it had to be said), there was more soccer on TV back home in New York. George would send the soccer-on-TV list every Thursday. He'd been in the country since the early 1990s and he was as staggered by the choices as I was. The list seemed to get longer every week.

If there was less soccer on TV in Zurich, at least there were two teams in town that were reachable in under twenty-five minutes without price-inflated food and drink concessions. Even to get to the beautiful new Red Bull Arena in Harrison, New Jersey, it still took me over an hour. And on this trip to Zurich, besides FCZ and Grasshoppers—I went to another derby on October 3—there would be something more: a soccer conference.

A Swiss contact put me on the e-mail list of a Zurich organization called the International Football Arena (IFA), in Zurich. It was hard to know exactly what they did or what its goals were. It held conferences in Beijing, Kuala Lumpur, and India. The conferences appeared to be made up of presentations, panel discussions, and networking for powerful figures within the sport. Was it a shadow FIFA? Or FIFA's outsourced rogue? Or an ideal of how FIFA should operate?

It appeared to be independent of FIFA, despite its Zurich address, and was a small, streamlined operation, judging from its website. Simon Kuper, the journalist and author beyond reproach that I so admired, was a regular attendee so it couldn't be that bad.

I went to find out. I sent an e-mail and some of my soccer writing, and expressed interest in attending its annual conference at Zurich's Dolder Grand Hotel, as a freelance journalist, although that

I had no assignment as yet to write about it. I received a response that said they had Googled my name (many others have the same name) and that I was approved and invited to attend. If I could write about the event, all the better, they said.

I can't say I went in without preconceived notions. I'd written about the Dolder Grand Hotel in 2008 for the *New York Times*. It was understated in that Zwingli Protestant way—but still an otherworldly luxury. I felt an unsettling mix of guilt, resentment, and gratitude for spending one night there. I'd written on Zurich, and other matters, including soccer, for the *New York Times* before, and when Sir Norman Foster had finished his redesign, an editor at the Travel section asked me if I wanted to write a short article on it. I said yes, but when I told them how much it cost for a night—$730 to $1,100—they said they couldn't afford it. I couldn't blame them, frankly, and was almost relieved. The cost seemed vulgar to me, especially considering the economic backdrop—for me, the United States, and the world, even Switzerland. But then they had second thoughts. They e-mailed me again and asked if I was still up for it. They'd pay for one night in the least expensive room and however much $400 would cover in meals (not much, believe it or not). I said yes, again. I'd spend a night where Winston Churchill, Arturo Toscanini, and the Rolling Stones had stayed. And the Shah of Iran—no wonder there was a revolution in 1979.

I found the place off-putting. There were millionaires (billionaires?) from Russia and the Gulf and a mainly young German staff—cheaper labor than the Swiss—that seemed terrified of them. I was diplomatic when I wrote the article, as you must be in the *Times*, but when I got down the hill the next day, I was happy to be out of there. So with the IFA conference staged at the Dolder, I wasn't the tabula rasa I should've been. I thought it could be a coming together of fatuous know-nothings with only their money and their talent to ingratiate. I thought it would be awash in booze and cheap, embellished women to provide these contented fools with sufficient eye candy.

I was wrong. Nor was it a shadow or rogue FIFA. It was a sober, serious affair, with the tone set immediately by IFA founder Marcel Schmid in his seven-minute opening remarks:

> Every time I'm asked to explain what type of conference the IFA actually is, I call it a business meeting. It's a business meeting about the huge global industry of football. . . . The IFA Conference is a gathering of people who are keen to talk about business opportunities, to get to know and understand each other, and to explore or discover new avenues. And yet despite this underlying agenda, let's never forget that football is a game after all. It's a game everyone understands and knows how to play, a game capable of bringing together rich and poor, tall and small, fat and slim, or dark- and light-skinned. The game of football is probably the most universal of all languages.

He then spoke about the film *Pelada*, a documentary on pickup soccer that he had recently seen: "*Pelada* has touched me emotionally because this film is a testimony to football's natural ability to move people and bring them together, demonstrating there is more to football than merchandising and broadcasting rights and ticket sales. This is what we should never come to disregard, not even at a business meeting."

I thought it was a rousing way to end his introduction, but it received only quiet applause from the full conference room, which to me seemed somewhat strange. But, to reiterate, this *was* a business meeting and it was sober.

There were three panels on the first day (the Future of Players' Agents, the Future of Football Communication in the Age of Social Media, and the Future of Football Stadiums) with several breaks for food and coffee, and two more on the shorter second day (the Future of Global Football Sponsoring and the Future of World Cup Hosts), with still more food and coffee.

I had hoped there would be one labeled the Future of the Fan, and though I wasn't a fan of later Michael Jackson, I began to hear his song "They Don't Care About Us" in my head.

When, during the first panel on the Future of Agents, the president of the European Football Agents Association, a Dutchman, said a new ruling would bring about "total chaos," the host—the quick, able, and incredibly dapper Darren Tulett, a Brit with Canal Plus—retorted, "First there was Total Football, now there's total chaos."

I burst out laughing. No one else did. I scribbled the following in my notebook: "about 250 people; all very well-dressed; mostly male; espresso machines every 20 feet, no exaggeration; and it's great espresso; food is remarkable; from the lunch buffet (I have rare entrecote, arugula, and grilled vegetables); good debate in a.m.; it's hard to say anything bad so far; and ah, the chocolate mousse."

There was a short one-man panel on social media and soccer, specifically the Bundesliga, and then the main event, the Future of the Stadium panel. There were architects from Foster and Partners; Gerkan, Marg, und Partner from Hamburg; Populous; and Manhattan Construction Group, which did Cowboys Stadium in Dallas, and was based not in Manhattan but across the South.

They talked of sustainability, being green, of contracting stadiums (so a Bristol City stadium can go from forty-five thousand to thirty thousand), of not leaving "white elephants," massive structures of no use after the World Cup or Olympics, and creating minicities around the stadium. One said it was important to balance "the iconic with the practical." The next architect made it a point of saying how he hates the word "iconic."

Only one, the American from the Manhattan Group, mentioned the bad economy. He said Jerry Jones wanted to pipe in the smell of popcorn into the new Cowboys Stadium, but that it couldn't be done. No one laughed. Markus Pfisterer of the Gerkan, Marg, showed slides of the Ukrainian and Polish stadiums he worked on for the upcoming European Championships. He used the word "iconic."

When they opened it up for questions, I asked one about Zurich, as I've felt more and more like a local, even down to complaining about the city's weather, size, and aloofness. What, I asked, would the panelists do about the current stadium crises at Hardturm, with essentially no "soccer specific" (my Americanism) stadium in Switzerland's largest city? The German from Hamburg said a soccer stadium should be built on the old Hardturm site and the two clubs should share it.

Fair enough—even if I like the English way of separate teams in separate grounds—but after the Q&A session was over, several Swiss journalists came up to me and said, in effect, You should do a story on how it's a scandal that FIFA doesn't build a stadium for us, that they give nothing back to this city, that they don't pay taxes, those so-and-sos. I shrugged. I had grown to love soccer in Zurich—and I, the only American writer in a room of almost 250, had asked the question, after all. But you are journalists, I said. There are three papers in Zurich; why don't *you* write about it? Why is it always the English and German press demanding answers from FIFA? And besides, I said, do you even want favors from FIFA? You need a twenty-thousand-seat stadium; you can find the money in Zurich, where legend has it there's gold stashed in vaults beneath the Bahnhofstrasse. If we could do it in Harrison, New Jersey, surely it could be done in Zurich.

Now I wanted to find the only other American there, the architect. I introduced myself, *my fellow American!*, and said I was a Vikings fan from New York City and asked if he'd been approached to do a stadium in the Twin Cities. No, he said, he prefers working in places like Dallas and the South, where he's comfortable. I think I get it.

Soon after there was the cocktail hour, and I came across a revolting character from England, a marketing specialist, who, as soon as I met him, was giving me a spiel that I didn't ask to hear and didn't even understand. He was young, made a lot more money than I did (as did every one of the guests), and had the world by the balls, but he had a frightened look on his face. He wasn't *not* smart; he was all PR cliché and a fraud, though I suspect he was aware of this. I wanted to get away from him as soon as possible, to shower preferably, but instead I found a table for dinner.

I sat with two Australian sports journalists, there to cover their country's presentation to host the 2022 World Cup. They were, like all Aussies I've ever encountered, great fun—like night and day from the marketer—and even had a great grasp of American sports. We three sat at an empty table for at least ten, by ourselves, when who joined us but about six of the very tall, very young, ridiculously beautiful hostesses in tight dresses that went to midthigh. With their hair slicked back, they look like the women from Robert Palmer's 1980s *Addicted to Love* video, which appeared probably before any of them were born.

The entire dining hall looked at us thinking, "You lucky bastards." We three kind of looked at one another, like *Holy shit, of the twenty or so tables, they sit at ours, what luck, what should we do?* We were all about the same age, grown men, but suddenly we were fourteen again. *Should we talk to them? You go talk to them. What should I say?* Both Aussies were married, with wives expecting phone calls, and my girlfriend was at the bottom of the hill expecting me back soon. Finally we did break the ice and they turned out to be approachable and fun and gave us gossip about the hotel and an infamous Zurich rich kid who lived there and raised all sorts of hell. One told us that her dream job was to work for FIFA.

I left about 11:00 p.m., the same way I came, via the Dolderbahn, a funicular railway that's part of the Zurich mass transit system. The station is in the back of the hotel, on another level. It was sitting there, with people inside waiting for it to depart. None of them were guests from the conference. They were plainly or poorly dressed, and I realized that they were hotel workers. They were immigrants who didn't have much, except this job, perhaps to clean up after the hell-raising rich kid.

I immediately felt for them. Their lives could be worse, they could be working poor in New York, but they could be much better, too. They look tired, their eyes downcast, faces expressionless, like the faces I used to see commuting back and forth from the Bronx. What were they thinking? I'm not from the working class, but I always felt at least a partial allegiance to them. Now, I decide, I'm with them, solidarity for life.

We got to the bottom of the hill and each of us went to catch a different tram. I waited for the No. 8. I was alone, the night was perfectly still. It had rained most of the day—there were puddles everywhere—but now the sky was clear in the darkness. While I waited in the tram shelter, my mind wandered in an attempt to process the long day. There was a newspaper on the bench with the recent FIFA bribery scandal on the front page. I looked at it, trying to translate it, when I became aware of an encroaching sound. It was a big street cleaner, with its huge brushes churning toward the curb, and a massive puddle, right beside me. There was nowhere for me to sidestep or run, I was in the corner of the shelter. The puddle was substantial, the driver was going fast. If he didn't slow down, I, and my nice clothes, the only nice ones I had, would get showered in whatever was in that puddle. I said, out loud, "No!" but it was too late. He didn't see me, or maybe did see me—he had to have seen me, the shelter was lit—and kept going.

Fuck the working class.

October 29, 2010
Press Conference
FIFA Headquarters
FIFA-Strasse 20
Zurich, Switzerland

On December 2 the long-awaited secret vote and announcement of who would host both the 2018 and 2022 World Cups would be made. The U.S.-Anglo press, I thought, had a sense of entitlement and assumed they would get the respective nods. They didn't. Instead it went to Russia and Qatar.

Odd, both, but not quite the scandal it became. No one thought the U.S. should have been awarded the 1994 World Cup and yet it was a great success that left a significant legacy. Australia seemed worthy, even if it would've meant kickoff times in the wee hours on the U.S. East Coast, which had made the 2002 tournament so hard to enjoy. (At the IFA conference, there had been a free copy of a *FourFourTwo* limited edition issue on Australian soccer and its 2022 bid, with Harry Kewell on the cover, a future collector's item I'd hang on to.) I had hoped Canada would have bid, but it didn't. I also thought a pan-Scandinavian bid would have been interesting or a London-only bid or Cameroon/Nigeria or Ghana/Cote d'Ivoire—but these were just my own personal musings, late at night when I couldn't get to bed, like when I was a teenager. Silly, I guess.

England had a more legitimate claim than did the United States, not having hosted since 1966, and there was likely an anti-England bias within the organization. But the Arab world did deserve a World Cup, though a shift to a January tournament to avoid the heat would have made more sense. Russia? Always a hockey country but you could make the argument that they could and should host. Turkey would have been more interesting, but it didn't bid nor was it awarded the 2016 European Championships. Sure, there were shenanigans, votes were traded, and money most likely changed hands. It was a dirty process, but somehow, I didn't share the apoplexy. So the Americans and Brits didn't get what they wanted. Boo-hoo. The U.S. got it in 1994—pretty recent in World Cup years—plus, although through a different organization, the Olympics in 1980, '84, '96, and '02. England had Euro 96 and would have the 2012 Olympics.

It seemed as if David Beckham, who, along with Prince William, was flown in for the vote, gave the same answer to the same question (How do you feel about the decision?) three different ways: Obviously, at the end of the day, we're disappointed; At the end of the day, we're disappointed obviously; We're disappointed, obviously, at the end of the day.

Even before the decision, there was steady chatter that the whole thing was rigged. Anticipating the storm, FIFA held a preemptive press conference—just a couple of days after the IFA

Conference—with Sepp Blatter and his closest lieutenants. I hadn't even known about it until one of the Australian journalists told me. (To reciprocate, I told him there was a midweek league match in town, FCZ-FC Luzern, and I got us press presses for the next day—a great 2-2 game—passing up a live Wayne Shorter concert.) FIFA granted me a credential for the press conference. It was a chance to see FIFA dysfunction and obfuscation up close—in a sumptuous leather chair.

The FIFA headquarters was easy enough to get to. It overlooks the city from the placid hill known as Zuriberg—where James Joyce and Elias Canetti are buried at Fluntern Cemetery—and is just steps from the last stop on the No. 6 tram.

I had been there once before, just to check it out. How could I not? And I was at the house, or one of the houses, that made up the old headquarters. I got the name of someone who worked on the website and tried to get an informational interview, which I did, but all I remember from it was someone in a French accent telling me what an exclusive part of Zurich this was, something that didn't impress me. (The happening part was down below and in the ugliest interiors of town, which is where my girlfriend and I lived.)

The new glass-and-black-granite building was impressive but also odd. It had only opened in 2007 and was designed by Zurich architect Tilla Theus, product—like Herzog & de Meuron, Santiago Calatrava, and Einstein himself—of the imminent technological institute Eidgenössische Technische Hochschule (ETH), about fifteen minutes away. FIFA's three-story glass façade is covered by translucent aluminum slats that suggest the netting of the soccer goal—an architectural interpretation of Tommy Smyth's "ol' onion bag"—and acts as a screen for the sun, not insignificant since this is known, famously here, as the "Gold Coast" side of Lake Zurich, the choice side, same as the Dolder, but perplexing, too, since most of the offices are in the five levels *below* ground. So much for the view; so much for transparency. It begs the question: Which came first, the bunker or the bunker mentality?

The building is set inside its own small park with trees and vegetation from all six continents—nice touch, that—and soccer fields that no one uses and rows of flags not unlike those on First Avenue at the United Nations, which at one point, I'd read long ago, had less member states than FIFA. (Whether that was good or bad, I'll leave to you.)

FIFA is separate. It's above, looks down, looks away—and maybe, in its private moments, looks over its shoulder or, one would hope, in the mirror. No matter how counterintuitive one's disposition, and no matter how much good the organization accomplishes—and it does a lot, especially the organizing and execution of under-the-radar tournaments in lands less traveled—it's difficult, especially after reading Andrew Jennings's 2006 exposé, *Foul! The Secret World of FIFA: Bribes, Vote Rigging and Ticket Scandals*, to defend it.

Still I was willing to hear FIFA out. Part of me wanted to see Sepp Blatter, from the oft-ridiculed southwestern region of the Valais, as an underdog outsider who got under the skin of the Zurich (and Parisian and Berlin and London and Milan) city slickers. A scientist I knew in Zurich told me that the Valais was noted for its ridiculous accent, for its provincialism, and scheming ways with money. So maybe Blatter had a chip on his shoulder for good reason. But then you'd see him in action.

After his initial comments in French, he fielded questions. The first was from the BBC and it was simple: How can you promise the football fans around the world that the votes for the 2018 and 2022 World Cups will be clean? There was a long pause—eight seconds, according to my tape recorder—and then, in English, Blatter said, "What do you mean by being 'clean'?" The questions kept coming, high and tight, and then, from a Brazilian journalist, a soft ball, about whether he was worried about the progress for the 2014 World Cup. He could exhale now. And that was it for the questions; the press conference was over. Then he left us with this: "Enjoy the game, but enjoy life—it's more important." It was farce—or maybe allegory. Near the exit, I stopped at the souvenir counter and bought a T-shirt, as a kind of remembrance.

A couple of weeks later, I tried reaching the head of FIFA's ethics committee, a former Grasshoppers player named Claudio Sulser. Sulser, from Ticino, had something incredibly impressive on his resume. He was the leading scorer in the 1978/79 European Cup in which Grasshoppers made it to the quarterfinal stage before being eliminated by eventual champion Nottingham Forest. Six of his goals may have been against Maltese champ Valletta, but one was away at the Bernabéu and two more against Real at Hardturm—the last one, which put them through on away goals, in the eighty-sixth minute. You couldn't help but admire that. And I told him so, in an e-mail. I called FIFA and asked to speak to him. I was told, very robotically, that he didn't have an office at FIFA headquarters, and that he worked out of his private law practice in Lugano. Fine, I said, Can I have his number? They said they didn't have it. I researched his law firm and tried him there. I left a message with the receptionist, left my numbers, and wrote a nice e-mail. She promised he'd call. I never got a reply.

November 3, 2010
FC Basel vs. AS Roma
Champions League
St. Jakob Park
Basel, Switzerland

After the conference at the Dolder and the drama at FIFA it was nice to get back to the actual game, something that often seemed beside the point. I'd been thinking a lot about the Champions League as it approached its twentieth anniversary since the rebranding. (God, did I hate that word.) Had it been watered down? Did it result in too many games? Were the quarterfinalists, say, and especially the semifinalists, in a small, elite league of their own? Could past winners like Ajax, Benfica, or Red Star Belgrade, once grand clubs, have a realistic chance of lifting the trophy? Had it all become too predictable? Could it be that, counter to conventional wisdom, the UEFA Cup, now the Europa League (speaking of rebranding), was a more interesting tournament to close observers, with more tactical experiments, more young talent, and more surprises? I wasn't sure, but another live game was, not in town, but nearby, in Basel, against, of all teams, my Roma. The train ride was only an hour and ten minutes but cost sixty Swiss francs, about fifty bucks. Steep, but I'd save on the ticket since I was granted a press credential.

I got there early and picked up a city map to reacquaint myself with Basel. As I looked down at it, I asked the woman at the tourist office to point out the Kunstmuseum, where I still had time to check out an Andy Warhol exhibit. She did. Then I asked her to point to the stadium. She looked surprised that I would be asking about both. Be careful, she said, there was some sort of hooligan alert because of the Italian fans. How do you know I'm not one? I asked. (I was a *Romanista*, but a Zuricher, too, and the Basel fans not only attacked an FCZ player once, but were a constant thorn to the Zurich police.) She was funny, I thought. I smiled and walked out toward the green trams of Basel.

Warhol always felt so American; I felt like I was home, at the Whitney Museum, say, for a couple of hours. Then I got to the stadium. Outside, still well before kickoff, there was a hawker with an 'Arry Redknapp accent selling game scarves with the Basel and Roma logos. Basel was on the Rhine—not the Thames—within walking distance of both Germany and France. What was a cockney doing here selling scarves? And then there were the riot police, hundreds of them, with helmets, face shields, and guns. Was this warranted? Were that many Roma *mammoni* actually going to travel north of Milan or Turin?

I had a wurst and went inside. It was nice to be back in this stadium. It was perfect for soccer. My seat in the press area was fourteen rows up, just off the midfield stripe. Close to perfect. Roma was warming up in front of me. I hadn't been this close to Totti since I'd seen him at the Guggenheim Museum. He looked like he needed to lose five to seven pounds. Basel, across the field, were engaged in high-intensity minigames; Roma, in front of me, did some light running. Basel, who beat Roma in the first leg, looked inspired and ready; Roma looked ill-prepared and lazy. The same for the fans. The Basel supporters sang the lilting melody of the song "Brazil" but substituted "Basel" instead. It's clever, and it sounds good. Roma *tifosi*—and they were to my left, what looked like a hundred or so fenced off in the corner of the upper deck—could only counter with the generic Italian chant of "Basile, Basile va fanculo!" Basel, fuck you! Grittier than "you suck asshole" at the Red Bulls game, but lacking in imagination. In the Basel curve there was a sign that read "You'll Never Walk Alone," the famous song/slogan of Liverpool. Whether this was an allusion to the 1984 European Cup final in which Liverpool beat Roma, in Rome by chance, where fan trouble ensued, I couldn't be sure. This could be a difficult night for Roma, but I was Press tonight and neutral. (Right?)

Just before kickoff Novak Djokovic, the tennis star in town for the Basel Open, is being interviewed on the touchline. Roger Federer, who is from Basel and is a real fan of the club, must be somewhere in the stadium.

When the game began, Basel came out flying; Roma were flat, as if they were still going through their lackadaisical pregame warm-up. They needed something to wake them up.

If there was one thing that troubled me about Roma games, and Roma fans, it was the fireworks they set off. Not the colorful sparklers that are, or were, a staple at all Serie A games, but what in my neighborhood we used to call m-80s and blockbusters (an older generation in New York called them cherry bombs). I'd be in my apartment in New York watching Roma on the Fox Soccer Channel and hear these explosions that brought back memories that made the Fourth of July a holiday to be avoided in my part of the Bronx. I'd often wondered what would happen if one of these explosives, whatever they were now called, went off right next to you? Would they damage your hearing for life? Why weren't they banned in the Olimpico?

And then in the sixth minute, far from Rome, one of these things goes off. I guess it's thrown from the section in the upper deck, the cage, where the Roma fans are, and lands near the corner flag, which isn't that far from me, maybe thirty or forty yards. It's so loud it feels as if the stadium shakes. Frankly, it scares the shit out of me, and I nearly jump out of my seat. The entire stadium starts to boo and hiss. I don't blame them. The journalist next to me is from a tiny paper in the French part of Switzerland and doesn't speak English (or Swiss-German). He looks at me and holds his nose, as if to say these Roma *tifosi* are real shit. As usual, I'm ambivalent. I always hated those fireworks, and the *tifosi*, to be honest, are acting like baboons in that cage up there, trying to tear down the fence and get at the Basel fans—or doing a good job of pretending to. You're from Rome, I want to tell them, act like princes, act the way you want to be treated. Maybe the woman at the train station was right; maybe that's why there were only 36,375 here, about two thousand short of a sellout. At the same time, I want to tell this nobody next to me to fuck the hell off back to his nothing French-speaking canton, learn Swiss-German, the language that makes your country's economy hum, and sit back and watch Roma, the team, wake up and teach you something about soccer.

Sure enough, the team does come back to life. Very much against the run of play—after Basel could be up 2–0—Roma score on a perfectly placed shot from Jérémy Ménez, the young Frenchman, who is so effervescent it might be his best game thus far for the club. I nearly jump out of my seat but contain myself. The cage with *tifosi* goes nuts; off goes another explosion. Six minutes later Ménez goes on a dazzling fifty-yard run that ends with a perfect back-heel pass in the area to John Arne Riise, who was legitimately fouled. A penalty was called, Totti converted, sucked his thumb, another firework goes off, Roma leads 0–2. Ha! Somewhere in Zurich, the FCZ fans are cheering.

I give Basel credit: they came out like wild dogs in the second half, and Alex Frei, whose single-mindedness and selfishness I admired in a striker, got one back in the sixty-ninth minute. But again, against the run of play, Roma got a third. The action was nonstop now, everything you'd want from a Champions League game. This was now the best live game I'd ever seen. Maybe my skepticism about the competition wasn't fair (or maybe it was and this was just a terrific game). Basel got a second, 2–3, and came pouring forth for an equalizer. It didn't happen. All the fans were left to do was jeer Totti, the best player on the field.

My friend Brian and I had always avoided discussions of Roma and Lazio and Totti, who he referred to as Tottina, the diminutive feminine. We didn't want the rivalry to come between our friendship. But the next day, we e-mailed. The day before I was at the Champions League, he was watching his other team, Schalke 04, in the Champions League on TV. After his soccer shop closed he was having a hard time and transitioned to the bar and running a telecom store in Koreatown. He wrote the following (and reminded me why I fell for soccer all those years ago):

Hi Michael,

I was so depressed two days ago that I was about to explode and hide myself from the rest of the world, but somehow I ended at Nevada Smiths to catch Tel Aviv—Schalke 04. While I was there all by myself in front of the set that showed the match, two guys around our age sat next to me and right before the start of the match they both pulled their blue scarves from their bags and hung them over their necks. Then realizing that we were all Schalke fans (I had Schalke's Libuda jacket on) we greeted and talked, finding out that they were from Schalke supporters club in Wilhelmshavn (a city from northern seas). We bought drinks for each other, they gave me their supporters' club scarf, and hung out after the match.

I had a really great time, it was like I have met some good old friends from childhood, as times past I understood most of the conversation and also spoke much better German. They were leaving the next day and have kept in touch with me. The reality has not changed a bit since but I sure do feel better and feel relieved at least not to feel more depressed. Hang on to yourself and let's try to see and think the brighter side of the world.

Ciao,
Bri

March 26, 2011
United States vs. Argentina
New Meadowlands Stadium
East Rutherford, New Jersey

It had been rare for the U.S. national team to play in New York and rare, too, for a major international power to come to town. Now the U.S. team was back, and seven and a half months after Brazil, Argentina was here, with the best player on the planet in uniform and expected to start. You had to go. I hated to be a prisoner of the moment, but my feeling on Lionel Messi was this: He was the best I'd ever seen and, yes, maybe the best ever. Maradona, who absorded much more of a beating, was right there, and Platini, even if he was never mentioned in the conversation, was a hair behind Diego. Pelé I'd only seen on tape and so much of his magic was not preserved on video. I'd also tell anyone who would listen that Messi was so special—and at the same time, so fragile—that we should watch, and savor, each performance as if it was the last, that all it took for it to end was a vindictive tackle.

On the way to the game, by bus again, even if there was now a direct NJ Transit stop at the Meadowlands, I overheard a conversation about Duke basketball, just over my shoulder. Today was the day of the Elite Eight, though Duke had been eliminated in the Sweet Sixteen. At least "It's alright, it's okay, you will work for us one day" wouldn't be heard for the rest of the tournament.

At the stadium there was a sign that said "No Vuvuzelas Allowed," which seemed already like an anachronism, yet so dictatorial. (*Why can't I blow my vuvuzela if I damn well please?!*) Not that I could've heard them if they had been allowed; I was in the press box. I wasn't necessarily complaining—it was a night game and it was cold, 35 Fahrenheit and windy, the stat sheet said—but the crowd, on the other side of the climate-controlled glass, seemed ready for a big occasion. In my notebook, just after the thirty-eighth minute, I scribbled "everyone in lower deck is standing." This was a very New York thing to do, but only on the biggest occasions: the last seconds of a Knicks game at the Garden; the last round of a big fight, when there were big fights; or in the late innings of a Yankee playoff game. This was a friendly. And this was before the goal, which finally happened in the forty-second minute and started with a Messi nutmeg of Carlos Bocanegra. In the thirty-third minute, I wrote in my notebook, it was "all Argentina, no goals, but they are schooling us." The South Americans were fluid in formation, Messi a free agent in orange boots. The press seemed obsessed with his footwear in reports the next day. Even the word "freelancing" in regard to Messi was becoming overused. His nickname was "La Pulga," the flea; I didn't know much about fleas, but in the warm-weather months, my apartment was loaded with mosquitoes; in vain, I followed, as best I could, their flight path. It was utterly unpredictable and, frankly, neurotic—up, to the side, down, sideways, up again. And then, light as air, they'd disappear in shadow. Then buzz around my ear; I was left smacking myself upside the head. This, to me, was Messi, and why the entire lower deck was standing, and why, on a cold night in March, for a meaningless game, there were 78,936.

As good as he was—and he played the entire game, something that made me, and probably everyone in Barcelona, ask why—there are eleven players on a team. At the half, Bob Bradley, still the coach, brought on the Colombian-born, New Jersey–raised Juan Agudelo. Fourteen minutes later, Agudelo tied the score. Late in the match, I scribbled in my notebook, "the U.S. getting better as game goes on." It ended 1–1. Schooled in the first half, maybe; redeemed in the second. A worthy night's work.

After the game, I went to the press room to listen to the coaches. Bradley—with another good result on his CV—was as media phobic as ever. Maybe I couldn't blame him. Again, I stayed on after most American journalists left to listen to Argentina's coach, Sergio Batista, who succeeded the perennial star of the show Diego Maradona, his 1986 World Cup teammate. The first question came from a young reporter; I forget from which publication. He was very nervous—his voice quivered and he spoke too quickly—and he prefaced his question with, and I paraphrase, I became a soccer fan because of you and your teammates who won the 1986 World Cup, and then he segued into his question, which I don't remember. But his sentiment, while maybe not the most professional and slightly out of the norm, I found sweet and soulful. It came from the heart. Why did these press rituals have to be predictable? Boring questions met with boring answers.

Batista's response was rude. I was having trouble with the batteries in my tape recorder and couldn't quite get it started, but he didn't even acknowledge the kind words. Bradley was dull; he wasn't the rock star the United States Soccer Federation was looking for to take them to "the next level," whatever that was. (A World Cup semifinal? That could take a lifetime—ask England.) But Bradley wasn't mean. Batista was, and worse, he showed no grace.

If I had been a World Cup winner—I wasn't even in that sphere, but if I were lucky enough to have been and to touch lives in whatever small way—I would have said this: "Well, thank you for the kind words. Yes, 1986, it seems like yesterday in some ways and long ago in others. It was a magical time that brought happiness to many people, including, it sounds like, to yourself. So for that

I'll always be grateful. But it's a new era now in soccer and for our national team, and tonight we illustrated many positives but we know there's still work to be done."

January 14, 2012
FC Basel vs. Feyenoord
Marbella Football Center
Marbella, Spain

At the end of 2011, Kim Jong-il, North Korea's dictator, died. I had been in touch with an editor at ESPN *Magazine* about a possible story on two FC Basel players, one from North Korea, the other from South Korea. It was his idea, a good one, and being that I knew the Swiss league, this editor wanted me to do it. The question was when. With the latest front-page news, his top editors decided they wanted it—and wanted it now, even if Swiss soccer was on its two-month winter break. Maybe they were influenced, too, by a recent front-page article in the *New York Times*. The October 21 piece was about how Fox and Telemundo had purchased the rights for the 2018 and 2022 World Cups, "demonstrating the steady and diverse growth of soccer in America." But it also had the following:

> This is what people have been talking about since the World Cup was held in the United States in 1994—is the U.S. a soccer nation? "Clearly, it is," said Michael Cohen, who was the executive producer for Major League Soccer and its marketing arm from 2001 to 2010. "You've got a whole generation of kids in their 20s, 30s and 40s who have grown up with soccer. And with the influx of immigrants coming to this country, soccer is their No. 1 sport. It is the perfect storm."

(Great I thought, but don't storms, especially perfect ones, have a tendency to leave trails of ruin?)

I still wanted to do the Basel-Korea piece but had reservations. My father, whom I was with for the holidays when the news from

North Korea came through, had grown more fragile. It was plain to see that there wasn't much longer for him. Since that time I had spent with him at the hospital in 2010, often while writing 2010 World Cup previews, he seemed to be on borrowed time.

My worst fear was that I'd be away in Zurich when he died and there would be some kind of weather delay that would keep me from getting to him. So when the editor called, I asked him if he was sure they wanted it. He said yes. We approached the club, and after a lot of wrangling, they said neither player would be available for interviews, nor would their teammates, only the head coach, Heiko Vogel, a young German who had only been on the job for three months after the previous coach, Torsten Fink, had left for Hamburg. Under Vogel, Basel had beaten Manchester United 2–1 in Champions League play—eliminating the giants from the tournament—and propelled themselves to the round of sixteen.

Not much to go on, but I was told to pursue it anyway. My father encouraged me, too. We never talked about his end; he would tell me when we'd watch *Charlie Rose* episodes at night, "I figure, I got another four, five years." He always encouraged me to write, even if there seemed to be fewer assignments for me, and, besides, he said, this was a story on soccer, a subject I loved, and about politics and Switzerland and international concerns, all topics I had written about.

So I went, not to Korea, North or South, or to Basel, but to, of all places, Marbella, Spain, where many northern and eastern European clubs would spend part of their winter break, to train and bond. It would be a feature in a major magazine. I needed the exposure and, of course, the money. They put me in a five-star resort hotel, a few steps from the beach, for the simple reason that it was where FC Basel was staying. Sounds nice, right? It wasn't. The Costa del Sol in January is better than Hamburg or Basel or St. Petersburg, but it's maybe 55 degrees, and being that it's beach towns strung together, pretty much deserted in the winter. I wasn't a beach or a pool or spa person, so the amenities would mean little to me.

I flew to Paris, where I made the connection to Málaga (along with the Hungarian club Videoton). From Málaga, I took a bus for about forty-five minutes along the coast to central Marbella. The hotel was nowhere near, and I needed a taxi, which would take another twenty minutes, to get to the middle of nowhere, with no town or street to walk on. Besides a group of German golfers and FC Basel, with its big blue-and-red bus parked outside, the hotel seemed mostly empty. It was patrolled by an armed guard.

I had a big room, one too big for one person; the bathroom was almost the size of my New York apartment. I wanted my girlfriend to join me from Zurich, but then told her it would best for her not to, that it would only be a distraction, as this was a virtual stakeout.

I had a few days before my only interview with the coach, and no one on the team, including the head of public relations, knew that I was there or what I looked like, so I was, in a way, under-cover, free to observe the two Koreans at the breakfast room, the dining room, and on the practice field, where they ran drills and had friendly games against other teams from Europe on retreat.

Joining me in Marbella was a freelance photographer. He met me at the hotel, and I found him instantly likable. He was an Irish-man who had been married to a Spaniard and lived in Madrid. If there was ever a stereotype of a good Irish storyteller, it was him. He loved to talk and I loved listening to him. He told me of his divorce, of his brother leaving journalism because there was no way to make a good living at it anymore, and of the financial crisis in Spain—but he managed to be funny. I should've turned on the tape recorder and just let it go. Luckily, he had a car—which it turned out you needed in these parts—and was fluent in Spanish. What he didn't have was a good sense of direction. We would drive to training sessions at the Marbella Football Center, another twenty minutes from the hotel, in the hills above the coast, which was dot-ted with ugly housing complexes and, as I put it in my first draft, cancerous with golf courses. In fact, when we would stop and get directions—his rental didn't have GPS—no one knew where it was, but when I chimed in with "muy cerca La Quinta Golf," only then were they able to direct us. These dusty hills were ground zero of Spain's, and Europe's, economic collapse: overdevelopment, greed unleashed, second houses no one needed, luxury God knows who could afford, supply and vanished demand.

The first day of training, and a friendly against Holland's NEC Nijmegen, we remained undercover. The rules from the team were clear: only the one interview with the coach, still a few days away, and no—absolutely no!—photos of the South Korean, Park Joo-Ho, and the North Korean, Pak Kwang-Ryong, together. This came from the North Korean government and was to be respected. Fine, but, I asked, why? I never got a straight answer. I even asked an academic on North Korean politics—I interviewed three scholars for deep background, also hoping to quote them directly in the piece if they had anything valuable to say. His answer was that it was likely because Pak, the North Korean, grew up poorly nourished—or not quite as well fed as Park, the South Korean, and was probably smaller and weaker in appearance, something that the paranoid North Korean government wouldn't want its people to see. Well, I said, that's not the case; the opposite is true. Pak was taller, over six feet, broad-shouldered, even better looking. Again, no good answer.

When we arrived back at the hotel, just after the team did—we got lost again—we got strange looks. The photographer decided he'd now stay for the next two nights—and there were plenty of rooms. He was originally in my wing of the hotel, the same as the players—the rooms surrounded an open arabesque courtyard with fountain—but when he was spotted with his photography equipment, he was informed, midshower, by the staff that he had to relocate to the opposite end of the hotel. He lost his Irish charm immediately and said he wouldn't move. Finally, they offered a free dinner, wine included, for him and a guest—me—and he accepted. By now, I had introduced myself to the head of PR, a large, sweaty, beleaguered man, who could turn from friendly to rude within seconds. He seemed especially under the gun since during the January transfer window many big clubs were looking to swoop in for Basel's young talent, particularly Xherdan Shaqiri—a cocky, squatty Kosovar, an odd mix of thug and diva, who kept giving me death looks.

I asked again for more interviews and, turning rude, he said no, a deal was a deal (true, it was) and besides, no one spoke English (that was a lie). What about Scott Chipperfield? I asked, referring to the Australian international midfielder who had played eleven years with the club. But Chipperfield can't communicate with the Koreans, as they are being taught Hochdeutsch (true) and Scott only speaks Schweizerdeutsch (possibly true, but highly unusual for a foreigner) since his wife is Swiss (true). But the Koreans speak a little English, I said (which was true), but, I was told, not enough to get through to Chipperfield (who knew?).

Alex Frei, the captain, must speak English, I asked. No, only French and German (maybe true). But, I said, Streller does (true, I saw him speak it on Swiss TV). No, I was told (untrue). And the Africans? No, they are from former French colonies (that was true).

I'd have the coach on Friday at the agreed-upon time, with the interview in German. I'd have to supply a translator—and remember, no photos of the players together.

But I kept showing up, at the breakfast room, at the training sessions, back in the hotel, at the dinner room, and he started to break down. I would speak some Swiss-German (*How do you know Swiss-German?*) and he called over Scott Chipperfield, who answered questions on the record; then a Nigerian assistant coach; then the team president, during a training session. He was absolutely candid and gave the name, number, and e-mail of the North Korean player's agent, a shady figure who was exporting players out of Pyongyang to Switzerland as a way station, with the hopes of getting them to bigger clubs. The Irish photographer, who was a freelancer specializing in soccer for the biggest papers in Spain, was now shocked at the access we were getting.

The coach, who had been eyeing me as suspiciously as Shaqiri—my hunch was they thought I was from the German or English press looking for a scoop on the midfielder's rumored move to Bayern Munich—was a joy to talk to. And his English was nearly perfect. I noticed it was his custom to have a late afternoon beer with his staff in the hotel lounge, and he did the same with me.

This was suddenly going very well. I reported back to my editor—as I did every day—and he was as ecstatic about the piece as I'd ever heard an editor. The consensus was that the two players got along, but because of political pressures had to stay in the closet, so to speak. That was fine, my editor said, it was what we had anticipated, even on the phone in New York before I left, and we couldn't make stuff up, even if the piece was slated for an issue on rivalries.

His enthusiasm was, like an editor's should be, infectious. The next friendly—or, as they say in German, *Testspiele*, which is actually more appropriate—was on a Saturday against Feyenoord. I had planned to make a pilgrimage to Sevilla and see a La Liga game that day, but I still didn't have a lead for my story, and work, this piece, came first.

The Dubliner/*Madrileño* and I were back up the hill—*Hola, bueno. Dónde está El Marbella Football Center? Muy cerca La Quinta Golf*—and to our surprise there were actual fans there. First, there were a group of Moroccans there to watch their national team train for the upcoming African Nations Cup. When the team bus arrived, the fans and players went through a routine that was new to me. As soon as the players—Arsenal's Marouane Chamakh, among them—stepped off the bus, a fan, with his arm already outstretched, would join the player in stride, the player instantaneously would put his arm around the fan, they would pause, and a friend would take a cell-phone photo. It was almost like a choreographed dance maneuver. No words were spoken, no fan was ignored, no player was above this. The Irishman said to me, "Look at that, the players accept it as part of their duty as national team players." It was a civilized ritual.

Not so civilized was the contingent of Feyenoord supporters. Shockingly, there were two or three hundred, with banners and beer.

It happened to be a nice day, bright and sunny, maybe approaching 60 degrees, but it wasn't beach or resort weather. Nicer than Rotterdam, surely, but if you had vacation time, wouldn't you have something better to do than watch your team play exhibition matches? They were loud and raucous and fat and ugly. And they were giving me all sorts of odd looks. Even though Basel was the opponent, they made it clear who they hated, and that was Ajax. When Shaqiri touched the ball, they either knew in advance he was a diva or sensed it immediately by his Ronaldo-esque haircut and chanted "Shakira, Shakira." Since I wasn't cheering for Feyenoord, wasn't in red, white, and black (or blue and red, for that matter), there must be something wrong with me, that maybe I was a spying Ajax fan. One asked me where I was from. New York City, I said. And everyone kind of turned around. *What are you doing here?* It's a long, long story, I wanted to say, involving Switzerland, a woman, love, soccer, love of soccer, if it was still love, and writing and still trying to prove myself as a writer to the powers that be. Instead I just said, "The Koreans."

Before I could explain, an older Feyenoord fan with a bit more polish said, "I love New York." I started rattling off all the Dutch names from the city's history—Spuyten Duyvil, Kill van Kull, Hellegat, Stuyvesant—and everyone laughed. I was able to relax a little and enjoy the virtual front-row seat I had at the training ground. I asked this nice man which players I should look out for. He said, without hesitation, John Guidetti, a young Swede, property of Man City. And he was right. Guidetti had size, strength, presence, finesse, finishing skill (he had two terrific goals), and vision (he assisted on another with a lovely back heel).

When the match was over—it ended 3–3—and Feyenoord was boarding its bus, not one but two legends were within feet of me: the recently retired Giovanni van Bronckhorst, now an assistant coach, and Ronald Koeman, the head coach. The first thing I remembered about each, both Barça legends, was van Bronckhorst's long-range wonder goal against Uruguay in the 2010 World Cup, and Koeman's free kick in extra time against Sampdoria in the 1992 European Cup final. If ever I needed the Irish photographer—and to do that Moroccan maneuver to pose for a snapshot—it was now. It wasn't Sevilla-Español, which was just an hour and a half away (or, if I stayed another week, the Sevilla–Real Betis derby), but it was a good afternoon.

I thought about detouring back to Zurich on the way home to New York, maybe do another long stay and be close to Basel if I needed to do follow-up reporting. But I came straight back home—best to be in the same time zone as my editor—and I could always do interviews over the phone. And I did, with the team's sporting director, who actually gave me the cell number of the South Korean player, whom we interviewed with the help of a translator.

But it still didn't satisfy my editor's editor. They then wanted more info on the North Korean player's family. One interview became ten, and this still wasn't enough. I asked the player's agent for his family story and he gave it to me. I got the feeling that I was supposed to get his North Korean mother on the phone. And if I got that, I felt I would've had to get Kim Jong-un (and if I got that, I joked with my editor, I'm sure I would've been ordered to get his father. *Oh he's dead? Well he's still on e-mail! Find him. No excuses.*) This piece wasn't going to run in the magazine, nor was it ever going to. I was only glad my father managed to stay alive.

February 26, 2012
Dia:Beacon
Beacon, New York

I had never been a fan of modern dance. I'd heard Robert Gottlieb speak with love and reverence about it on *Charlie Rose*, I once enjoyed a performance by Paul Taylor at City Center, and I knew the important names: Martha Graham, Merce Cunningham, Alvin Ailey, Pina Bausch. Maybe I'd never given it a proper chance or seen enough of it live. Jazz, one of my loves, is always better live, I told people, especially free jazz.

Maybe a change was about to happen. Ever since *The Goalie's Anxiety at the Penalty Kick*, I would see anything by Wim Wenders. Most of it I liked, some I didn't, like an exhibition of his still photos at Galerie Judin in Zurich, beside the Sihl River. Wim was there, and looked approachable, and, yes, I was tempted to ask him about his Peter Handke adaptation, but didn't.

At the end of 2011, I went to his film *Pina*. It was the most original piece of filmmaking I'd seen in years—I couldn't remember how long, maybe since *Russian Ark*—and the best documentary I'd seen since *Man on Wire*. So when my girlfriend suggested that we take a ride to Beacon, New York, up the Hudson, to see a performance by the dancer and choreographer Yvonne Rainer, I said sure. I was up for more dance. I only knew Yvonne Rainer by name, and as my girlfriend reminded me, any performance by Yvonne Rainer was a must-see event. The Friday *New York Times* said it was the one cultural event you couldn't miss that weekend. My girlfriend already had the tickets bought on the Wednesday. I'd missed Pina Bausch when she was alive; I would not miss Yvonne Rainer.

The train from Grand Central was filled with city folk—with eyeglass frames Le Corbusier would approve of—nerds, art and media elites, or art wannabes. Dia:Beacon was as I remembered it when we, the two of us, first ventured up soon after it opened: exciting and magnificent.

We got there with just a few minutes to spare and had no time to read the short program. Just as well, as I liked to be surprised and leave it to myself to figure things out. The third piece was called "Spiraling Down" and out came four of Rainer's dancers in sweats, college T-shirts, and sneakers—to the grand, and grandly clichéd, "Bolero."

The theme was participatory sports, and what appeared to be a send-up and appreciation all at once of the notion of "the week-end warrior." At certain points, Ravel was lowered and one of the dancers went to a lectern and began reading a text about jogging. Over the last couple of years, I was running more and more. I didn't get running—never did, really. For me, it was about convenience and practicality. It was often torture, sometimes exhilarating, but always a mystery. There were dozens of books on running, but none seemed especially interesting or daring except for Haruki Murakami's *What I Talk About When I Talk About Running*.

By chance, I had just started reading it, and when this member of Rainer's company took to the lectern and began reciting a text, one by a runner who was also a novelist and who lived in Japan, I realized it was from the same book I was in the middle of reading. Then she would stop, "Bolero" was cranked back up, and the dancers continued their movements, all done within a square about the size of a boxing ring.

I looked closely at the movements and damn if they didn't suggest soccer. Not obvious soccer moves, kicking, heading, dribbling. No, they were far more subtle, or maybe it was just my imagination. But it appeared as if they were pantomiming the act of juggling, my favorite thing in the game, maybe because it's so graceful and so beside the point. But as I continued to stare, mesmerized, the dancers did more than pretend to juggle with their feet. They bent their thighs at the knee, and then again with the other leg, as if they were juggling the ball off their thighs, as I first saw done in the movie *Victory*. And then they would make short, staccato movements with the upper arm that seemed to simulate a difficult juggling maneuver, for show-offs only, with the shoulder. And then they'd thrust out their sternum, as if executing a chest pass. Was I seeing things? If I was interpreting this correctly, if there even was such a thing as a "correct" interpretation, Yvonne Rainer might be not only a fan of soccer, but a careful aficionado of the sport, so careful that she studied players' preparation and technique while training and goofing around. Wow, I thought.

Was I projecting? Was that allowed? Was I misreading this? Even if I wasn't, was she making fun of them, of us? Her dancers didn't have the perfect form of professional players, but maybe that was the point. Maybe it was about the beauty in all of us, even the Sunday park player—or the accomplished dancer as the Sunday park player.

When "Bolero" came to its crescendo, as irresistible as Torvill and Dean in Sarajevo 1984, and the lights were raised, I remained in my seat to process what I'd just seen. After a few moments, I looked through the small program guide that I didn't have time to read when I arrived. Thanked for inspiration was, yes, Haruki Murakami. And Ted Shawn and Preston Sturges and Lilly Tomlin and Pierre Boulez and Gene Kelly and Sylvia Plath, and the New York Philharmonic and Vaslav Nijinsky. And there, ha ha! Mané Garrincha. Not just Garrincha, but Mané Garrincha. And Pelé!

June 9, 2012
Argentina vs. Brazil
MetLife Stadium
East Rutherford, New Jersey

What years before—even just the *year* before—was something special—a Brazil or Argentina coming to town—was now becoming routine. Twice each for both teams in the last two years, this time without even playing the U.S. national team, but each other. Ticket prices for this game were astronomical, into the four figures for a great seat. Even if I wanted to sit among the fans, I couldn't afford it. But I applied for a press credential and got one.

I considered *not* going. I had hurt my back and though it was getting better, it was still hard for me to move around as I normally would. Still, I had to go. It was Argentina versus Brazil, Messi versus Neymar. And there was a chance to write something about the game for a new venture.

The previous year, I'd met George Quraishi, who was starting a new soccer magazine. An English book editor in New York (and an Inter fan) told George that I was working on a soccer book and that he should contact me as a possible contributor. I was flattered, of course, and even more so when George invited me to a Red Bulls game on the otherwise melancholy day of September 10, 2011, versus the Vancouver Whitecaps and its two Swiss I'd seen play so many times, Davide Chiumiento, from FC Luzern, and especially FCZ's Eric Hassli. George Q had season tickets—upper deck, behind the goal—and laid out his vision. He was delightful company, young, enthusiastic, a Yale grad, smart about soccer, sans the typical media elite take on the sport, and open to all stories, great and small, from any and all parts of the world, not just England and Barcelona. His father had played in the NASL in the 1970s for the Tampa Bay Rowdies so George was weaned on the sport. He wanted to edit a literary soccer magazine that would combine great writing with great art and design. He would do it with his friend Mark Kirby, and they would launch it with a Kickstarter campaign. They'd use social media to spread the word, but the magazine would be analog, an oversized book that looked beautiful, something you'd want to buy and collect. Old world and new—what was not to like?

A few months later he had me start on a piece on AS Roma. The first issue wasn't due out until fall of 2012, but it already was getting notice, and he was commissioned to do an app-only game program for the Argentina-Brazil game. He was covering the game for the *Guardian* but asked if I might contribute a scene piece.

The talent on the field was staggering, even if Brazil "only" brought its Olympic team: Marcelo, Pato, Oscar, Neymar, Juan, Hulk; and on the other side, Zabaleta, Gago, DiMaria, Aguero, Higuain, Lavezzi, Mascherano, Messi. (The coach, Sergio Batista, had already been replaced after just a year.) So despite the ticket prices and the fact that it was on the same day as the Belmont Stakes, Mets versus Yankees in the Bronx, the New Jersey Devils in the Stanley Cup finals nearby in Newark, not to mention a track-and-field event on Randall's Island, and a 10k in Central Park, it attracted 81,994, the largest soccer attendance in New Jersey history.

It almost felt scripted, like Beckham's first game against New York at Giants Stadium. This was a 4–3 for Argentina, which on its own seems fantastical, but on top of that, Messi scored a hat trick. So much had been written about Messi that writers were trying to outdo one another with their hyperliterary descriptions, myself included. But I'd had enough. I didn't know what to say anymore; he was beyond superlatives and almost transcended words. (In that sense, Messi approached the level of art. I still maintained that athletics and art were separate, but if anyone had come ever so close it was him.) So with the game tied in the eighty-fourth minute, when he received the ball near the midfield stripe far on the right, he appeared to decide that this match should be won here and now. He took off on a solo run and just outside the penalty area, let go of a left-footed shot that curled into the top left-hand corner. It was the finest goal I'd ever seen live, and I said out loud, in the press box, with George next to me, "Oh my God. Oh my God!"

Epilogue

....

Everything I know about
morality and the obligations
of men, I owe to football.
ALBERT CAMUS

August 8, 2012
Real Madrid vs. AC Milan
Yankee Stadium
Bronx, New York

On March 2, my father fell into a coma. Thankfully, I wasn't on a
wild-goose chase in Marbella. My mother called me in the early
afternoon and by early evening I was there. The next day, my birthday, he was pronounced dead. I held my father's hand and said
"thanks for everything." Just two months before, he had encouraged
me to do the story because I loved soccer, I loved to write, that it
could lead to bigger and better things, that I shouldn't worry about
him. A watered-down version of the piece ran on the Internet, but
it was held and held and held, even after Basel shocked Bayern on
February 22 in the first leg by winning 1–0. It was only posted a
couple of weeks later, about sixteen hours before the second leg,
which Basel lost 7–0. It got all sorts of play on social media, but
my father never did get to read it.

I couldn't help but think of him on this August night. It was exactly thirty years and one day ago that he took me to my first soccer game, the FIFA-UNICEF World All-Star Game at Giants Stadium. I'd always be grateful, for that and so many other things.

I took the subway up to Yankee Stadium with the hope of getting a ticket, face value, for Real Madrid vs. AC Milan. Death is awkward, for me still a mystery, and everyone handles it differently. I had avoided dealing with the loss of my father, instead trying to help my mother and sister, and focus on finding work. And then, on the No. 4 subway, on the way up to the Bronx, my home, thinking about that game thirty years ago, yeah, I began to sob. I stood there—I always preferred to stand in subways, leaning against the door—weeping.

But my father was never one for sappy endings or Hollywood tearjerkers—he was New Wave—and this is about soccer, right, *this is about the joy.* So on to 161st Street and River Avenue. Instead of walking left, south, to Yankee Stadium, as per conditioning, I/we walked right, to the new Yankee Stadium (new stadiums were everywhere). The game was sold out, and I hadn't applied for a press credential, but I thought I'd snag a single ticket somewhere, somehow. I didn't really want to pay scalper prices, nor could I afford them, so I went to the box office thinking they'd sell tickets from no-shows or cancellations. It had worked before, at concerts and sporting events. Maybe I'd be lucky and someone would sell below face value. If I didn't get in, I could live with it. I still had my doubts about these preseason friendlies.

At the very least, I thought, I'd run into people I knew. George, the Mexican American at the chicken place in my neighborhood, whom I ran into at U.S.-Brazil, was a Real fan and his sister bought him a ticket for his birthday. Brian wasn't going, but several friends he made from the soccer store, guys I knew, were going. Paul Gardner would be there, David maybe, and probably Steve, who also happened to be a big Yankee fan. Maybe John my former co-worker, originally from Kearny, if he wasn't working late. Or Bakary, from

Mali, who I also met at Brian's store and who delivered groceries at one of the supermarket chains. We'd have long discussions on soccer in the middle of the street with his delivery wagon. He was part of the recent wave of African immigrants who had settled into the Bronx. He had a ticket. I'd run into someone, surely.

Instead, I didn't see anyone I knew. The only person I recognized was T.I., the rapper. He and a small entourage of a couple of body-guards and a blond woman picked up their tickets at the window where I stood. He was in shorts, maybe light green, with violet socks (or vice versa)—but designer shorts, designer everything, the socks, the loafers, the eyeglass frames, the checkered shirt, and sweater vest. Some fans whispered to their friends and tried not to stare. One said, "That's not T.I." I couldn't help myself and chimed in, "Guys, of course, it's T.I. Who else would have the guts to dress like that?" That seemed to convince them.

I waited and waited, but no one was selling. And soon it was game time. I wasn't the only one who didn't get in, and felt espe-cially bad for a guy in his forties with his son, about ten. Even if I'd found a ticket, I think I would've given it to them. We chatted for a few minutes, they were Real and Argentina fans, had been for a while. I told them not to worry, that there would be more games, a lot more games, and we shook hands and went our separate ways. Soccer wasn't just for us outsiders (or were we insiders?) anymore.

I walked toward Macombs Dam Park, newly refurbished with its own misty cooling station. Twenty, thirty, forty years ago, this was a scary place. Now people threw footballs, jogged around the track, speed walked, someone skipped rope, someone else shadow boxed. There was a homeless man with a shopping cart. And there was soccer. Africans juggled the ball; another group played four on four. From the stadium, I heard a roar, the unmistakable sound of a goal. About ten minutes later, the same roar, someone scored again. Ronaldo? Robinho? There was soccer inside Yankee Stadium and now outside. I smiled, walked out of the park, across 161st Street, and back to the No. 4 train.

Lightning Source UK Ltd.
Milton Keynes UK
UKHW03f0625290318
320223UK00001B/21/P

9 781496 205971